2159

THE
MY LAI
INQUIRY

THE
MY LAI
INQUIRY

Lt. Gen. W. R. Peers, USA (Ret.)

W · W · NORTON & COMPANY
NEW YORK   LONDON

Library of Congress Cataloging in Publication Data
Peers, William R
The My Lai inquiry.

Includes index.
1. My Lai-4, Vietnam—Massacre, 1968.
I. Title.
DS557.8.M9P43   1979   959.704'34   78-14242
ISBN 0-393-01184-4

1 2 3 4 5 6 7 8 9 0

For all the American soldiers
(officers and enlisted men)
who fought and died in Vietnam.

Contents

III. The Aftermath

Documents and Charts

NOTE: There are maps throughout Chapters 5, 15, and 16.

Photographs will be found following page 120.

Introduction

The My Lai incident was a black mark in the annals of American military history. In analyzing the entire episode, we found that the principal breakdown was in leadership. Failures occurred at every level within the chain of command, from individual noncommissioned-officer squad leaders to the command group of the division. It was an illegal operation in violation of military regulations and of human rights, starting with the planning, continuing through the brutal, destructive acts of many of the men who were involved, and culminating in aborted efforts to investigate and, finally, the suppression of the truth. The pain caused by the My Lai affair will not soon be forgotten.

The leadership failures may be divided into two broad categories. The first concerns the unit level, a composite organization known as Task Force Barker with three subordinate companies of infantry, where leadership was lacking in the planning of an illegal operation and in its execution, with the senseless killing of hundreds of innocent women, children, and old men. This kind of activity would be manifestly wrong in any civilized society. The other category relates to the reporting and investigative process. Directives and regulations in force at the time provided ample, if not detailed, guidance for reporting serious incidents and insuring that they were properly investigated by competent, disinterested authority, but none of them was followed. As a result, the integrity of the Army was jeopardized.

This kind of coverup is not unique to the military services. In the political arena we have seen it in Watergate, with people acting above the law and using various subterfuges and deceptions to conceal their activities. We are still seeing many elected and appointed officials cited for using their offices to their personal advantage. Hence, the lessons to be learned from My Lai in responsibility, honesty, and integrity are applicable to all government officials. In a similar sense they may be applied to business and labor leaders.

My Lai was a gruesome tragedy, a massacre of the first order. Some of the soldiers participating in the operation did not become involved in the killing, raping, and destruction of property, and should not be considered in the same light as those who committed the atrocities. Similarly, a few men were outraged and tried to report the incident through proper channels, but their efforts were stifled by lack of attention, erroneous interpretation, and improper leadership. These men are to be commended.

The Army acted courageously in investigating the incident and reporting its findings to the American public and the world. Although the My Lai incident damaged the image of the Army and the integrity of its officer and noncommissioned officer corps, the investigation and reporting did much to restore faith in the Army and its institutions. The failure to bring to justice those who participated in the tragedy or were negligent in following it up, however, casts grave doubts upon the efficacy of American justice— military and civilian alike. These shortcomings must be corrected.

part I

The Preliminaries

chapter 1

The Beginning

My introduction to the My Lai incident came with unexpected suddenness on Monday, November 24, 1969, when I was called to a meeting with General William C. Westmoreland, the Army Chief of Staff. He told me that he and the Secretary of the Army, Stanley C. Resor, had been discussing the My Lai operation and had come to the conclusion that it was necessary to conduct a formal investigation.[1] He wanted to find out what had gone wrong with the reporting system; why, in his position as commander of U.S. forces in Vietnam at the time, he had not been fully informed; and whether the operation had been investigated. He wanted me to head the inquiry panel.

This came as quite a shock to me. I knew practically nothing about My Lai. In fact, my knowledge was limited to what I had read about it in the Washington newspapers, and most of that concerned the court martial charges that had been filed against Lieutenant William L. Calley. Of course, I had talked about it briefly with other officers; we had found it hard to believe that an atrocity of the magnitude being reported could really have happened.

At the time I was serving as chief of the Office Reserve Components,

---

1. Recently General Westmoreland told me that he had been thinking about an investigation for some time. However, he had encountered considerable resistance from within the Department of Defense, which he strongly suspected had originated in the White House. Finally he had met with General Alexander Haig, assistant to President Nixon, and informed him of what was going on; if the obstruction did not cease, he said, he was going to invoke his prerogative as Chief of Staff and report directly to the President. Evidently that did the job, as thereafter there was no further resistance to the investigation.

working with the Army Reserves and the Army National Guard, both of which were having severe problems because of the war in Vietnam. They had enough people in their units but the training was ineffective because so much of their equipment was being used to replace losses in Vietnam. They needed help badly, and I was devoting all of my time and energy to that end. Frankly, I was not exactly overjoyed with the prospects of this new assignment, but when one is asked to do something by the Chief of Staff and the Secretary of the Army one doesn't quibble about it; one just gets on with it and does the best job possible.[2]

Then General Westmoreland showed me a copy of a letter from Ron Ridenhour, an ex-GI who had been in Vietnam in 1968. This letter had triggered the Army's decision to look into the My Lai incident. It was a very startling letter, and should be quoted in full.

Phoenix, Arizona
March 29, 1969

Gentlemen:

It was late in April, 1968 that I first heard of "Pinkville" and what allegedly happened there. I received that first report with some skepticism, but in the following months I was to hear similar stories from such a wide variety of people that it became impossible for me to disbelieve that something rather dark and bloody did indeed occur sometime in March, 1968 in a village called "Pinkville" in the Republic of Viet Nam.

The circumstances that led to my having access to the reports I'm about to relate need explanation. I was inducted in March, 1967 into the U. S. Army. After receiving various training I was assigned to the 70th Infantry Detachment (LRP), 11th Light Infantry Brigade at Schofield Barracks, Hawaii, in early October, 1967. That unit, the 70th Infantry Detachment (LRP), was disbanded a week before the 11th Brigade shipped out for Viet Nam on the 5th of December, 1967. All of the men from whom I later heard reports of the "Pinkville" incident were reassigned to "C" Company, 1st Battalion, 20th Infantry, 11th Light Infantry Brigade. I was reassigned to the aviation section of Headquarters Headquarters Company 11th LIB. After we had been in Viet Nam for 3 to 4 months many of the men from the 70th Inf. Det. (LRP) began to transfer into the same unit, "E" Company, 51st Infantry (LRP).

In late April, 1968 I was awaiting orders for a transfer from HHC, 11th Brigade to Company "E," 51st Inf. (LRP), when I happened to run into Pfc "Butch"

---

2. I have often been asked why I was selected for this job. Since I felt it was improper to ask, I can only offer this excerpt from General Westmoreland's book, *A Soldier Reports,* published in 1976: "To head the board the Secretary and I selected the former I Field Force commander, General Peers, who had a reputation of objectivity and fairness. Ray Peers had also been a division commander in Vietnam and was thus thoroughly familiar with the conditions; he had never had jurisdiction over any activity in Quang Ngai Province. Because he had entered the Army through ROTC at the University of California at Los Angeles, there could be no presumption that ties among brother officers from West Point would be involved."

Gruver, whom I had known in Hawaii. Gruver told me he had been assigned to "C" Company 1st of the 20th until April 1st when he transferred to the unit that I was headed for. During the course of our conversation he told me the first of many reports I was to hear of "Pinkville."

"Charlie" Company 1/20 had been assigned to Task Force Barker in late February, 1968 to help conduct "search and destroy" operations on the Batangan Peninsula, Barker's area of operation. The task force was operating out of L. F. Dottie, located five or six miles north of Quang Nhai city on Viet Namese National Highway 1. Gruver said that Charlie Company had sustained casualties; primarily from mines and booby traps, almost everyday from the first day they arrived on the peninsula. One village area was particularly troublesome and seemed to be infested with booby traps and enemy soldiers. It was located about six miles northeast of Quang Nhai city at approximate coordinates B.S. 728795. It was a notorious area and the men of Task Force Barker had a special name for it: they called it "Pinkville." One morning in the latter part of March, Task Force Barker moved out from its firebase headed for "Pinkville." Its mission: destroy the trouble spot and all of its inhabitants.

When "Butch" told me this I didn't quite believe that what he was telling me was true, but he assured me that it was and went on to describe what had happened. The other two companies that made up the task force cordoned off the village so that "Charlie" Company could move through to destroy the structures and kill the inhabitants. Any villagers who ran from Charlie Company were stopped by the encircling companies. I asked "Butch" several times if all the people were killed. He said that he thought they were, men, women and children. He recalled seeing a small boy, about three or four years old, standing by the trail with a gunshot wound in one arm. The boy was clutching his wounded arm with his other hand, while blood trickled between his fingers. He was staring around himself in shock and disbelief at what he saw. "He just stood there with big eyes staring around like he didn't understand; he didn't believe what was happening. Then the captain's RTO (radio operator) put a burst of 16 (M-16 rifle) fire into him." It was so bad, Gruver said, that one of the men in his squad shot himself in the foot in order to be medivac-ed out of the area so that he would not have to participate in the slaughter. Although he had not seen it, Gruver had been told by people he considered trustworthy that one of the company's officers, 2nd Lieutenant Kally (this spelling may be incorrect) had rounded up several groups of villagers (each group consisting of a minimum of 20 persons of both sexes and all ages). According to the story, Kally then machine-gunned each group. Gruver estimated that the population of the village had been 300 to 400 people and that very few, if any, escaped.

After hearing this account I couldn't quite accept it. Somehow I just couldn't believe that not only had so many young American men participated in such an act of barbarism, but that their officers had ordered it. There were other men in the unit I was soon to be assigned to, "E" Company, 51st Infantry (LRP), who had been in Charlie Company at the time that Gruver alleged the incident at "Pinkville" had occurred. I became determined to ask them about "Pinkville" so that I might compare their accounts with Pfc Gruver's.

When I arrived at "Echo" Company, 51st Infantry (LRP) the first men I looked for were Pfc's Michael Terry and William Doherty. Both were veterans of

"Charlie" Company, 1/20 and "Pinkville." Instead of contradicting "Butch" Gruver's story they corroborated it, adding some tasty tidbits of information of their own. Terry and Doherty had been in the same squad and their platoon was the third platoon of "C" Company to pass through the village. Most of the people they came to were already dead. Those that weren't were sought out and shot. The platoon left nothing alive, neither livestock nor people. Around noon the two soldiers' squad stopped to eat. "Billy and I started to get out our chow," Terry said, "but close to us was a bunch of Vietnamese in a heap, and some of them were moaning. Kally (2nd Lt. Kally) had been through before us and all of them had been shot, but many weren't dead. It was obvious that they weren't going to get any medical attention so Billy and I got up and went over to where they were. I guess we sort of finished them off." Terry went on to say that he and Doherty then returned to where their packs were and ate lunch. He estimated the size of the village to be 200 to 300 people. Doherty thought that the population of "Pinkville" had been 400 people.

If Terry, Doherty and Gruver could be believed, then not only had "Charlie" Company received orders to slaughter all the inhabitants of the village, but those orders had come from the commanding officer of Task Force Barker, or possibly even higher in the chain of command. Pfc Terry stated that when Captain Medina (Charlie Company's commanding officer Captain Ernest Medina) issued the order for the destruction of "Pinkville" he had been hesitant, as if it were something he didn't want to do but had to. Others I spoke to concurred with Terry on this.

It was June before I spoke to anyone who had something of significance to add to what I had already been told of the "Pinkville" incident. It was the end of June, 1968 when I ran into Sargent Larry La Croix at the USO in Chu Lai. La Croix had been in 2nd Lt. Kally's platoon on the day Task Force Barker swept through "Pinkville." What he told me verified the stories of the others, but he also had something new to add. He had been a witness to Kally's gunning down of at least three separate groups of villagers. "It was terrible. They were slaughtering the villagers like so many sheep." Kally's men were dragging people out of bunkers and hootches and putting them together in a group. The people in the group were men, women and children of all ages. As soon as he felt that the group was big enough, Kally ordered an M-60 (machine-gun) set up and the people killed. La Croix said that he bore witness to this procedure at least three times. The three groups were of different sizes, one of about twenty people, one of about thirty people, and one of about forty people. When the first group was put together Kally ordered Pfc Torres to man the machine-gun and open fire on the villagers that had been grouped together. This Torres did, but before everyone in the group was down he ceased fire and refused to fire again. After ordering Torres to recommence firing several times, Lieutenant Kally took over the M-60 and finished shooting the remaining villagers in that first group himself. Sargent La Croix told me that Kally didn't bother to order anyone to take the machine-gun when the other two groups of villagers were formed. He simply manned it himself and shot down all villagers in both groups.

This account of Sargent La Croix's confirmed the rumors that Gruver, Terry and Doherty had previously told me about Lieutenant Kally. It also convinced me that there was a very substantial amount of truth to the stories that all of these men had told. If I needed more convincing, I was to receive it.

It was in the middle of November, 1968 just a few weeks before I was to return to the United States for separation from the army that I talked to Pfc Michael Bernhardt. Bernhardt had served his entire year in Viet Nam in "Charlie" Company 1/20 and he too was about to go home. "Bernie" substantiated the tales told by the other men I had talked to in vivid, bloody detail and added this. "Bernie" had absolutely refused to take part in the massacre of the villagers of "Pinkville" that morning and he thought that it was rather strange that the officers of the company had not made an issue of it. But that evening "Medina (Captain Ernest Medina) came up to me ("Bernie") and told me not to do anything stupid like write my congressman" about what had happened that day. Bernhardt assured Captain Medina that he had no such thing in mind. He had nine months left in Viet Nam and felt that it was dangerous enough just fighting the acknowledged enemy.

Exactly what did, in fact, occur in the village of "Pinkville" in March, 1968 I do not know for *certain*, but I am convinced that it was something very black indeed. I remain irrevocably persuaded that if you and I do truly believe in the principles, of justice and the equality of every man, however humble, before the law, that form the very backbone that this country is founded on, then we must press forward a widespread and public investigation of this matter with all our combined efforts. I think that it was Winston Churchhill who once said "A country without a conscience is a country without a soul, and a country without a soul is a country that cannot survive." I feel that I must take some positive action on this matter. I hope that you will launch an investigation immediately and keep me informed of your progress. If you cannot, then I don't know what other course of action to take.

I have considered sending this to newspapers, magazines, and broadcasting companies, but I somehow feel that investigation and action by the Congress of the United States is the appropriate procedure, and as a conscientious citizen I have no desire to further besmirch the image of the American serviceman in the eyes of the world. I feel that this action, while probably it would promote attention, would not bring about the constructive actions that the direct actions of the Congress of the United States would.

Sincerely,

Ron Ridenhour

I was stunned by this letter. At first I found it hard to believe that an incident such as Ridenhour described not only could have happened but could have remained hidden for so long. In fact, I thought that maybe Ridenhour was just a disgruntled Vietnam veteran trying to attract attention. After getting into the investigation and discovering the true facts of the incident, however, my view of Ron Ridenhour changed to one of admiration. His letter proved to be the key to uncovering the tragedy, and had he not sent it, it is conceivable that the My Lai incident would have remained hidden to this day. For this reason, the Army and the American people owe him a vote of thanks.

General Westmoreland said the letter had taken him by surprise, too, and he had been greatly disturbed by it. Although he had been aware of the operation by Task Force Barker and remembered that it had been quite successful—128 Viet Cong were reported to have been killed—there had been no indication that civilians had been involved in any way, much less that atrocities or war crimes had been committed. I could well understand General Westmoreland's position. His headquarters at the time, the Military Assistance Command, Vietnam (MACV), received dozens of operational reports every day, and he was briefed only on the outstanding or unusual ones. He could not possibly have been expected to know all the details of every operation; that was the responsibility of the MACV general staff. Now, however, he was personally concerned about the possibilities of a coverup.

After receiving the Ridenhour letter, the Army had checked with headquarters, U.S. Army, Vietnam (USARV), which had responded by confirming that Task Force Barker had conducted an operation against My Lai-4 on March 16, 1968, but had no knowledge of any atrocities having been committed; there were no indications that the incident had been investigated. Since this told them almost nothing, in late April 1969 General Westmoreland had directed the Army Inspector General to conduct a preliminary investigation.

This investigation was carried out by Colonel William V. Wilson, who traveled extensively throughout the United States interviewing a large number of people who had taken part in or knew about the My Lai operation. By July Colonel Wilson had gathered enough evidence to indicate that some criminal acts had taken place. After being briefed on Colonel Wilson's report, in August General Westmoreland had transferred the responsibility for further investigation of possible war crimes to the Criminal Investigation Division (CID) of the Office of the Provost Marshal General. The CID continued to locate persons connected with the incident and to take sworn statements from them. By September they had assembled a great deal of information, especially concerning the activities of the platoon that had been commanded by Lieutenant William L. Calley. This information was forwarded to Fort Benning, Georgia, where Lieutenant Calley was stationed, and shortly thereafter court martial charges were filed against him, alleging that he was responsible for the deaths of 109 civilians at My Lai-4 on March 16, 1968.

But while the CID was continuing its investigation into possible war crimes and atrocities, General Westmoreland was still very concerned about the possibility of a coverup of what had happened at My Lai. The inquiry I was to head would be limited to checking into the reports and investigations of the incident; our work was not to interfere with the CID's but we were expected to establish a working liaison with them.

General Westmoreland stressed the importance of my assignment and the effect it would have on the image of the Army in the eyes of the American public. He also emphasized the urgency of getting the investigation under way and completing it as soon as practicable. Since it had been over seven months since the receipt of the Ridenhour letter he felt that the Army might be accused of dragging its feet. He left no doubt in my mind that it would be a full-time job. As a final thought he said that regardless of whom I selected to serve with me on the panel, he wanted me to know it would be I—and only I—who would be held responsible for the findings and recommendations of the Inquiry. This put the responsibility squarely on my shoulders.

In some respects General Westmoreland had been quite specific, but in others my instructions were rather vague. I had served in the Army for more than thirty-two years and knew that one should not rely on verbal guidance; it often leads to misunderstanding and confusion. Moreover, regulations specified that instructions be issued in writing by the appointing authority before an investigation can be undertaken. Accordingly, I asked General Westmoreland to have a written directive prepared. He agreed and said he would inform Secretary Resor and that they would have both the military and civilian members of the Army staff prepare one.

It turned out that I also became involved in the preparation of the directive. The concerned staff agencies wanted to make sure that it would fulfill my requirements and I, of course, wanted to make sure that it would not tie my hands. The initial draft was too long and too specific, but finally on November 26, it was honed down, coordinated, and accepted by the Army staff. It was then sent to General Westmoreland and Secretary Resor for their approval and signatures.[3] Then we had the authority to go to work.

The day after I met with General Westmoreland, I contacted Colonel Wilson, who had conducted the original investigation for the Office of the Inspector General. He told me he had interviewed fifteen to twenty men, some of whom had been involved in the incident and others from within the chain of command, and was convinced that serious war crimes had been committed during the assault on My Lai-4. Colonel Wilson had been considerably impressed with Colonel Oran K. Henderson, who had been the commander of the 11th Infantry Brigade at the time of the incident and had provided him with a copy of a Report of Investigation dated April 24, 1968. Colonel Henderson had said that there was yet another Report of Investigation, which would provide considerably more detail, and Colonel Wilson was hopeful that it could be found. I was looking forward to seeing it when the Inquiry got under way, because if such a report existed it could possibly provide the Inquiry with guidelines as to how to proceed.

Another person who had made a good impression on Colonel Wilson was Warrant Officer Hugh Thompson, the pilot of an aero scout helicopter, who

---

3. Document 1–1: Directive for Investigation (November 26, 1969). See page 259.

had been observing in and around the My Lai-4 area on the morning of the incident. He had had a close view of the action, and had tried to do something about stopping it. Colonel Wilson also had talked with Ron Ridenhour, but his statement, as was his letter, was totally hearsay and could be accepted only in that light.

We talked at length about his interrogations and his impressions of people, places, and things. I kept his report—which included the sworn statements of the persons he had interviewed; a copy of Colonel Henderson's April 24 Report of Investigation; several maps and charts; and his findings and conclusions—and studied it to see if it would provide some clues as to what we might do.

These early days were a continuous whirlwind. There seemed to be a million things to be done and little time in which to do them. Much of this period has become blurred in my memory. There was no precedent to follow in recent U.S. military history—an investigation of allegations that a U.S. combat unit had killed a large number of civilians. Thus any action we took would be like plowing new ground. I felt that all of my decisions had to be correct in their beginning.

Very soon after the panel members were assembled, the philosophy of the Inquiry was clearly established. We agreed that the keys had to be absolute integrity and objectivity on the part of all members of the panel. No matter what any of us might feel, it was our job only to ascertain and report the facts, to let the chips fall where they may. It was *not* our job to determine innocence or guilt of individuals, nor to be concerned about what effects the Inquiry might have on the Army's "image" or about the press or public's reaction to our proceedings. When completed, our report, with its conclusions and recommendations, was to be submitted to the Chief of Staff and the Secretary of the Army, and it would be up to them to decide what to do thereafter. This was a hard line for us to follow. After all, the military members of the panel were all Regular Army officers; it was not beyond the realm of possibility that any one of us might subconsciously adopt a protective attitude toward the Army and not want to put it in a bad light. However, once the guidelines for strict integrity and objectivity were firmly established they were followed meticulously by all members of the panel. We never found it necessary to discuss this matter again.

Our guiding document, Army Regulation 15-6, which defines the procedures for conducting an investigation, was causing me considerable consternation. As I read it, we would be required to designate a respondent or respondents—that is, one or more persons who might actually have committed an offense, the accused, so to speak. Early in the Inquiry, we had no solid evidence that there had been any failures in reporting or investigating the incident or, if there had been, who was responsible. It was fortunate that two legal experts were on the panel. Both of them assured me that we did not have to follow precisely the provisions of the regulation but could deviate from them as necessary, provided we did not violate its spirit. They checked with the Judge Advocate General's office to see if this interpretation was still applicable. They found that it was, and that we were not required to name respondents.

The directive asked that I provide an expected completion date for the Inquiry. Thus, on November 30 I responded by sending a memorandum to Secretary Resor and General Westmoreland outlining our concept of operation and organization as well as giving a tentative schedule of events and the expected date of completion.[4]

The concept of operations remained valid throughout the Inquiry. A review of the paragraphs on organization and the tentative schedule, however, shows how little I knew of the situation at that time. As the account of the incident and its investigations unfolded, the size of the panel expanded several times over, the thirty to forty expected witnesses increased to over four hundred, and the six weeks' completion time became closer to fourteen. Clearly, at that stage I was a bit naive and overly optimistic.

In the memorandum, I recommended that the Inquiry be given an official title and that it be disseminated to the appropriate commands with instruction to provide requisite assistance to the panel. Thus, in the Office of the Chief of Staff we were bestowed with the official title "The Department of the Army Review of the Preliminary Investigations into the My Lai Incident" and given a shorter title to be used in communications: "the Peers Inquiry."

4. Document 1–2: Memorandum on Concept, Organization, and Schedule of Inquiry (November 30, 1969). See page 260.

chapter 2

The Panel

General Westmoreland had assured me that I would be supplied with all the people, funds, and anything else needed for the investigation. I could select the people I wanted to serve with me on the investigation regardless of their rank, their position, or whether they were in the United States or overseas. He had also said that he and Secretary Resor wanted to have civilian representation on the panel, and suggested that Bland West, an assistant general counsel of the Army, act as my deputy. I had not met Mr. West but knew him by reputation, and I had no objection. As it turned out, Bland West was a retired Army colonel who had served in the Army's legal department, called the Judge Advocate General (JAG). He was a calm and highly effective person and proved to be a tower of strength throughout the Inquiry. A better man could not have been selected.

A matter that required immediate attention was obtaining Army staff support. I knew that once the Inquiry got under way we would be too busy to worry about such administrative details as personnel needs, office space, office equipment, and the like. Colonel G. W. Everett of the Secretary of the General Staff's office was selected to set up and head such a group. In addition, we arranged for contacts within each of the Army staff agencies so that whenever members of the Inquiry or Colonel Everett's group needed support or information they would always be dealing with the same persons. This arrangement proved to be particularly effective and relieved the Inquiry of a large part of its administrative burdens. Major Dilworth, of General Westmoreland's office, was especially helpful.

I also had a long discussion with Bland West about the composition of the Inquiry panel. He agreed with me that we should keep the number of persons to an essential minimum. He felt we should have at least one other civilian on the panel and suggested someone from the Office of the General Counsel. As for the military members, I felt that Colonel William V. Wilson, with his experience and knowledge from the Inspector General's investigation, would be most helpful and could assist in providing continuity from his original investigation.

We also needed the best military legal assistance we could possibly obtain, and finally decided upon Colonel Robert W. Miller, chief of the international division of the Judge Advocate General's office. He was described to me as being knowledgeable, hard-working, and hard-nosed, perhaps the best-qualified person within the JAG corps for such an assignment. I found this assessment to be absolutely accurate; Bob's only problem was that he worked too hard and his hours were too long.[1]

To maintain liaison with the CID, we chose Major E. F. Zychowski, an experienced investigator with the Office of the Provost Marshal General, who also served as a member of the Inquiry panel. He was most useful throughout our investigation in obtaining copies of the CID's testimony and in the exchange of other information pertaining to the incident.

Because the issues were so complex, we needed a skilled administrative officer who also had a thorough knowledge of combat operations. We finally chose Lieutenant Colonel James H. Breen, who was with the Office of the Deputy Chief of Staff for Operations. Lieutenant Colonel Breen served throughout the entire Inquiry and proved to be one of the finest and most capable officers I have ever met.

We also needed an officer to serve as the recorder, who would not be a participating member of the Inquiry but would be responsible for the handling and swearing in of the witnesses and monitoring the preparation and taking of testimony. Major Clyde D. Lynn was selected for the assignment, and he too proved to be highly capable and a fine team member. Initially, I thought two military court reporters would be sufficient for the task, but Bland West strongly suggested that we request four. Little did I know at the time what our eventual requirements would be; ultimately, we were to have a total of sixteen.

Our offices were set up in the Army Operation Center in the basement of the Pentagon. It was a small area but at the time appeared adequate, and it provided good security and a degree of isolation from reporters and curiosity seekers.

Because of the interest in the My Lai incident and the Calley case, during the first few days of the Inquiry whenever I left the Operations Center I was confronted by newspaper and television reporters and cameramen. While I wanted the public to be informed of the progress of the investigation, I

---

1. Colonel Miller died in the spring of 1974 following a long illness after a brain tumor operation.

simply did not have the time to be giving daily press interviews. I had always tried to maintain good relations with the press; as commander of the 4th Infantry Division in the Central Highlands and of the First Field Force, I had made it a policy to be as helpful to the news media as possible, which included providing food and lodging, helicopter lifts to front-line units whenever space was available, and whatever other needs they had. From this I knew several of the reporters who were covering the Inquiry, and felt they would accept the conditions I had to impose.

I explained that because of the confidential nature of the investigation I would be unable to give them any firsthand information about the testimony or the views of panel members. Lieutenant Colonel Dan Zink, who had been my information officer with the 4th Infantry Division and was now with the Office of the Chief of Information, would keep them informed of the progress of the Inquiry and, when possible, give them the names of witnesses scheduled to appear. The press would be permitted to interview each witness before he testified, but we would instruct the witnesses not to discuss their testimony with anyone after they had appeared before the Inquiry. Once these ground rules were established, I was no longer stopped to discuss My Lai. The reporters seemed to understand, and we maintained cordial relations for the duration of the investigation.

The first meeting of the Inquiry panel took place on November 27, Thanksgiving Day. Among other things, I wanted the panel members to become thoroughly acquainted with one another. Even though I was to be solely responsible for the investigation and its conclusions and recommendations, the task would require a coordinated team effort.

We decided that we would meet at about 8:00 A.M. each morning to review the plans for the day, and again after the Inquiry session to review progress, go over what had to be done that evening, and make plans for the next day. Some of these meetings lasted for several hours. We habitually put in a six-day week, and the average working day was from twelve to sixteen hours, and sometimes longer. Many of our people voluntarily worked seven days a week. Other procedural matters included designating Bland West as the coordinator (chief of staff) to pull all the loose ends together.

There was a great amount of work to be accomplished during the first few days to prepare for the first witness. Each member had to study Colonel Wilson's Inspector General's report and discuss its critical points with him. They also had to review the CID interrogation reports, which by this time had grown to considerable volume, and become familiar with our basic guidance document, Army Regulation 15–6.

On November 29 General Westmoreland asked me how I would feel about a civilian lawyer or jurist to observe our proceedings—to act more or less as the "public conscience." I told him that at the moment I was not too warm to the idea. I knew what was wanted and was prepared to do the job, and I did not want anyone looking over my shoulder, raising questions that might muddy the waters or slow down the process of the Inquiry. Later in the day, however, I told General Westmoreland that I had given the matter very serious thought and agreed with him that a civilian counsel would serve a useful purpose if we could get the right person, someone who would serve actively on the panel. He said they would leave the matter to my judgment and that I would have a hand in his selection. Thus the next day I sent a memorandum to Secretary Resor and General Westmoreland that said, in part:

> As you are aware, intense interest has been expressed in Congressional quarters and by the public as to whether the preliminary inquiries into My Lai-4 incident involved a "coverup by the Army." I intend to conduct the investigation as directed by the above reference in a completely impartial manner. However, I believe that the public recognition of the inquiry and its effectiveness would be prompted if I had available to me a distinguished jurist of impeccable integrity. It is visualized that he would observe and appraise the investigation as it progresses and provide assistance and guidance as to the proceedings and any legal matters related thereto.
>
> Accordingly, I recommend that you solicit the services of such an individual and designate him to serve as my legal counsel.

Three days later the Under Secretary of the Army, Thaddeus R. Beal, invited me to his office to meet Robert MacCrate, who was being considered as the civilian legal counsel to the Inquiry panel. Mr. MacCrate was a senior partner in the New York law firm of Sullivan & Cromwell. He had served as a law secretary to Justice Dowd W. Peck, and between 1959 and 1962 had been Governor Rockefeller's counsel, so he was not unfamiliar with the ways of government. Most importantly, he had had extensive experience as an attorney in complex private litigation, and from 1943 to 1946 had been active in the Naval Reserve.

After giving him background about our progress so far, I told him that if he joined the Inquiry he would become an active member of the panel and take part in questioning the witnesses. I was pleased when he answered that this was the only way he would even consider serving with us. He didn't want to be a figurehead off in a corner reviewing progress and offering advice from time to time; he wanted to get into it on a full-time basis and participate fully.

Then he asked if we would consider having Jerome Walsh, a young lawyer with whom he had worked closely at Sullivan & Cromwell, on the panel. He felt that Mr. Walsh, who was now a partner in his own New York firm of Walsh and Frisch, would be a great help to him and to the rest of the panel. Neither Mr. Beal nor I had any objection. The next day both men joined the panel and stayed with us all the way.

Bob MacCrate and Jerry Walsh were tremendous assets. The entire panel and administrative staff functioned as an integrated team, and they fit right in. They had unlimited energy and were tireless workers. I normally left the office between eight and nine o'clock each night, and they were usually still there, reviewing testimony, preparing for the next day, or discussing some aspect of the law or testimony with other panel members. Each Saturday evening they caught the 6:00 o'clock shuttle flight to New York and by 7:30 Monday morning were again hard at work in the office.

The office space we gave them must have come as quite a letdown. Instead of the large, well-appointed offices, reference libraries, and comparative peace and quiet they were accustomed to, with us they shared an eight-by-ten-foot office furnished with two small metal desks in the midst of the noise and confusion of a conglomoration of administrative personnel, military lawyers reviewing testimony, telephones, and typewriters. However, they seemed to thrive on it.

In some ways Bob and Jerry were very much alike. Both were hard-liners who followed the principle that right is right, wrong is wrong, and one cannot be just a little bit dishonest. Both had extensive knowledge of civil law. In other ways they were quite dissimilar. Bob, who was then fifty, tended to be soft-spoken, calm, and reserved, although he could come down forceful and hard if necessary. Jerry, who was then thirty-seven, was more dynamic and forceful in his approach, and sometimes his Irish temperment flared up. He had had some military experience, having enlisted in the Army in 1952. Following basic training he had entered Officers' Candidate School and had been commissioned a 2nd lieutenant in August 1953. Subsequently, he had qualified as a parachutist and been assigned to the 82nd Airborne Division, first as a platoon leader and later as a battalion intelligence officer, until his discharge in 1954.

Bob and Jerry worked together well, each complementing the other. They were quick to pick up the nuances and differences in civil and military law and worked exceptionally well with the panel's military lawyers. It took them some time, however, to become familiar with military terminology and jargon relating to organization and tactics. Even Jerry needed a refresher, as the Army had changed considerably since 1954 and the war in Vietnam had brought about many modifications in military terminology. But after some special help the first few days, they became most adept in this area.

As the Inquiry progressed and we realized we would have to take the testimony of ground troops, I knew we would have to add others to the panel who understood combat operations in the kind of tactical environment that had existed in the My Lai area. The people selected for the panel up to that time were well qualified in their own fields but lacked tactical experience. After some negotiating, I was able to obtain Colonel Joseph R. (Ross) Franklin, who was with the Office of the Deputy Chief of Staff for Operations. He had had experience in South Vietnam under combat conditions very similar to those in My Lai. We also took on Colonel Thomas F. Whalen, an exceptionally fine officer whom I had known well in South Vietnam. We badly needed someone to coordinate the collection of documents, and Colonel Whalen was given the task. In addition, we already had plans to visit South Vietnam, and he was an ideal person to set up an office in the Military Assistance Command headquarters, make arrangements for our trip, and act as liaison with the commands we wanted to visit.

I also approved the selection of Lieutenant Colonel James H. Patterson both to serve on the panel and to assist in the collecting and handling of documents. In view of the need to interrogate persons involved in the ground operation, a witness section was created under the direction of Major Joseph I. Apici. His job was to locate witnesses, many of whom had been separated from the service, arrange for their travel, schedule their appearances before the panel, and take care of administrative details. This section was later to expand to a total of seven.

As the Inquiry progressed its scope was expanded and the number of people assigned to it increased many times over. For example, several other highly qualified officers with combat experience in Vietnam were added; the number of officer court recorders was increased from one to three and enlisted court recorders from two to sixteen; and comparable augmentation occurred in the legal review, editing, and administrative sections. By the time the Inquiry was completed in March 1970, the overall panel and staff had reached a total of ninety-two.

Each of these persons had been carefully selected as an expert in his particular field, and yet they cooperated with each other as a team. They worked under cramped, pressured conditions and yet never complained. They all recognized the importance of the Inquiry to the Army and to the nation and were totally dedicated to their task. They were one of the finest groups of people with whom I have ever been associated, and I have nothing but admiration for them.

chapter 3

Other My Lai Investigations

It was perhaps by sheer coincidence that a well-documented article appeared in the December 5, 1969, issue of *Life* magazine, shortly after we had started taking testimony. It included some color photographs taken during the My Lai operation by former Army photographer Ronald L. Haeberle. They were extremely bloody and sensational, with several scenes of dead women and children, buildings being burned, and foodstuffs being destroyed. The article also included several statements by men who had participated in the operation. Needless to say, *Life* magazine's wide distribution and the nature of the article did much to focus the attention of the American public upon My Lai.

Thus ours was not the only inquiry being conducted into the My Lai incident at that time.

The court martial of Lieutenant William L. Calley Jr. has been well documented elsewhere, and although he was the focus of most of the public's attention on My Lai he played almost no role in our investigation. During the time of our inquiry he was undergoing preliminary investigation on the court martial charges, although the trial itself did not take place until November 1970 to March 1971. He appeared before us on December 5, 1969, accompanied by a civilian lawyer, George Lattimore, but elected to remain silent except for answering one question. He said, "To the best of my knowledge and recollection, I was never asked any questions concerning the My Lai operations by either Colonel Henderson or Lieutenant Colonel Barker."

As has been mentioned earlier, the charges against Lieutenant Calley grew out of an investigation by the Criminal Investigation Division, whose inquiries into possible war crimes in connection with My Lai were continuing during our Inquiry. The CID is the criminal investigative arm of the Army. Comparable to the FBI, it uses field agents to contact possible witnesses or participants in criminal actions and take sworn statements from them. It has no power to question civilians except on a voluntary basis, and it is not a prosecutorial body. If the information collected by its agents indicates that an offense has been committed, this material is turned over to the proper authority for courts martial or other appropriate action. War crimes like those allegedly committed at My Lai are not subject to a statute of limitations; a person may be brought to trial at any time under the Uniform Code of Military Justice (UCMJ) as long as he is still in the military service. If a suspect has been discharged from the service, the CID's information is turned over to federal authorities for prosecution through civilian courts.

If charges are preferred against someone still in the service and a trial by general court martial seems warranted, yet another investigation is required in accordance with Article 32 of the UCMJ, known as an Article 32 investigation. The general officer who has jurisdiction over the case appoints another officer, senior to the accused, to conduct the investigation. This officer reviews all available information, may obtain additional facts by taking sworn statements, and makes recommendations to the commanding general as to whether or not the suspected person should be brought to trial. The final decision rests with the commanding general.

Inevitably, with the news generated by Lieutenant Calley's pretrial investigation and the announcement of the Army's My Lai Inquiry, things began to heat up on Capitol Hill. Several committees of the Senate and the House of Representatives were vying for the right to conduct an investigation into the incident, but it settled down to the Senate and House Armed Services committees under the chairmanship of Senator John C. Stennis and Congressman L. Mendell Rivers, respectively. It would appear that the House Armed Services Committee (HASC), with its investigation subcommittee, had the higher prerogative.

Just after our investigation got under way the Army received a request from the House Armed Services Committee to brief them on the My Lai operation, which was passed to the deputy chief of staff for military operations, Lieutenant General Richard G. Stilwell. The briefing was rather rudimentary since there was at that time little reliable information as to what actually had happened at My Lai, but General Stilwell was able to present a geographic orientation, the planned scheme of maneuver for Task Force Barker, and the reported results of 128 Viet Cong killed and three weapons captured.

Then, on December 5, 1969, I was asked to appear before the House Armed Services Committee early the following week. Although we were only a week into the Inquiry, we had interrogated several of the key witnesses and had a reasonably good grasp of the nature of the My Lai incident. We were far from having sufficient data upon which to draw any conclusions, but I felt confident we could meet their requirements for background information.

Bob MacCrate and I appeared before the committee on December 9. We were not put under oath; Chairman Rivers said they merely wanted to have a report on our investigation to date and that the session would be as informal as possible. I described how the Inquiry had come into being and told them about the directive from Secretary Resor and General Westmoreland. I explained that initially I had expected the Inquiry to last only a few weeks and that we would interrogate only about thirty-five people but that we had taken testimony from ten persons to date and it was apparent that the number of witnesses would increase to seventy or more. We had already had to expand our staff, I said, and two of those added were Bob MacCrate and Jerry Walsh, who would serve as the Inquiry's "public conscience" as well as being active members of the panel.

Since some congressmen had expressed strong reservations about the Army creating its own Inquiry, I wanted to make my views of the investigation abundantly clear. I told them I recognized that, to a degree, the Army was investigating itself; my position could be ambiguous and the Army subjected to severe criticism if our investigation were not handled properly. Therefore, I said, I would make sure we maintained maximum objectivity and conducted the Inquiry in as fair and impartial a manner as possible. We then responded to a number of questions from committee members.

It was clear that the HASC was going to conduct some kind of an investigation of the My Lai incident but its ground rules had not yet been established. In any case, since our Inquiry was under way and was classified, I expressed the hope that no witness would be called by the committee before our panel had had an opportunity to interrogate him. There did not seem to be any objection to this procedure by any of the members present. I later discussed this with Bob Jordan, the Army General Counsel, and he agreed with me. He then discussed the matter with Secretary Resor, and subsequently it became the official Army position. I mention this because this issue was later to become one of the sore points between the HASC and the Department of the Army. That day, however—although it is difficult to determine how this kind of session is received—Bob MacCrate felt that it had gone well. Certainly there had been no hostile questioning.

As we were leaving, Chairman Rivers asked me to meet with him in his office two days later at 7:00 A.M. When I arrived, the Rayburn Building was like a morgue, with nobody in the halls. But Mr. Rivers was in his office, and it was obvious from the papers on his desk that he had been there for some time. I have always admired Mr. Rivers; he was vitally interested in national security and always supported the men and women in uniform. That was his life and he was dedicated to it.

We had quite a discussion. He spoke of the difficulty of identifying a VC hidden within the population and of the fact that women and children often helped the VC by planting mines and booby traps, acting as lookouts, picking up weapons, and the like. It was clear that he had a far better than average knowledge of the VC and their tactics. Then, while we were talking about the My Lai operation, he said, in effect, "You know our boys would never do anything like that."

I was somewhat taken aback. This statement could be taken in several different ways. On the one hand, it could imply a tendency to whitewash the investigation or be too lenient; on the other, it could indicate that he thought the information had been falsely reported. I told him that even at this early point in the investigation I was convinced that something had gone drastically wrong in the operation; it had been a bloody affair in which a large number of civilians were killed, which I could not justify. Also, there were strong indications that something was amiss in the reporting system. As far as I was concerned, I said, I had been given a directive, and I could see no course of action other than to execute it as honestly and objectively as I knew how. I expected to examine all sides of the issues and be fair to all concerned: the men, the units, the Army, and the country.

When I left, I felt it had been a good meeting. It was clearer than ever to me that I had an unenviable assignment and that I could do justice to it only be being as impartial and unbiased as possible. Also, our discussion may have influenced Chairman Rivers' views, for certainly the directive he issued to F. Edward Hébert on December 19, 1969, to form a subcommittee to investigate the My Lai incident was forthright, complete, and left no room for vacillation:

. . . Your Subcommittee will examine all pertinent documents and take the testimony of such witnesses as might be necessary to permit you to make a full report to me as soon as possible. Such report should cover the following:

1. What was the nature of the military action on March 16, 1968 at My Lai, South Vietnam, conducted by Company C, Task Force, of the Americal Division?
2. What were the orders under which the said Company was operating on that day?
3. What was the result of the Company's action?
4. Did such action result in the deliberate killing of innocent South Vietnamese civilians by U.S. forces, or the unnecessary destruction of private property?
5. What investigation of the allegations was made by the Army?
6. To what level of command can knowledge of the allegations be traced?
7. Did the investigation conform to the rules and regulations in effect at that time? If not, in what respect was it deficient?
8. At the time of the alleged incident, what were the Rules of Engagement and MACV Directives and Orders with respect to the protection of Vietnamese civilians and property?

9. How and to what extent were the aforesaid Rules and Directives usually enforced during the period of the alleged incident?

All during the investigation we sat on the sidelines of a constitutional dispute between the My Lai Incident Subcommittee of the House Armed Services Committee, on the one hand, and Department of Defense and Department of the Army, on the other. Each had its constitutional responsibilities to discharge, but these responsibilities overlapped somewhat, so perhaps some heated exchanges were inevitable. Staff interviews of witnesses began shortly after the My Lai subcommittee was formed, but it was not until April 15, 1970, that the subcommittee began its formal hearings.

In mid-December we received an informal request through Major General William Becker, chief of the Army Legislative Liaison Division (ALLD), to have several witnesses appear before the subcommittee, some of whom we had not yet questioned. I thought it had been agreed, even if tacitly, that the subcommittee would not question witnesses until after we had done so. I certainly did not want to become embroiled in any argument with the subcommittee; we did not have time and, more importantly, it was not our responsibility. So I asked to General Becker to take it up with the Army Secretary and the Army staff, which he did, and thereafter we were advised by the Secretary's office that it would respond to all such requests, which took the heat off of me and the panel. However, we were still involved to a degree. Although requests for information were normally funneled through ALLD, our administrative officer received periodic calls from subcommittee staff members, which he, of course, had to refer to ALLD for action. In addition, sometimes we were asked directly for lists of prospective witnesses and documents, and again we referred these to the Army Secretary.

In its final report, the HASC subcommittee took the Army Inquiry to task for its alleged lack of cooperation in these matters. The subcommittee had had no time limit on its investigation, whereas we most definitely had, and I could never understand why the matter had become so heated on their part. I do know, however, that we of the Inquiry certainly did not deliberately try to impede the HASC investigation—nor do I think the Army actually did so.

chapter 4

Orientation

In order to put the My Lai incident into greater perspective, it may be helpful to understand something about the command structure, the composition and training of the operative units, tactical operations, and the regulations and directives covering noncombatants during the Vietnamese conflict.

As the commander of the U.S. Military Assistance Command, Vietnam (MACV), General Westmoreland wore several hats. He commanded all U.S. forces (Army, Navy, Air Force, and Marines) and in relation to the U.S. Army, Vietnam (USARV), he retained operational control at MACV headquarters; the administrative and logistical functions of USARV were directed by a deputy. Although General Westmoreland did not directly command Vietnamese or other allied forces, he was able to exert a great deal of influence on their activities through MACV's coordination of the planning and conduct of their operations, the training of their personnel, and the provision of essential supplies and equipment. He was also responsible for assisting in the development of Vietnamese civil-operations and rural-development programs; this function was actually carried out by a civilian deputy with the rank of ambassador, but General Westmoreland was ultimately responsible for the coordination of these activities with military operations.

Because of the multinational character of the allied command in South Vietnam, the fact that enemy forces included both local Vietnamese (Viet Cong) and North Vietnam regular army units, and the requirement to assist the South Vietnamese in civilian as well as military activities, the overall U.S. organization in Vietnam was highly complex. The accompanying chart

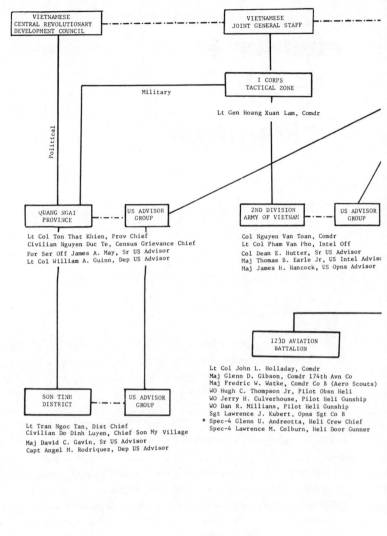

```
┌─────────────────────┐                              ┌─────────────────────┐
│     VIETNAMESE       │                              │     VIETNAMESE       │
│ CENTRAL REVOLUTIONARY│ ─ ─ ─ ─ ─ ─ ─ ─ ─ ─ ─ ─ ─ ─  │ JOINT GENERAL STAFF  │
│  DEVELOPMENT COUNCIL │                              │                      │
└─────────────────────┘                              └─────────────────────┘
```

Military

Political

┌──────────────────┐   ┌──────────────┐   ┌──────────────────┐
│ I CORPS   │
│ TACTICAL ZONE   │
└──────────────────┘

Lt Gen Hoang Xuan Lam, Comdr

┌──────────────┐   ┌──────────────┐
│ QUANG NGAI   │   │ US ADVISOR   │
│ PROVINCE   │─ ─ ─│ GROUP   │
└──────────────┘   └──────────────┘

Lt Col Ton That Khien, Prov Chief
Civilian Nguyen Duc Te, Census Grievance Chief
For Ser Off James A. May, Sr US Advisor
Lt Col William A. Guinn, Dep US Advisor

┌──────────────────┐   ┌──────────────┐
│ 2ND DIVISION   │   │ US ADVISOR   │
│ ARMY OF VIETNAM │─ ─ ─│ GROUP   │
└──────────────────┘   └──────────────┘

Col Nguyen Van Toan, Comdr
Lt Col Pham Van Pho, Intel Off
Col Dean E. Hutter, Sr US Advisor
Maj Thomas B. Earle Jr, US Intel Advisor
Maj James H. Hancock, US Opns Advisor

┌──────────────────┐
│ 123D AVIATION   │
│ BATTALION   │
└──────────────────┘

Lt Col John L. Holladay, Comdr
Maj Glenn D. Gibson, Comdr 174th Avn Co
Maj Fredric W. Watke, Comdr Co B (Aero Scouts)
WO Hugh C. Thompson Jr, Pilot Obsn Heli
WO Jerry H. Culverhouse, Pilot Heli Gunship
WO Dan R. Millians, Pilot Heli Gunship
Sgt Lawrence J. Kubert, Opns Sgt Co B
* Spec-4 Glenn U. Andreotta, Heli Crew Chief
Spec-4 Lawrence M. Colburn, Heli Door Gunner

┌──────────────┐   ┌──────────────┐
│ SON TINH   │   │ US ADVISOR   │
│ DISTRICT   │─ ─ ─│ GROUP   │
└──────────────┘   └──────────────┘

Lt Tran Ngoc Tan, Dist Chief
Civilian Do Dinh Luyen, Chief Son My Village
Maj David C. Gavin, Sr US Advisor
Capt Angel M. Rodriquez, Dep US Advisor

* Deceased

```
Command                      ─────────────────────
Coordination & Cooperation   ─ · ─ · ─ · ─ · ─ · ─
Administration & Logistics   · · · · · · · · · · · ·
```

┌──────────────┐
│ A COMPANY   │
│ 1/3 INFANTRY │
└──────────────┘

Capt William C. Riggs, Comdr

CHAIN OF COMMAND IN RELATION TO MY LAI INCIDENT

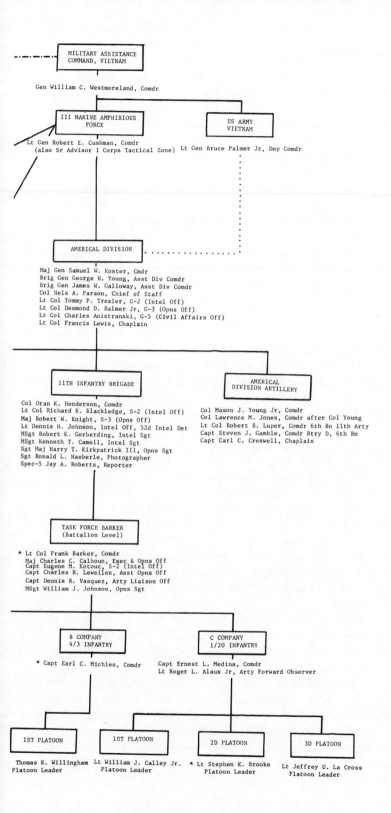

MILITARY ASSISTANCE
COMMAND, VIETNAM

Gen William C. Westmoreland, Comdr

III MARINE AMPHIBIOUS
FORCE

US ARMY
VIETNAM

Lt Gen Robert E. Cushman, Comdr
(also Sr Advisor I Corps Tactical Zone) Lt Gen Bruce Palmer Jr, Dep Comdr

AMERICAL DIVISION

Maj Gen Samuel W. Koster, Cmdr
Brig Gen George H. Young, Asst Div Comdr
Brig Gen James W. Galloway, Asst Div Comdr
Col Nels A. Parson, Chief of Staff
Lt Col Tommy P. Trexler, G-2 (Intel Off)
Lt Col Desmond D. Balmer Jr, G-3 (Opns Off)
Lt Col Charles Anistranski, G-5 (Civil Affairs Off)
Lt Col Francis Lewis, Chaplain

11TH INFANTRY BRIGADE

AMERICAL
DIVISION ARTILLERY

Col Oran K. Henderson, Comdr
Lt Col Richard K. Blackledge, S-2 (Intel Off)
Maj Robert W. Knight, S-3 (Opns Off)
Lt Dennis H. Johnson, Intel Off, 52d Intel Det
MSgt Robert K. Gerberding, Intel Sgt
MSgt Kenneth T. Camell, Intel Sgt
Sgt Maj Harry T. Kirkpatrick III, Opns Sgt
Sgt Ronald L. Haeberle, Photographer
Spec-5 Jay A. Roberts, Reporter

Col Mason J. Young Jr, Comdr
Col Lawrence M. Jones, Comdr after Col Young
Lt Col Robert B. Luper, Comdr 6th Bn 11th Arty
Capt Steven J. Gamble, Comdr Btry D, 6th Bn
Capt Carl C. Creswell, Chaplain

TASK FORCE BARKER
(Battalion Level)

* Lt Col Frank Barker, Comdr
Maj Charles C. Calhoun, Exec & Opns Off
Capt Eugene M. Kotouc, S-2 (Intel Off)
Capt Charles R. Lewellen, Asst Opns Off
Capt Dennis R. Vasquez, Arty Liaison Off
MSgt William J. Johnson, Opns Sgt

B COMPANY
4/3 INFANTRY

C COMPANY
1/20 INFANTRY

* Capt Earl C. Michles, Comdr

Capt Ernest L. Medina, Comdr
Lt Roger L. Alaux Jr, Arty Forward Observer

1ST PLATOON

1ST PLATOON

2D PLATOON

3D PLATOON

Thomas K. Willingham
Platoon Leader

Lt William J. Calley Jr.
Platoon Leader

* Lt Stephen K. Brooks
Platoon Leader

Lt Jeffrey U. La Cross
Platoon Leader

is a simplified representation of the command lines from MACV headquarters through the various echelons down to the platoon level in Task Force Barker. (It depicts only those units and individuals having a direct relationship with the My Lai operation; all others have been omitted.)

The South Vietnamese had two chains of command paralleling that of the U.S. forces. Their military forces were under the command of the Joint General Staff in Saigon. Civil affairs were handled by the province chiefs, who received instructions on political or administrative matters from the Central Revolutionary Development Council, headed by the prime minister, and military guidance from the Corps Tactical Zone commanders. General Robert E. Cushman, commander of the Third Marine Amphibious Force (III MAF), served as the senior advisor to General Hoang Xuan Lam at I Corps. The U.S. advisory groups with the 2nd ARVN Division and at Quang Ngai Province reported directly to III MAF headquarters. The key Vietnamese and U.S. advisory personnel affected by the My Lai incident are also shown on the chart.

It will help to understand the My Lai incident to have some background on the 11th Infantry Brigade. It was activated in Hawaii in 1966 as part of the 6th Infantry Division, with Colonel Oran K. Henderson as its commander. In July 1967, when it was learned that the brigade was to be sent to South Vietnam as a separate light infantry combat brigade, Colonel Henderson was replaced by Brigadier General John H. Hay Jr.; Colonel Henderson remained as deputy commander. General Hay was in turn replaced by Brigadier General Andy Lipscomb, who directed the completion of the brigade's training in Hawaii, prepared it for overseas movement, and accompanied it to South Vietnam in December 1967.

In early September 1967 Colonel Henderson headed a planning group, consisting of some of the unit commanders and brigade staff officers, that visited USARV headquarters, Task Force Oregon (which was later replaced by the Americal Division), and the 3rd Brigade, 4th Infantry Division, at Duc Pho. The visit was considered both informative and profitable in preparing the 11th Brigade for its later deployment. During the trip numerous regulations, directives, and brochures were collected and later used for training within the brigade.

Although the brigade had been quite well trained by mid-1967, many of the men assigned to it had too little time remaining in service to be sent to South Vietnam; thus more than thirteen hundred new replacements were brought in, many of them arriving only a few days before the unit was to leave Hawaii. Even so, it was still short by over seven hundred men when it shipped out. Many of the men hardly knew one another, and there was a lack of cohesion in all the units. Additional confusion and turmoil resulted from a decision to send the brigade to South Vietnam in December 1967 instead of January 1968 as originally planned, which meant cutting the final training period from eight to four weeks. The unit was issued M-16 rifles only about two weeks before it was to leave Hawaii; thus each man had to become familiar with the weapon and be given range practice, which further detracted from unit training. All in all, when the 11th Brigade (consisting of the 3rd Battalion, 1st Infantry; 4th Battalion, 3rd Infantry; and 1st Battalion, 20th Infantry[1]) was finally shipped to South Vietnam it was not a very stable organization and was in a poor state of training.

The brigade arrived at the port of Que Nhon in Binh Dinh Province and from there moved north to Duc Pho in southern part of Quang Ngai Province. The 3rd Brigade, 4th Infantry Division, had been directed to assist in the orientation of the 11th Brigade, and particularly to acquaint its personnel with the area of operations and tactics that had been used successfully there. The orientation period had been scheduled to last for nearly a month, but, because the 3rd Brigade was needed further to the north as soon as possible, it was cut to about a week. To make up somewhat for the shortened training period in Hawaii, MACV granted the 11th Brigade additional training time in South Vietnam to become familiar with airmobile tactics, operations against VC villages, the detection and handling of booby traps, and other pertinent operating techniques. Even so, personnel turmoil, as new replacements arrived, continued to plague the brigade.

It was General Lipscomb's decision to organize a task force to control the eastern portion of the Muscatine Area taken over from the Korean Marine brigade. To create this task force, General Lipscomb took one company from each of his three battalions (reportedly the best companies); Battery D, 6th Battalion, 11th Field Artillery, with four 105-mm. howitzers in lieu of the normal six; and some other smaller detachments to round out the unit. Lieutenant Colonel Frank A. Barker, the brigade operations officer, was selected to command the task force (hence the name Task Force Barker) and was assigned an extremely austere staff to assist him in its operations.

When the 11th Brigade arrived in South Vietnam it was assigned to the Americal Division (officially titled the 23rd Infantry Division), which had been organized with a small headquarters to direct the activities of three attached light infantry brigades. When it was later decided to convert the division to a standard division type of organization, Colonel Henderson again assumed command of the 11th Infantry Brigade, taking over from General Lipscomb on March 15, 1968, the day before the My Lai operation.[2]

---

1. A fourth battalion (4th Battalion, 21st Infantry) was added in November 1967 but remained in Hawaii for training until April 1968.
2. Normally, separate brigades, with their attachments, represent about five to six thousand men and are commanded by brigadier generals. Brigades of a standard infantry division have a strength of approximately three thousand to thirty-five hundred and are commanded by colonels. The brigades are assigned directly to the division; aviation, artillery, engineer, signal, and other elements of the brigades are consolidated under division control and the brigade staffs are reduced in size while the division staff is enlarged. The standard division provides greater flexibility and effectiveness in that it allows the division commander to shift his forces

In the interim between the wars in Korea and South Vietnam the development of the helicopter and airmobile operations occasioned numerous changes in strategic and tactical doctrine and military terminology. The helicopter became a highly versatile vehicle to be used in a wide variety of roles—troop movement, supply and logistics, aerial gunfire, and observation, among others. Strategically, it was used to move large groups of men and equipment over long distances to bring maximum effort to bear quickly. Tactically, it provided a means by which ground forces could be moved into a crucial area with little or no warning. This type of operation, known as an air assault, was normally used by forces from platoon (thirty to fifty men) to battalion (five to six hundred) size and required detailed planning and precise timing in execution.

The first requirements of an air assault are to establish the objective, determine the size and capability of the enemy, designate the friendly forces to be used in the operation, and then—by map, photo, or air reconnaissance—to plot the exact location where the troops are to be landed. This is known as the landing zone, or LZ. (Some of the LZs used by larger formations were later converted to fire bases for artillery or used for other purposes; this was the case with those referred to in the following pages as LZ Dottie and LZ Uptight.) Normally, before the first flight of troop-carrying helicopters is landed, the LZ is thoroughly covered by an artillery preparation to clear it of enemy forces, destroy mines and booby traps, and cause nearby enemy troops to seek cover. The amount of artillery used depends principally upon the strength and location of enemy forces and the size of the LZ.

Before the air assault, the commander of the assault force assembles the commanders or representatives of all units that are to participate to review every aspect of the assault, including such matters as the assignment of helicopters, timing of the artillery prep, and the use of helicopter gunships. Normally the assault-force commander controls the operation from a command helicopter with radio contact to all concerned units so that he can make adjustments if necessary. The artillery prep is scheduled to lift immediately—not more than a minute—before the initial flight of troop-carrying helicopters set down in the LZ. The landing itself requires only four or five seconds, with the helicopter barely touching the ground while the troops get out and move to secure the LZ while other troops are landing. If enemy fire is received during the assault, the LZ is referred to as "hot"; if not, it is designated "cold." The gunships assisting in the assault are used to subdue any enemy forces that oppose the landing. When the LZ has been

---

about as may be required by the tactical situation. When the Americal Division was standardized, the brigade command position was downgraded to colonel. The assignment of colonels to brigade command spots was strictly controlled by division and higher headquarters, and all officers assigned as brigade commanders had outstanding military records. Accordingly, it would appear that in early 1968 Colonel Henderson was in line for possible promotion to brigadier general.

secured and sufficient forces landed, efforts are directed toward the objective area. Upon completion of the operation the troops are often extracted from the field by helicopter, an operation that also requires careful execution to make sure that the final elements to be taken out are not overwhelmed by superior enemy forces.

To meet the needs of the situation in South Vietnam, MACV headquarters published numerous regulations and directives. One group, known in general terms as Rules of Engagement, covered the employment of artillery and mortar fire, air operations, helicopter gunfire, and ground operations, among other matters. In every instance that I am aware of the intent was unquestionable: to minimize noncombatant casualties and prevent the destruction of property. For example, the rule covering ground forces specifically prohibited firing into homes or buildings of any kind unless enemy fire was being received from it. Fire zones were defined in the rules covering artillery fire; a no-fire zone was exactly as stated; a specified-strike zone could be fired into only with the approval of the provincial headquarters, but even with such approval artillery was not to be fired into villages or other areas where noncombatants might be located; free-fire zones were generally located in the remote areas of jungle or mountains and required no prior approval before being fired into, but if it was known or suspected that noncombatants might be present fire was to be withheld. The problem with these and other comparable regulations, however, was that it was difficult to define rules to cover every possible situation and have them understood by all the troops, and it was even more difficult to make sure they were implemented. The constantly changing situation and the rapid rotation of personnel magnified the problem in South Vietnam.

One set of terms that bears discussion concerns the type of operation to be conducted, specifically "search and clear" and "search and destroy."

Search-and-clear operations were analogous to a police roundup. Military forces reinforced with interrogation teams moved through an area or cordoned it off to isolate individuals suspected of being Viet Cong, who were then turned over to the interrogation teams for additional screening and questioning. Such operations were sometimes accompanied by medical teams and other civic-action-oriented personnel to gain the support of the people.

Search-and-destroy operations, despite their name, were never intended to obliterate settlements, but were focused upon enemy base camps, with their stores of weapons, ammunition, other military equipment, and foodstuffs. These were normally located in jungle or mountain areas, although occasionally they were near or even in population centers. In such cases, weapons and other military equipment were removed or destroyed on the spot. Under no circumstances did search-and-destroy missions include the wholesale destruction of dwellings or the killing of noncombatants. However, if the term were used by commanders who did not fully understand it, or who did not explain its meaning to the men in their units, it could lead to misunderstanding.

One term that was badly mangled during the South Vietnam conflict, especially by the news media, was "body count." It certainly was not a new concept; in most battles throughout history a count of enemy and friendly killed in action was made to determine the ratio of casualties. To my knowledge it was done in World War II and the Korean conflict as well as in Vietnam. Generally, the larger ratio favored the victor, but not always, as sometimes it was necessary to sustain casualties in order to seize key objectives. In Vietnam, the news media blew up the daily "body count" out of all proportion and made it sound as though killing VC and members of the North Vietnamese Army was somehow a bad thing. The problem was that, with improper leadership, "body count" could create competition between units, particularly if these statistics were compared like baseball standings and there were no stringent requirements as to how and by whom the counts were to be made.

Most of these terms are not in the *Dictionary of Military Terms,* but one that is to be found there, and that will be referred to many times in this book, is Standing Operating Procedures (SOP). An SOP spells out the ground rules for operations under a wide variety of conditions. Normally, it is quite detailed in its guidelines for subordinate units, covering intelligence, rules of engagement, handling of prisoners and civilians, psychological operations, and other matters. These may be expanded by the addition of annexes; for example—and very relevant to the My Lai operation—Section 10, "Civil Affairs and Civic Action," of the 11th Brigade SOP stated:

General Policies:
1. Maximum effort will be made to minimize noncombatant battle casualties during tactical operations.
2. Troops will be informed of the importance of minimizing civilian casualties and the destruction of property, including livestock.
3. Destruction of dwellings and livestock as a denial measure is the responsibility of GVN authorities, or ARVN military units unless specifically authorized by this headquarters.

There was nothing in the directive establishing our Inquiry requiring us to look into the policies and regulations governing the treatment of noncombatants, but in order to evaluate the adequacy of earlier investigations of My Lai it became necessary for us to review the U.S. national policy and implementing instructions as they related to the My Lai situation. This was covered separately in the Inquiry's final report, the highlights of which are noted in the following paragraphs.

The United States is a signatory to both the Hague and Geneva conventions governing the conduct of warfare between civilized nations. The provisions of these conventions are referred to in a broad sense as the Law of War. We are also party to the unwritten (or customary) Law of War, which is generally well understood and followed by civilized nations. One of the primary objectives of the Law of War is to protect both noncombatants and combatants from unnecessary suffering and to safeguard their fundamental human rights. Each signatory of the 1949 Geneva Convention agreed to enact legislation to provide for appropriate penal penalties against any persons found guilty of committing acts in violation of the Law of War.

The United States specifically recognized the application of the Law of War to the Vietnamese conflict and stated its intention to observe the law. To this end, the Department of Defense issued directives to the military departments spelling out U.S. national obligations under the conventions and requiring them to train all military personnel in these principles.

The Department of the Army developed a series of regulations and training manuals to insure that each individual understood not only the principles of the conventions but his own responsibility to protect prisoners of war and civilian noncombatants. Specifically, during a soldier's initial training he was given one hour of instruction about the meaning of the conventions, the rights of combatants and noncombatants, and his duties and obligations. Thereafter, a refresher training session was given annually to each individual by competent legal officers, and entries were to be made in each man's service record showing that he had received this instruction.

MACV and USARV headquarters were highly sensitive to the requirements to protect noncombatants and prevent the destruction of property. In 1964, well before the introduction of U.S. combat forces into South Vietnam, regulations had been published outlining the individual's duties and obligations under the Law of War. By 1967, a complete body of regulations had been developed covering all aspects of military operations as well as unit and individual training. In addition, this topic was discussed at all senior commander conferences. General Westmoreland's closing comments at such a conference on December 3, 1967, are illustrative: he directed each commander to reduce firing incidents, report all accidents and incidents to MACV, and make sure that all troops understood the rules governing their conduct.

MACV's most pertinent directive regarding war crimes was published in April 1967 as Number 20–4,[3] paragraph 5 of which required any person having knowledge or receiving a report of a war crime to report it to his commanding officer. This was further strengthened by a message to all field units in February 1968 stating that "all known, suspected or alleged war crimes" were to be investigated.[4] MACV also prepared hand cards to be issued to each soldier to carry in his wallet or field jacket as a reminder of

3. Document 4–1: Extracts from MACV Directive 20–4. See page 261.
4. Document 4–2: MACV Message, "Mistreatment of Detainees and PW." See page 263.

his obligations; these included "Nine Rules,"[5] "The Enemy in Your Hands,"[6] and another reminder prepared for all unit commanders.[7]

The Third Marine Amphibious Force implemented the MACV directives and regulations with a series of force orders applicable to all of its subordinate commands, including the American Division. These orders closely paralleled those of MACV and the wording left no doubt as to the intention of controlling firepower and minimizing noncombatant casualties and the destruction of property.

The American Division did not have its own set of regulations at the time it assumed control from Task Force Oregon, so it followed its predecessor's policies and directives until it could formulate and publish a set of its own. The one exception was the SOP published by Division Artillery on December 1, 1967, outlining the procedures for employing artillery. These covered obtaining approval from the proper authorities before firing into an area, maintaining safety procedures, reporting civilian casualties, and other related matters.

On March 16, 1968, the day of the My Lai operation, the American Division published a regulation (525–4) for the control of firepower. Drafts of the document, however, had been reviewed by all subordinate commands well before that date. Among other things, it emphasized the necessity to keep noncombatant casualties to an absolute minimum and required subordinate commands to publish implementing instructions.

While in Hawaii the 11th Brigade had developed a training SOP, presumably based on that of Task Force Oregon, that was applicable to combat in a counterinsurgency environment. It was a well-conceived policy containing numerous references to the protection of civilians and their property, and was still in effect on the day of the My Lai incident.

Another pertinent document of the 11th Brigade was its Regulation 525–1, "Combat Operations, Rules of Engagement," dated January 30, 1968, providing guidance for the application of firepower and reduction of civilian casualties. In one paragraph a very serious error had been made; it stated: "Commanders will exercise utmost care to insure *maximum* noncombatant casualties and property destruction" (italics added). A few days later this obvious error was corrected by a directive substituting "minimum" for "maximum," and Task Force Barker of course received both the original version and its revision. Hence, the task force was doubly aware of brigade's desire to protect civilians and property.

Although all members of the 11th Brigade were supposed to have been issued copies of "Nine Rules" and "The Enemy in Your Hands" upon their arrival in Vietnam, because of an administrative error only about half the

5. Document 4–3: MACV Pocket Card, "Nine Rules." See page 264.
6. Document 4–4: MACV Pocket Card, "The Enemy in Your Hands." See page 264.
7. Document 4–5: MACV Pocket Card, "Guidance for Commanders in Vietnam." See page 266.

number required were immediately available, and it was almost two months before the remainder were distributed. In any case, many of the cards were not read or were lost or discarded. The "Guidance for Commanders in Vietnam" card was widely distributed within the brigade, but it was handled routinely and not given proper emphasis.

The government of South Vietnam encouraged its leaders to work with the people, to expedite redevelopment, and to do everything possible to prevent loss of civilian lives and the destruction of property. Such objectives were included in the joint U.S./South Vietnamese combined campaign plans, which were upgraded and republished each year, and were also included in the combined plans prepared at the Vietnamese corps and U.S. field force levels. But here the problem was one of application; on the Vietnamese side it varied greatly from corps to corps and province to province. Some Vietnamese military and civilian authorities had great concern about the welfare of civilians and did everything possible to assist them. Others were not so sympathetic, which was especially true in VC-controlled areas. For example, in the My Lai area, some of the Vietnamese authorities felt that all civilians were VC sympathizers, were there of their own choice, and should therefore suffer the consequences. Even though U.S. forces had to obtain approval to operate in the My Lai area or to fire artillery into it, it was generally known that the Vietnamese considered it a free-fire zone and thus approval was automatic.

This review of official directives and regulations should make it clear that whatever happened at My Lai, whatever orders were issued by unit commanders before the operation (as we will see, there was considerable disparity in the testimony as to what these actually were), and whatever the problems of enforcement or training, indiscriminate killing or atrocities were in no way sanctioned, explicitly or implicitly, by higher headquarters or U.S. government policy.

This brings us to one of the most serious overall problems in dealing with the tragedy of My Lai, and that is the subject of illegal orders. Very little was said on this subject in regulations and training manuals, and what was said was couched in terms that only a lawyer could understand. On the one hand, a soldier was told not to obey an order that was manifestly illegal, but was provided with only very limited guidance as to what he was to do in such a case. On the other hand, he was instructed that if he disobeyed (or refused to obey) an order it was at his own risk, and he could be subject to disciplinary action if he did so. This left the soldier in a dilemma. A specific problem was: To whom should a soldier report a war crime when his immediate commander was personally involved in the conduct of the crime? Obviously, the entire approach to the problem of illegal orders needed review, clarification, and improvement.

chapter 5

The Setting:
Quang Ngai Province

At the beginning, we had to learn as much as we could about the geography of the My Lai area, place names, and the kinds of military tactics that might be used there. Although few of the panel members knew much about My Lai, I at least was familiar with the terrain. While commanding the 4th Infantry Division in 1967 our 3rd Brigade was operating just south of My Lai under the operational control of the Third Marine Amphibious Force and later under Task Force Oregon. The brigade headquarters was located at Duc Pho, which later became the headquarters of the 11th Infantry Brigade in Quang Ngai Province. Although the 4th Infantry Division did not control the 3rd Brigade's operations, it was responsible for providing administrative support, and so I visited them periodically to see how they were getting along.

I always found these visits most interesting because essentially I was a student of guerrilla and special warfare, and this area of Quang Ngai Province was a Viet Cong stronghold. In the central highlands the 4th Infantry Division was engaged with regular elements of the North Vietnamese Army, which fought in uniform and used tactics similar to those employed by the Japanese in the jungle and mountains of Burma. Our tactics, of course, were designed to counter theirs: offensive operations to find the enemy forces, pin them down, and then use our tremendous firepower to engage them and inflict maximum casualties. There were a few local Viet Cong units in the highlands but they were small and insignificant as a threat.

For the 3rd Brigade in the coastal lowlands of Quang Ngai Province, the situation was nearly the exact opposite. There the enemy forces came mostly from the local population. Some fought in military uniform while others wore the familiar "black pajamas." Some were organized into formalized units, generally up to battalion strength, which would withdraw to the greater safety of the mountains to the west to reorganize and regroup when they were under heavy pressure from U.S., Vietnamese, or Korean units. There were also smaller local-force units of five to ten or perhaps up to thirty men who lived and fought in the vicinity of their hamlets and villages. All the local-force units, regardless of their size, were skilled in the use of booby traps, mines, and camouflage.

When the 3rd Brigade moved into Quang Ngai Province in early 1967, they found it difficult to pin down the enemy. They would be engaged in a fairly good size firefight when suddenly the enemy would disappear into thin air. No matter how long or how carefully the men searched, they could not locate the elusive VC. This went on for some time before the brigade forces discovered the cause. One day one of the soldiers noticed a large hollowed-out tube of dried bamboo sticking up in the middle of a clump of live bamboo. When he dropped a smoke grenade into the tube, three black-pajama-clad VC popped out of a nearby hole. It turned out that there was an underground cavern, about six feet wide, eight feet long, and high enough for a man to squat or kneel, which held from three to eight men. The bamboo tube served as an air vent, and entry was through a trap door that when closed blended perfectly with the surrounding terrain.

With this knowledge, the brigade developed a tactic called "hole hunting." Whenever the enemy disappeared, the brigade forces searched in nearby bamboo clumps for a breathing tube. If they found one, they used a portable smoke generator to pump smoke into the tube, which quickly flushed the enemy out. If they could not locate a breathing tube, they looked for the trap door or used long sharpened sticks to probe the ground to locate the hollowed-out area, which could then be exposed by a bit of digging. These tactics put them on more equal footing with the local forces. Within a few weeks they were able to kill or capture over three hundred VC, initiate some effective civic-action programs, and return many villages to the control of the government of South Vietnam.

But even with this experience and my knowledge of the area, I was as confused as everyone else when, during the Inquiry, we began hearing different names to identify various villages and hamlets. Although we were using the standard U.S. Army maps we soon found that their identifications and terminology did not always coincide with those shown on Vietnamese maps. It was not until we made the trip to South Vietnam in late December 1969 that we were able to clear up the discrepancies.

For military purposes, South Vietnam had been divided into four corps tactical zones, normally referred to as CTZs, with I CTZ in the north and IV CTZ in the south (Map 5–1). I CTZ consisted of five provinces, analogous to small states; Quang Ngai Province, the scene of the My Lai incident,

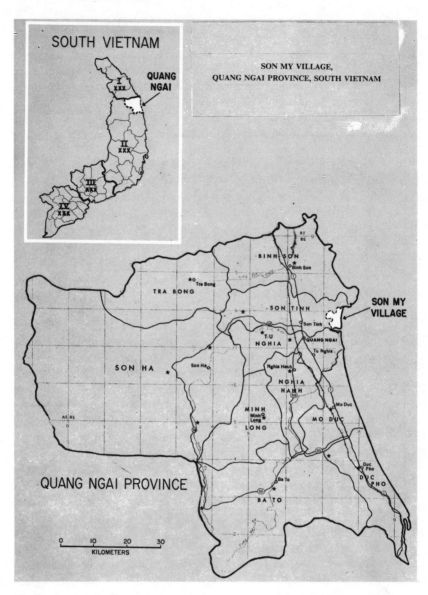

Map 5–1

was the southern most. Each province was further subdivided into districts, of which there were eleven in Quang Ngai. The My Lai incident took place in Son My Village (still another subdivision) in Son Tinh District.

Scenically Quang Ngai Province is a beautiful area. It is bounded on the east by the South China Sea, whose deep blue color contrasts sharply with the white sands of gracefully elongated beaches, which in turn are lined with groves of palm trees. Several large rivers drain the highlands area in the west and run eastward into the South China Sea. Over the centuries the alluvial silt carried by these rivers has created areas of flat delta land. Numerous hills rise out of the delta lands, adding to the beauty of the area. To the west the land rises gradually into a piedmont region of low hills and mountains and finally into the heavily forested mountains of the central highlands.

In earlier times the area now known as Quang Ngai was part of Central Vietnam, called Annam, and was ruled by an emperor with his court in Hue. Its people, although Vietnamese, were somewhat different both physically and culturally from those to the north and to the south. Quang Ngai has a long history of revolt and rebellion. Before World War II it was one of the principal centers of resistance to French rule, and this resistance intensified during the war with France. Ho Chi Minh regarded the capital, Quang Ngai City, as the focal point for the Viet Minh. Duc Pho, farther to the south, became the principal rest and reorganization area for the Viet Minh forces. Although many of these forces moved to North Vietnam after the Geneva Accords in 1954, others remained behind to control both the underground organization and the local population. Many of those who went north were given extensive training in guerrilla and resistance tactics and later were infiltrated back into Quang Ngai to become part of the National Liberation Front (NLF).

The government of South Vietnam's Strategic Hamlet Program of 1962 further alienated the people of Quang Ngai. Throughout South Vietnam many of the smaller settlements were combined, ostensibly to weaken the control of the NLF and to provide a more effective protection. This was accomplished by forcibly moving many villagers from their homes and then destroying the settlements. Not surprisingly, the program proved to be an utter failure, was very costly, and in the end did much more harm than good, especially in areas such as Quang Ngai, where there was a great deal of sympathy with the Communist cause.

When the 11th Infantry Brigade arrived in South Vietnam in December 1967 to become part of the Americal Division it assumed operational control of the southern coastal area of Quang Ngai Province, designated as the 11th Brigade area of operations (Map 5-2), with headquarters at Duc Pho. The southern section of the brigade's area had previously been controlled by elements of the 3rd Brigade, 4th Infantry Division. The 2nd Army of Vietnam (ARVN) Division was responsible for the central portion of the coastal littoral and also conducted operations to the west.

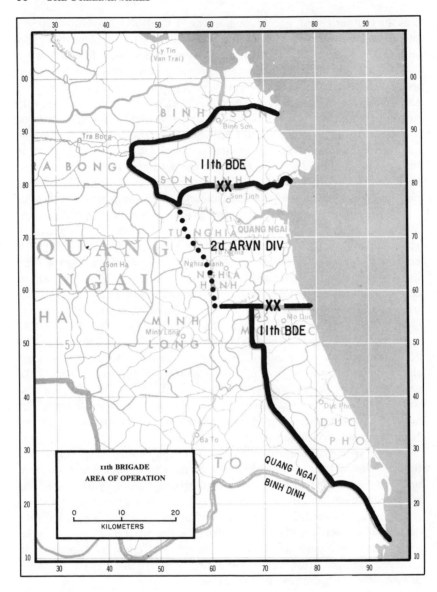

Map 5–2

The Republic of Korea 5th Marine Brigade had been located north of the 2nd ARVN Division in an area known by the code name Muscatine. When the Korean brigade was moved further north, the Muscatine area was assigned to the 11th Brigade. Thus, the 11th Infantry Brigade was responsible not only for a huge geographical area—roughly sixty kilometers long and about fifteen kilometers wide—but it was also physically split by the 2nd ARVN Division. This created a difficult command and control situation for the brigade, along with additional problems of coordinating operations with the 2nd ARVN Division. Since the southern sector of the brigade area of operations was far from "pacified," two of the brigade's three battalions were needed there, leaving only one battalion to deal with the extensive Muscatine area to the north. On top of all this, the brigade arrived at a time when the Americal Division was being reorganized. Taken all together, the difficulties facing the brigade commander assumed immense proportions.

Because of the size of the Muscatine area of operations, Brigadier General Andy Lipscomb, then commander of the 11th Infantry Brigade, decided to bolster it with some additional troops. The 4th Battalion, 3rd Infantry, was assigned responsibility for the western sector, and to meet the requirements in the eastern portion he organized a task force under the command of Lieutenant Colonel Frank Barker (Map 5–3).

In general, Task Force Barker's area of operations consisted of rolling hills extending westward from the South China Sea and the Batangan Peninsula. It was bounded on the north by the 198th Infantry Brigade of the Americal Division and on the south by the 2nd ARVN Division. Highway 1 and the railway formed the boundary on the west, shared with the 4th Battalion, 3rd Infantry. Task force headquarters was located at Landing Zone Dottie, named for Lieutenant Colonel Barker's wife. Normally, two of the rifle companies operated out of LZ Dottie. The task force artillery battery was located to the east at LZ Uptight, and the third infantry company operated out of this landing zone and also provided security for the artillery battery.

The Batangan Peninsula was the most active portion of Task Force Barker's area of operations. Since this area was sparsely populated, the task force staff assumed that most of the Viet Cong came from the coastal area to the south controlled by the 2nd ARVN Division, where the VC 48th Local Force Battalion was based. The task force did not have many engagements with the VC, but when they did the enemy always seemed to slip away, and the commanders felt the VC were using the southern coastal area as a sanctuary. Accordingly, the task force wanted to destroy the 48th Battalion, and on two occasions in February 1968 had requested that the Muscatine area of operations be extended into of the 2nd ARVN Division's area. Both requests were approved. A three-day operation against My Lai-4 and My Lai-1, starting on February 13, resulted in three U.S. soldiers killed in action and fifteen wounded, with eighty VC reported killed; no enemy

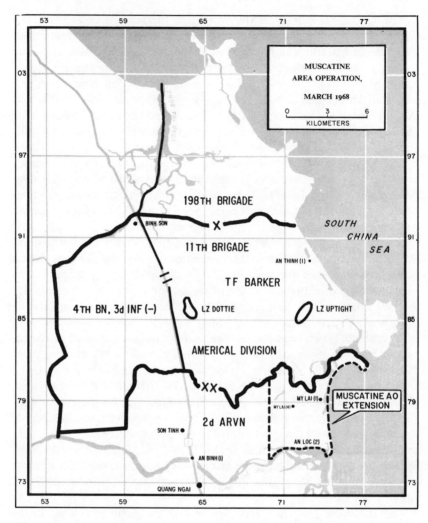

Map 5–3

weapons were captured. As a result of a later operation started on February 23, three U.S. troops were reported killed and twenty-eight wounded, with seventy-five VC killed, one captured, and six weapons seized.

The most difficult problem we encountered in terminology related to the names of the various places within the extension of the Muscatine area, the setting of the Task Force Barker operation that began on March 16, 1968 (Map 5–4).

France had ruled Indo-China, including Vietnam, for over a hundred years, and South Vietnam was still organized and governed through the French canton system. Thus the village of Son My was subdivided into four hamlets. Located in the northeast was the hamlet of My Lai and, moving clockwise, Co Luy, My Khe, and Tu Cung. Each of these hamlets was further divided into subhamlets. Tu Cung Hamlet, for example, contained five subhamlets. Confusion arose, to give just one example, because a subhamlet would be shown on Vietnamese maps as Thuan Yen, referred to by local inhabitants as Xom Lang, and identified on U.S. Army maps as My Lai-4. To compound the misunderstanding, in years past the area of My Lai-1, located to the east of Thuan Yen or My Lai-4, had had a population of several thousand people and had covered a fairly large area. On U.S. maps made by the Corps of Engineers, the area of My Lai-1 was colored pink, and gradually this area and the outlying subhamlets became fused together in the minds of the GIs, who referred to them collectively as Pinkville.

As the Inquiry progressed we found that the events we were concerned with were not limited to the subhamlet of My Lai-4 but also extended into some of the adjacent subhamlets. (For purposes of clarity and uniformity, hereafter only the name My Lai-4 will be used to identify this subhamlet.) We also discovered that Task Force Barker's March 1968 operation had spilled over into the hamlets of My Lai, Co Luy, and My Khe; in fact, they affected nearly all of Son My Village. For this reason, on January 21, 1970, I sent a memorandum to Secretary Resor and General Westmoreland requesting that the scope of the Inquiry be expanded to include all of Son My Village. Approval was received on February 2.

My Lai-4 is only a tiny spot on even the largest map, since it is only about 400 meters wide from east to west and between 150 to 250 meters long from north to south. For several years the population of My Lai-4 had been about four hundred. The residents worked in the surrounding area, which consisted almost entirely of rice fields, each separated by an earthen wall a foot and a half to two feet high and about a foot wide. During the winter months these fields are filled with water from the monsoon rains. In the spring they are laboriously planted by hand with individual rice plants that ripen for harvest in the late summer or early fall, thus producing the rice that is the basis of the Vietnamese diet.

Within the settlement each family has a small plot where it grows vegeta-

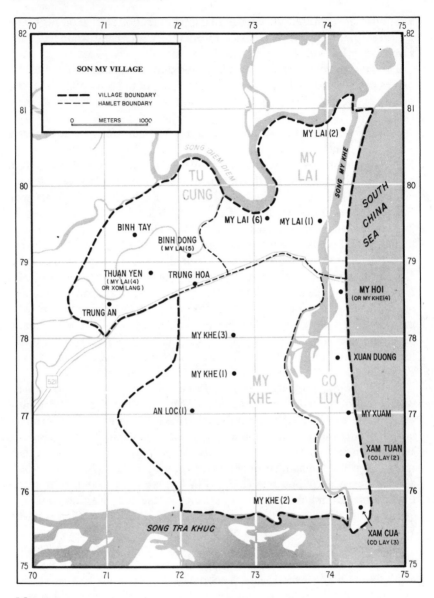

SON MY VILLAGE

- — — — VILLAGE BOUNDARY
- – – – – HAMLET BOUNDARY

0   METERS   1000

SONG DIEM DIEM

TU CUNG

MY LAI

SONG MY KHE

MY LAI (2)

SOUTH CHINA SEA

BINH TAY

MY LAI (6)   MY LAI (1)

BINH DONG
(MY LAI (5))

THUAN YEN
(MY LAI (4)
OR XOM LANG)

TRUNG HOA

MY HOI
(OR MY KHE (4))

TRUNG AN

MY KHE (3)

XUAN DUONG

MY KHE (1)

MY KHE

CO LUY

AN LOC (1)

MY XUAM

XAM TUAN
(CO LAY (2))

MY KHE (2)

XAM CUA
(CO LAY (3))

SONG TRA KHUC

521

Map 5-4

bles, used either to supplement its diet or to trade in the village market. Families tend to be large—six to ten children are not uncommon. In addition, there are many water buffalo and oxen, used to plow the fields, as well as pigs, ducks, chickens, and always a large number of dogs. All these people, animals, and fowl together in such a small area means there is almost continuous activity in every Vietnamese settlement.

part II

The Inquiry

chapter 6

Final Preparations
for the Inquiry

We had a great many issues to consider in relation to calling witnesses and handling the testimony as it was taken. Our directive stipulated that we were to look into the reports and investigations of the My Lai incident but not to concern ourselves with the criminal aspects of it, which meant we would be concentrating on officers and commanders rather than on the men who were actually carrying out the operation. The officers we were going to interrogate were familiar with the plans for the Task Force Barker operation and had a broad knowledge of the action as it had been reported to them. None of them had been physically present on the ground to observe, however, and they had no firsthand knowledge of the activities of the troops, enemy resistance, if any, or other details we needed to know.

So one of our problems was: How were we to determine the adequacy of a report or an investigation of something when we did not know what that something was all about, how it had occurred, who had taken part in it, and what had really happened? It would be like trying to determine the effectiveness of a sports broadcaster without knowing what game he was reporting. Clearly, we would need considerable information concerning the incident itself—not to determine who was at fault or who had committed possible crimes, but so that we would have a basis for judging the quality of reports and investigations and whether or not there had been any attempt to pull a cloak of secrecy over the operation.

It was obvious that in order to obtain this kind of information we would have to talk with the men who had actually participated in the ground action. Even though this might infringe upon the part of our directive specifying that we were not to interfere with the CID's investigation of possible war crimes, it was the only course of action open to us. After lengthy discussions with General Westmoreland and Army General Counsel Robert K. Jordan III, we were given authority to determine the details of the operation and call as witnesses men who been directly involved in it.

Another problem confronting us was whom to call as the first witness. We realized that the testimony of the early witnesses would be somewhat exploratory in nature, but we hoped to gain sufficient background to serve as a basis for future interrogations. Also, we wanted to select somebody within the chain of command who might have been responsible for reporting or possibly investigating the incident, which limited us to only a few people. From the bottom of the chain of command to the top would have included Captain Ernest Medina, the commanding officer of C (Charlie) Company, 1st Batallion, 20th Infantry, the company reported to have committed the atrocity at My Lai-4; Lieutenant Colonel Frank Barker, the overall commander of the task force that conducted the operation; Colonel Oran Henderson, the commander of the 11th Infantry Brigade; and finally Major General Samuel Koster, the commanding general of the Americal Division. Others in positions of responsibility, such as the assistant division commanders, were considered but ruled out as very early witnesses because they had not been in command positions and thus could not be held directly accountable.

The man I would like to have called was Lieutenant Colonel Barker, who would have known a great deal about the operation and any investigations. Unfortunately, he and Captain Earl Michles, who had commanded B (Bravo) Company of the 3rd Batallion, 4th Infantry—another element of Task Force Barker—had been killed in a plane crash a couple of months after the My Lai incident. Considering all this, and recalling Colonel Wilson's experience with several of the candidates during the Inspector General's investigation, we finally selected Colonel Oran Henderson to be the first witness. As commander of the 11th Brigade he was fully informed about the operation—he had, in fact, submitted a report about it that Colonel Wilson had seen, and he had been cooperative during the earlier investigation.

Then we finalized the procedures we would use in interrogating the witnesses. Major Lynn, the court recorder, would first swear in the witness. Then I would explain the purpose, scope, and authority of the Inquiry and point out that the proceedings were confidential, although they might be made public at a later date. Colonel Bob Miller would inform the witness of his rights—essentially, that he could make a sworn statement, in which case his testimony might be used against him in the event of a court martial; he could make an unsworn statement; or he could elect to remain silent. Further, if at any time during the proceedings the witness elected not to give further testimony he could choose to remain silent on the grounds against self-incrimination found in either the Fifth Amendment of the U.S. Constitution or Article 31 of the Uniform Code of Military Justice. After each interrogation I would again remind the witness of the confidential nature of the Inquiry and direct him not to talk with others who were to be called before the Inquiry or discuss his testimony with anyone.

I was to lead off the questioning of each witness. The first part of the interrogation would be purely routine—name, rank, serial number or social security number, station and duty assignment. Then would follow questions to find out where the witness had been and what he was doing on March 16, 1968. Finally, of course, would come questions to determine the witness' involvement in, or knowledge of, the incident. This would serve as a basis for questioning by other members of the panel.

As the work of the Inquiry progressed we became acutely aware of the magnitude of our undertaking. The small number of witnesses we had anticipated calling expanded into the hundreds. Accordingly, we enlarged Major Apici's witness section so it could more effectively contact and handle the prospective witnesses. Five or ten minutes—the time required to inform each witness of the purpose and organization of the Inquiry—may not seem very long, but when multiplied many times it consumes a considerable amount of time. To simplify matters, we assigned this task to the witness section, which decided to have each witness read the introductory remarks and sign a certificate stating that he understood them.[1]

Despite the persuasiveness of Major Apici and his assistant, Specialist-5 Richard F. Machusick, they encountered some resistance and, from some prospective witnesses, outright refusals to testify. With the authority of military law, the Inquiry could direct any person still in the military service to appear, even though he might later elect to remain silent. In the case of those who had left the service, however, we had no authority to require them to appear. This led to some discussions with Bob MacCrate, Jerry Walsh, Bland West, and Colonel Miller as to whether we should convene a Court of Inquiry instead of an investigatory panel. Such courts may be called by any officer having authority to appoint a general court martial, and consist of three or more officers, with the senior one acting as president. They are purely fact-finding bodies to assist the convening authority in determining what further action should be taken, and are often utilized when the matter to be investigated is of grave importance and testimony is expected to be difficult to obtain. The Army rarely makes use of a Court of Inquiry, whereas the Navy does so quite often, as for example with the *Pueblo* incident and accidents involving ships at sea.

The principal advantage of a Court of Inquiry over an investigation is that it has the same authority to summon witnesses to appear as does a court martial, where prospective witnesses who are in military service are simply directed to appear and civilians are served summonses by U.S. marshals.

1. Document 6–1: Purpose of the Inquiry as Read by Witnesses. See page 267.

Our lack of authority to summon civilians was causing us difficulty in obtaining pertinent evidence and that, of course, is why we started checking into alternative ways of proceeding.

But although having this authority would have been helpful, the necessity to designate "parties" (persons whose conduct is subject to inquiry), as required by a Court of Inquiry, would have caused us untold difficulties. Parties are designated by the court (individuals may also request to be so designated) and have the right to be present during all proceedings, to have counsel, and to cross examine other witnesses. Given the huge number of persons involved in the My Lai incident and its aftermath, such a procedure would have turned the Inquiry into a three-ring circus, pure pandemonium. In other respects the conduct of a Court of Inquiry and of an investigation is quite similar. In both, the convening authority, after receiving the findings, can take action against anyone still in the military service suspected of wrongdoing, and the Army can turn over evidence to the U.S. Attorney General to use in prosecuting, through the federal courts, those outside of military jurisdiction.

After discussing all the pros and cons with Army General Counsel Jordan, his deputy, Kenneth Webster, and Major General K. J. Hodson, the Judge Advocate General, we all agreed that having to designate parties was too great a drawback to the Court of Inquiry alternative. Also, our own Inquiry was already under way and any change would have meant considerable loss of time. However, we realized that if there were ever another incident as serious as My Lai a better way would have to be found to insure that all pertinent testimony was obtained so that all those who might be guilty of war crimes could be brought to justice.

It was in mid-January 1970, when we were well into the Inquiry, that Colonel Miller and Bland West brought the statute of limitations to our attention. The crimes we were investigating were generally referred to as military offenses—such things as negligence, dereliction of duty, failure to report, false reporting, and misprision of a felony—for which the statute of limitations was two years. If charges were not filed against a person suspected of committing such a crime within two years after the date on which it was committed, they could not be filed later.

This was crucial to us because on March 16, 1970, the statute of limitations would run out on the My Lai incident. Thus we had only two months to finish the interrogations, complete the documentation, prepare and submit our report, and have charges prepared against anyone whom we suspected had committed military offenses. In short, everything had to be completed by March 15. Then an odd quirk came to light when it suddenly dawned on us that there was a time difference between the United States and South Vietnam: the 15th in the United States would be the 16th in Vietnam. Thus we had to change our target date for completion from the 15th to the 14th.

As the Inquiry progressed, testimony grew to alarming proportions. In typed form, an hour's testimony represented about fifty pages, and many witnesses were on the stand for five or six hours, and some even longer. The workload began to be more than our court reporters could handle, even though they worked night and day. Fortunately, we were assigned additional reporters, which helped considerably. Even so, we never seemed to have enough of them, even when their number increased to sixteen near the end of the Inquiry. Backing up the reporters, we had a disc type of tape recorder to take down everything that was said by each witness.

At the end of the day the reporters would type a draft of the testimony, which was then reviewed by one of the senior officers who had been present during the interrogation of the pertinent witness. After a batch of testimony was reviewed it was retyped and then given to a group of four editors to put into readable form. They often had to replay the recordings many times to make sure the final version was consistent with what had actually been said. It would then go to another group of four captains from the Judge Advocate General's office, who prepared a summary of each witness' testimony.

As the volume of testimony increased the amount of typing and retyping became more than even our augmented staff of reporters could handle. Lieutenant Colonel Charles J. Bauer, a member of the Inquiry, suggested using Magnetic Tape/Selective Typewriters and machine printers, by which means the original draft could be put on tape. Thereafter, changes, deletions, and additions could be made without having the entire testimony retyped. It was a complicated procedure to become familiar with, but it proved to be extremely helpful. We eventually had four machines and eighteen operators working around the clock preparing what turned out to be nearly twenty thousand pages of testimony.

Anyone interested in checking the testimony of a particular witness had a number of options: he could refer to (1) the finished version of the report, (2) the reporter's original draft with editorial markings, or (3) the disc recording. In the process of editing we certainly did not want to alter the witness' stated intent, but it was nevertheless essential to present the testimony in readable form, so some changes were made to this end.

The contradictory nature of some of the testimony gave led us to consider using polygraph (lie detector) tests, as the Army regulation under which we were operating permitted it if all parties agreed to have it entered as evidence. Since we had no respondent, however, this would be difficult. Our legal advisors felt it would be inadvisable and inappropriate for us to use the polygraph. They discussed it with the Army General Counsel and the Judge Advocate General, who also advised against it. Accordingly, I accepted their legal judgment and the polygraph was not used during any phase of the investigation.

But all of that was in the future when we began the formal part of the Inquiry with our first witness, Colonel Oran Henderson.

chapter 7

Colonel Henderson's Testimony

I n his first appearance before the Inquiry, Colonel Oran K. Henderson, who had been the commanding officer of the 11th Infantry Brigade at the time of the My Lai incident, appeared to be quite straightforward and candid. It seemed to me that he was eager to tell his story to get it off his chest. He was told of his rights and advised that he could retain legal counsel, either military or civilian, but he elected not to.

On the afternoon of March 15 Lieutenant Colonel Barker assembled his unit commanders at LZ Dottie to brief them on the operation to be conducted in the My Lai area the following morning. Henderson was aware of the briefing plan, he said, so he flew to LZ Dottie to review the concept of the operation and to have a few words with Barker and his staff and commanders. He reminded them that the former brigade commander, General Lipscomb, had not been pleased with their previous operations, primarily because of their failure to maintain contact and their lack of aggressiveness. So Henderson said he had "made it a point of telling the company commanders that once they made contact with the enemy . . . they were to maintain contact." He didn't mention this in his testimony, but other witnesses later said that Henderson implied that the Viet Cong 48th Local Force Batallion would be present and that this would be their chance to wipe out the batallion once and for all. As I saw it, he had given them a short pep talk to prepare them for the operation; he acknowledged this, but wanted to make it clear to the panel that he had given no orders, nor implied any, that My Lai-4 was to be burned. He had not stayed to hear Barker's briefing to his commanders.

He had intended to observe the heliborne air assault by Captain Medina's unit—Charlie Company—which was to take place starting promptly at 7:30 A.M. on the 16th. However, there were some radio problems with his helicopter and he was late in getting off. With him in the helicopter, in addition to the pilot and co-pilot, were Command Sergeant Major Joseph W. Walsh Jr.; Major Robert W. McKnight, the brigade operations officer; Lieutenant Colonel Robert B. Luper, the commander of the artillery battalion that supported the 11th Brigade; Air Force Lieutenant Colonel William I. Mac-Lachlan, who would coordinate air strikes if it became necessary; and Sergeant Michael C. Adcock, the radio operator.

By the time they arrived in the area of My Lai-4 the artillery preparation had been completed and all the combat elements of Charlie Company were on the ground and proceeding with their attack. Although Henderson did not see the artillery preparation, he said he later talked to Barker and Medina about it and had been assured that all the rounds had landed in the area of the landing zone, that none had landed in the village, and that no white phosphorus rounds (which have an incendiary effect) had been used. In addition, he said, he later asked Lieutenant Colonel Luper to check into the matter, and said that Luper had assured him that none of the rounds had impacted on My Lai-4. (In his testimony, Luper denied that he had ever been asked to make such an investigation.)

They circled the area a few times at about fifteen hundred feet, somewhat above Barker's helicopter, which was also circling so that Barker could direct the operation on the ground. Henderson had radio access to all the units involved in the operation; he could listen to conversations between Barker and Medina on the ground, between Medina and Task Force Barker headquarters at LZ Dottie, and between the helicopter units supporting the operation. He could not monitor them all simultaneously but could switch from station to station, and if he wanted to talk with one of the commanders he could do so. After he heard the pilots of the gunships (known as Sharks) supporting the air assault on My Lai-4 that morning say they had killed a couple of armed VC north of My Lai-4, Henderson descended low enough to see the VC lying in the rice fields. He instructed Barker to recover their weapons, and his helicopter circled at the lower elevation until he saw some of the U.S. forces leave the village to carry out his order.

Then they flew a mile or so to the east to observe the air assault of Bravo Company, commanded by Captain Michles. It was a well-executed operation, Henderson said. The entire company was put safely on the ground in two flights of eight or nine helicopters each, and there did not seem to be any enemy resistance.

Upon returning to the My Lai-4 area Henderson saw a large number of civilians leaving it and the other nearby settlements, moving west along Highway 521 toward Quang Ngai City. He also saw six to eight bodies of what he thought were civilians, some on the road and some in rice paddies. He said he had wanted to land nearby so that he could inspect the bodies but his pilot could not do so because there were too many trees and bushes in the area and because of the slope of the ground.

A little later, three men dressed in black clothing suddenly darted out of the column of civilians and fled into a rice field. Henderson thought they were Viet Cong and directed the aero scout unit to intercept them. An aero scout observation aircraft cornered two of them in a rice paddy with their hands up, and Henderson's helicopter landed nearby. Sergeant Adcock searched them for weapons but found none; then they were taken into the helicopter and told to sit in a corner of the passenger compartment where they could be watched. Henderson said he then flew to LZ Dottie to talk with Barker and have the two VC interrogated by the Military Intelligence detachment.

Major General Koster, the Americal Division commander, arrived in the My Lai area in his command helicopter and flew over and around My Lai-4 a couple of times at an elevation that Henderson estimated to be about two thousand feet. Koster also landed at LZ Dottie, where he conferred with Henderson and Barker, who arrived a few minutes later and gave them a short rundown on the operation; Barker felt things were going quite well. Henderson told Koster about the large number of civilians leaving the My Lai-4 area, the two VC suspects he had apprehended, and the six to eight bodies he had thought were civilians. General Koster told him to "find out how they'd been killed."

Meanwhile, the Military Intelligence men established that the suspects were not VC but ARVN Regional Force soldiers who had been captured by the Viet Cong and held prisoner in My Lai-4. They had no information about the 48th Local Force Battalion. Colonel Henderson was greatly disappointed by this, as he had expected to learn a great deal about the location and activities of the Viet Cong in the area.

After the meeting Henderson again flew over the My Lai area at his normal operating altitude to observe the activities on the ground. He saw some smoke and a few buildings (hootches, he called them) on fire, which greatly concerned him. He contacted Lieutenant Colonel Barker, who said he thought the burning was being done by the squad of Vietnamese National Police that was accompanying Charlie Company on the operation. Henderson told Barker that no matter who was doing it to get it under control. He did not see any additional bodies in or around the village.

As the new brigade commander, he felt obliged to make some official calls on Vietnamese authorities, and flew to Quang Ngai City to keep an eleven o'clock appointment with Colonel Nuyen Van Toan, commander of the 2nd ARVN Division. This courtesy call lasted only about thirty minutes, but they had time to discuss the Task Force Barker operation. Henderson told Colonel Toan that everything was going according to schedule and that he felt quite good about it. He returned to Duc Pho for lunch and in the afternoon flew to the headquarters of the 4th Battalion, 3rd Infantry, which was operating to the west of Task Force Barker.

As he flew from place to place he monitored the radio traffic to keep abreast of the Task Force Barker operation. He knew, for example, that early in the afternoon Charlie Company had begun moving east from My Lai-4 to join up with Bravo Company in the area of My Lai-1. General Koster's admonition concerning civilian casualties had bothered him considerably, he said, and he had been thinking about it during his visits to the other battalions. He returned to LZ Dottie once or twice during the afternoon to confer with Barker about the operation and to try to determine the number of civilian casualties. Barker told him that to the best of his knowledge, twelve to fourteen civilians had been killed. Henderson told the Inquiry: "I directed [Barker] to get me a count by body—by male, female, woman, or child—and exactly how they'd been killed—I wanted to know if they had been killed by artillery, gunships, or small arms fire."

After Henderson returned to his headquarters at Duc Pho, Barker called to tell him that twenty civilians had been killed and that he would get the details. Henderson then telephoned General Koster to give him this information. Although we later learned from other witnesses that Captain Medina had already told the general that twenty to twenty-eight civilians had been killed, Henderson said Koster had been greatly surprised when he called, and had said he wanted to know all the details. Henderson said he passed this message on to Barker, as he wanted Barker to be aware of General Koster's personal interest and concern.

The next morning—Sunday, March 17, 1968—Henderson said, he returned to LZ Dottie, where he met Major Fredric W. Watke, commander of the Aero Scout Company, who told him one of his warrant officers had a story Henderson should hear. The young man, Warrant Officer Hugh Thompson, had been the pilot of the observation helicopter during the preceding day's operation. Henderson found Thompson to be highly emotional and almost in tears; he probably had not seen much combat and was so visibly upset he hardly made sense during their meeting. Henderson told the Inquiry that Thompson had seen a captain (this could only have been Medina, who was the only captain in the My Lai-4 area that day) shooting and killing a woman. Thompson also said that at one point he had landed his helicopter to pick up a group of civilians caught in a crossfire and had had them flown to safety. Thompson told Henderson "there was a lot of wild shooting going on" and "there were bodies all over the place," but he did not mention having seen any large numbers of dead civilians. Thompson did say, however, that he had seen several wounded civilians whom he had marked with smoke grenades, thinking they would be given medical aid. Instead, he said, small teams from Charlie Company had come over, throwing hand grenades and firing M-79 grenade rounds.

Henderson said he recorded Thompson's story in a notebook so that he would be sure of what he had been told. When the Inquiry asked to see the notebook, Henderson said that before leaving South Vietnam he had destroyed all his notebooks, including that one. It seemed incredible to me that he had taken the trouble to keep a set of notebooks—diaries, in effect—and then had destroyed them, but he insisted he had done so, and there was nothing to be done about it.

After talking with Thompson, Henderson immediately flew to Charlie Company's field location. Since the company was on the move, he contacted Captain Medina by radio and arranged to meet him. Henderson and Lieutenant Colonel Blackledge, the brigade intelligence officer, met with Medina while Henderson's helicopter was circling overhead. Henderson recalled the situation most vividly. They were in enemy territory, near an old cemetery, and to keep out of view they lay on the ground behind one of the burial mounds while they talked. The helicopter was making so much noise they practically had to shout in order to hear each other.

Medina told him that, to his knowledge, twenty to twenty-eight civilians had been killed, but he was not sure of the exact figure. Henderson asked for more details, but Medina was unable to supply any. Henderson also asked him about the young woman whom he heard Medina had shot. Medina told him that at one point he had been about two hundred yards south of My Lai-4 checking on some bodies in the rice fields when he found a young woman he thought was dead. As he turned to walk away, he said, out of the corner of his eye he saw her move her arm as if she were going to throw a grenade and he had instinctively whirled and fired a burst of M-16 into her, killing her instantly. Henderson told the panel that although he still had some doubts about the civilian casualties, he had been satisfied with Medina's explanation of the young woman's death. After this discussion he flew to LZ Dottie to confer with Barker again. En route he flew over My Lai-4 once more, observing the area with field glasses, but he said he had not seen any bodies or anything unusual. (If this was true, Henderson must not have been looking too closely. From later testimony we learned that by this time nearly all the buildings in My Lai-4 had been burned or otherwise destroyed, and that just to the east there was a sizable area of raw earth from the graves in which a large number of the civilian casualties had been buried.)

Colonel Henderson said he had remained uncertain as to the number of civilian casualties and had been suspicious of the body count of 128 VC killed in action, thinking that some of them might have been civilians. So when he returned to LZ Dottie that day—the 17th—he directed Barker to have Charlie Company return to My Lai-4 to make another body count and determine not only how many civilians had died but also their ages, sex, and how they had been killed.

Colonel Henderson assumed that his order had been carried out but later that afternoon learned it had been countermanded by General Koster. He flew once more to LZ Dottie, arriving, he said, just as Charlie Company was being returned from the field by helicopter. When the first flight landed, Henderson asked to speak to the men. He told the Inquiry that they were proud—"their heads were high, [they were] standing tall and in good spirits." He asked them as a group if they had seen anything unusual or any unnecessary killings at My Lai-4. No one answered, so he specifically asked four or five of the men, including some noncommissioned officers. Each of them responded with a resolute "No sir." He said he had looked each of them straight in the eye—"gave them the eye ball" as he called it—and since none of them averted their eyes he felt sure they were telling the truth. He told them, "I think you have done a damn fine job, and again I deeply appreciate everything."

Then Henderson went to the tactical operations center to talk to Lieutenant Colonel Barker about General Koster having countermanded his order. Barker was busy elsewhere, however, so instead Henderson spoke with Major Charles Calhoun, the operations officer, who told him that General Koster had not wanted to subject the men to possible mines and booby traps at My Lai-4. Further, the aircraft being used to bring the men back to LZ Dottie would be available that afternoon, but would be tied up for the next two or three days; if Charlie Company didn't leave the field that day they would have to come back on foot. Henderson told the Inquiry that he would not have minded having the troops walk out, but he could understand Koster's rationale.

I asked Henderson if it was normal procedure within the division to countermand an order without discussing it with the brigade commander. He said it was not. Later he discussed the matter with Brigadier General George H. Young, the Americal Division's assistant division commander for operations. Young told him that Barker had told General Koster he could not find Henderson, and Barker did not want the troops to return to the landing zone on foot. Then Koster had said, "Well, go ahead. Go through your extraction, but notify Colonel Henderson that I have approved your plan immediately, as soon as you can get in contact with him."

Henderson was correct in directing Charlie Company to return to My Lai-4 to make a body count of civilian casualties; if Charlie Company or any other unit had returned on the 17th they would have found a large number of bodies. Some of the dead had been removed by relatives and buried the night of the 16th, but it was several days before all of them were buried. Some were moved to family burial grounds a mile or so away but most of them were buried in hastily dug graves about two hundred yeards east of My Lai-4.

However, Henderson's account of the event was later found to be full of holes. Specifically, the order for Charlie Company to return to My Lai-4 and General Koster's countermand occurred on the 16th, not the 17th, and the extraction of Charlie Company did not take place until the 18th.

That evening, Henderson said, he talked with Major Glenn D. Gibson, the commander of the 174th Aviation Company, which was stationed at Duc Pho and provided aviation support to the 11th Brigade, and asked him to "survey all of his pilots that had participated in the operation and to find out from any individual or any pilot if any of them had observed any wild shooting or the killing of noncombatants and to advise me if there was any truth to this. I also informed him what the allegations were." According to Henderson, a day or so later Major Gibson reported that he had talked with all his pilots and had found no evidence that civilians had been killed or that there had been any wild or indiscriminate shooting by members of his unit. (Gibson, in his testimony, said Henderson had not asked him to talk to the pilots and that he had not done so.)

Henderson said he had also been concerned about the small number of weapons captured, six or seven as he recalled, in comparison to the large number—128—of VC reported to have been killed. In the four months the brigade had been in operation the percentage of weapons captured to enemy killed was approximately 75 percent—"some 1200 to 1400 enemy and 1000 to 1100 weapons," Henderson told us. Later in his testimony he indicated his doubts were based upon the system used by Charlie Company in its body count, which "led me to believe that there was possibly some overlap between platoons and competition within platoons, to report anything and everything that they saw whether it was in their area or not. This was my suspicion, not that anything unnatural had occurred and certainly not anything of a nature of an atrocity or a massacre."

When asked why he had done all this checking, and if in fact he had been conducting an investigation, he said no, it had really not been an investigation. Rather, it was a commander's inquiry to see if anything had gone wrong that might require a formal investigation. But, he said, he had found no evidence that would warrant such an investigation. With respect to the twenty to twenty-eight civilians Captain Medina had reported being killed, Henderson said he had already informed General Koster about this, and Lieutenant Colonel Barker was getting the details for Henderson to give to Koster.

When Barker got this information together he put it on a three-by-five-inch card and gave it to Henderson. On the card were listed twenty civilians who had been killed along with their sex, their ages, and the manner of their death. About all that Henderson could tell the Inquiry about this information was that most of the casualties had been caused by artillery fire or fire from the gunships.[1] Henderson said that on March 19 he relayed the information on the card to General Young, and also told Young that Major Gibson had said the helicopter pilots had not seen any indiscriminate

---

1. The killing or even wounding of Vietnamese civilians by artillery fire should have prompted an Artillery Incident Report to USARV headquarters. Similarly, casualties from other sources should have been reported to MACV/USARV by submitting a Serious Incident Report.

shooting. Young told him to report his findings to General Koster.

Henderson met with General Koster on March 20 and gave him the card that Barker had prepared. He also told the general that he could not substantiate Warrant Officer Thompson's allegations of indiscriminate shooting, and that he had accepted Captain Medina's explanation of the killing of the young woman. He said Koster had "let me know in no uncertain terms that this number of civilians [casualties] in an operation like this, regardless of the intensity of fire, was unacceptable." Koster gave him no additional instructions, however, so Henderson had felt that no additional action was necessary on his part.

Through Military History channels the Inquiry had obtained the Combat Action Report of the My Lai operation, dated March 28, 1968, and signed by Lieutenant Colonel Barker.[2] Although it was addressed to the commanding officer, 11th Brigade, Colonel Henderson claimed he had never seen it and had no idea why it had been prepared. He simply could not explain it, he told the panel. Barker's report is most interesting. It makes no mention of civilian casualties, and in light of what actually happened at My Lai-4 the two final paragraphs covering the evacuation of wounded civilians and population control are nothing short of ludicrous.

Then we got down to Henderson's Report of Investigation of April 24, 1968.[3] At the request of Colonel Wilson during the Inspector General's investigation, Henderson had obtained a copy of this report from Vietnam. He had thought it would probably be found in the safe of the intelligence or operations section of the 11th Brigade, where it had been put for safekeeping. After several days and some difficulty it was finally found in the intelligence section and a copy sent to Henderson. This was an unusual place to store such a document. Normally, it would have been kept in the brigade central file, and would have been logged in by title, date, and security classification, which had not been done.

As far as I was concerned, this document did not look like any Report of Investigation I had ever seen before. In the first place, one does not conduct an investigation of one's own unit; rather, a disinterested officer is appointed in writing to direct it and is given the necessary instructions. Additionally, a properly conducted Report of Investigation would include sworn statements from the persons interviewed, which was not the case in this report.

Appended to the report was an unsigned, unidentified "statement" dated April 14, 1968,[4] in reference to a letter from the Son Tinh District chief to the Quang Ngai Province chief about allied forces having killed civilians in

2. Document 7–1: Lt. Col. Barker's Combat Action Report (March 28, 1968). See page 268.
3. Document 7–2: Col. Henderson's Report of Investigation (April 24, 1968). See page 272.
4. It took us over a month to locate an original copy of this statement and to ascertain where it had been prepared and who had signed it. We were never able to find out who had deleted the signature from the copy attached to the report.

Son My Village on March 16, 1968. That letter was *not* appended, but a two-page translation of a propaganda message prepared by the Viet Cong National Liberation Front was. Henderson concluded his report by stating that twenty civilians had inadvertently been killed when caught in preparatory fires and crossfires between U.S. and VC units; that no civilians had been gathered together and shot; and that the Viet Cong broadcast message accusing U.S. forces of killing four to five hundred civilians was obviously propaganda. To rectify the situation he recommended a counterpropaganda campaign against the Viet Cong in Son Tinh District.

The panel wanted to know all about this report. What had prompted its preparation? Did Henderson actually consider it to be a Report of Investigation? Who had typed it? How had it been marked for distribution and how had it been delivered? Where had the copies been filed? Why all the secrecy about it? Where had the enclsoures come from?

In response, Colonel Henderson said that some time about mid-April his intelligence officer, Lieutenant Colonel Blackledge, had brought him a piece of VC propaganda that had been picked up by the 11th Brigade liaison officer in Quang Ngai City. It was in Vietnamese, but Blackledge pointed out that even though the operation was not correctly identified and was placed in the wrong district, the allegations that American troops had killed civilians referred to the My Lai operation. Henderson had Blackledge get it translated by the Military Intelligence detachment, and when it was returned to Henderson the unsigned statement was attached to it.

Since the statement referred to a letter from the Son Tinh District chief to the Quang Ngai Province chief, Henderson first went to see Colonel Nguyen Van Toan, commander of the 2nd ARVN Division, who was usually well informed about everything that went on in the province. Henderson told Colonel Toan he was very concerned about the VC allegations, and offered to make available a battalion of troops from the 11th Brigade to help check into the matter. Henderson said that Toan had refused his offer, saying, "No—this is VC propaganda. There is no truth to this," but that he had directed Lieutenant Colonel Ton That Khien, the Quang Ngai Province chief, to look into it.

Then Henderson, accompanied by Lieutenant Colonel William D. Guinn, deputy senior advisor and senior military advisor to Quang Ngai Province, met with Lieutenant Colonel Khien to discuss the matter. Again, Henderson said, he offered U.S. troops to help the Regional Forces/Popular Forces check into the VC accusations, but Khien, like Colonel Toan, did not think an investigation was necessary. Khien showed Henderson a copy of the letter he had received from Lieutenant Tran Ngoc Tan, the Son Tinh District chief, which had been referred to in the statement attached to Henderson's report. It was based on information given to Tan by the Son My Village chief alleging that U.S. forces had gathered together and killed 470 Vietnamese civilians on March 16, 1968. (Henderson told the panel that he was not given a copy of Lieutenant Tan's letter at that time but later did receive a copy of it.) Khien told Henderson that the village chief did not actually live in the village and reported only those things the Viet Cong told him to report, and that he—Khien—was going to conduct a propaganda campaign to counteract this information. As he left, Henderson told Khien that he wanted to get the facts and would help in any way possible.

The VC propaganda greatly disturbed Henderson, so he sent a copy of it, with an English translation, to the Americal Division by courier. A few days later General Young told him that, in response to the VC propaganda, General Koster wanted Henderson to put his oral report of March 20 in writing. Henderson asked if this meant he was to conduct a formal investigation, but General Young's response had been, no—that "this VC propaganda message had tripped [Koster's] memory here a little bit, and he just wants some backup in the files here in case anything further should develop on the matter. So provide him with a written report."

Using the data he had written in his notebook, Colonel Henderson prepared his Report of Investigation. He did not make any further investigation, but he did talk to Lieutenant Colonel Barker and several others in the task force about the VC propaganda, and they vigorously denied the allegations. He said he had never told anyone to keep quiet about this, but he did tell them he felt it would be best if they kept the matter somewhat confidential, for morale purposes, unless the allegations were substantiated.

The report was typed and signed on April 24, and Henderson himself took it to the division Chief of Staff, Colonel Nels A. Parson. He told the panel that he had not had the report entered into the brigade log because he had felt it was a personal communication between himself and General Koster. He did not know whether or not it had been logged in at division headquarters, but he left a file copy of the report with Sergeant Gerberding, the brigade intelligence sergeant, and assumed that Gerberding would keep it in his safe along with the other classified documents.

Several days after he had submitted his report, Henderson told us, General Young visited him at Duc Pho to tell him that General Koster had seen the report and "was satisfied that this issue was now dropped and that the thing had been put to bed and there was no evidence supporting the allegations."

A week or so after the My Lai operation, Henderson was wounded by a fragment of a grenade thrown by a VC suspect. His leg was in a cast for about three weeks, and because of this he was able to remember quite clearly what he did during that period. He was appreciative of the fact that General Koster had let him retain command of the brigade under those circumstances.

I was eager to find out about the other Report of Investigation Colonel Henderson had mentioned in his testimony to Colonel Wilson during the Inspector General's investigation. When asked about it, Henderson said that on about May 10, 1968, General Young had told him that General Koster had been thinking about the My Lai incident and now wanted a detailed report, in writing—a "formal investigation and report." (This, to any senior Army officer, would mean an investigation in accordance with Army Regulation 15–6: that official orders would be published appointing the investigating officer, sworn testimony would be taken, and an official report would be filed through channels.)

In April 1968 Task Force Barker had been inactivated and Lieutenant Colonel Barker had returned to the brigade as executive officer. Henderson said he appointed Barker as the investigating officer with the concurrence of General Young, but had not issued written orders to this effect because he thought division headquarters would do so. He gave Barker rather detailed verbal instructions, he said, to insure that the investigation would be complete, proper, and formal. After making inquiries, Barker concluded that approximately twenty civilians had been killed in the exchange of fire between VC and U.S. forces. The report, Henderson said, was three or four pages long, and attached to it were sworn, signed statements from fifteen to twenty of the men involved in the incident, including Captain Medina, Captain Michles, and some platoon leaders, pilots, and enlisted men in Bravo and Charlie companies as well as some of the men working in the Task Force Barker operations center. Since the task force had been disbanded and the rifle companies had returned to their parent battalions, Barker had had to visit several units to obtain the statements. Henderson was not certain whether statements from Lieutenant Calley and Warrant Officer Thompson had been included.

In the statements, Henderson said, each man acknowledged that he had been warned of his rights and had participated in the Task Force Barker operation at My Lai. None of them mentioned having witnessed or participated in an atrocity or massacre, and they all said they had not purposefully killed any civilians, nor had they seen anyone else do so. Henderson said he had concurred with Barker's findings because they were consistent with the results of his own personal inquiry, so he endorsed the report, recommending that it be accepted. Three unclassified copies—not even marked "For Official Use Only"—were typed up, and some time in late May he hand-carried all three copies to division and personally delivered them to the division Chief of Staff. No file copy was kept at the 11th Brigade; Henderson could not explain why one hadn't been.

At some later date Henderson discussed this report with General Young, but he said he had never talked about it with General Koster. He assumed it had been accepted by division, but to his knowledge division never returned an approved file copy.

When asked why he had designated Barker to conduct the formal investigation—in effect, to look into the activities of his own men—Henderson said he had thought it was all right because Barker was to investigate a subordinate unit, and—as he had already mentioned—he had cleared this with General Young, who had offered no objections.

Then the Inquiry panel got down to some nitty-gritty questions. Colonel Henderson said he did not think he had seen MACV Regulation 20–4 covering the reporting of war crimes, but he acknowledged that his ignorance of the specifics of the directive did not negate his responsibility to know of any atrocities that might have been committed and to conduct a proper investigation. He was certain that the brigade had a copy of the division Standing Operating Procedures (SOP) and, of course, the brigade had its own SOP. Both of these documents covered the treatment of civilians, handling of prisoners of war, and reporting of casualties. When asked why, in his operations report or by some other means, he had not reported the civilian casualties to higher headquarters, he said he felt those deaths had occurred during the normal conduct of war, in a firefight, and did not necessarily need to be reported. Besides, he said, he had given this information to the division commanding general, which he felt had fulfilled his reporting requirement.[5]

Colonel Henderson was shown the official black-and-white photos taken by Sergeant Ronald D. Haeberle of the 11th Brigade Public Information Office during the My Lai operation. He did not recall having seen them but acknowledged that some of them might have been included in the photo packet prepared for him on his departure from the brigade. As for Haeberle's color photos, he had seen only those which had appeared in the December 5, 1969, issue of *Life* magazine. Any photo showing any kind of atrocity should have been called to his attention by his public information officer, he said, but he had never been shown any of these.

He was fully aware of and supported General Koster's prohibition against deliberately burning Vietnamese houses. During the operation on March 16, he said, he had seen three or four grass hootches (houses) burning in My Lai-4 but had thought it was the result of the firefight in the hamlet. From its review of some of the CID interrogation reports the Inquiry had learned that not only had most of My Lai-4 been destroyed but that on the following day Bravo and Charlie companies had burned out five or six other hamlets. When confronted with this information, Henderson was greatly

5. To my knowledge, other large U.S. units in Vietnam did not function in such a lackadaisical manner. For example, within First Field Forces, which commanded all U.S. combat forces in the Vietnamese II Corps area, the subordinate commanders knew the requirements for reporting as cited in MACV and USARV regulations. They knew that if an artillery round so much as nicked a civilian it was to be reported. Also, all such incidents, regardless of whether they involved Vietnamese or Americans, were to be investigated by a disinterested officer appointed in writing by the division Staff Judge Advocate and an official report filed. These reports were to be analyzed and then forwarded to higher headquarters with appropriate comments and recommendations. This process served the purpose of letting subordinate commanders know that there must be no indiscriminate shooting, and that if there were any, action would be taken against the responsible party.

surprised and found it difficult to believe.

Colonel Henderson voluntarily told the Inquiry that after he had returned to Fort Monroe, Virginia, in 1969 he had spoken by phone to a *Washington Post* reporter who had just talked to Lieutenant Colonel Guinn. Guinn had claimed he was the first person to alert Henderson to the allegations that there had been a massacre in Quang Ngai Province. According to Guinn, he had given Henderson information from a Quang Ngai Census Grievance Committee[6] report alleging that U.S. forces had killed more than a thousand persons in the My Lai area. Henderson denied this to the reporter and then called Guinn himself. Yes, Guinn said, he had given such an informal report to Henderson in Duc Pho two or three weeks after the My Lai operation. Henderson told the Inquiry that this had simply not happened.

Colonel Henderson said he would swear under oath that according to the information available to him after the incident there had been no massacre. But, he said, "I feel that if it did occur, it was the result of some rash acts on the part of, perhaps, members of [Charlie] company and that, perhaps, Captain Medina then seeing that it had occurred, knowing he could not stop the thing once it had already happened—yes, a coverup. A coverup I'm confident was at that level if there was a coverup." Nevertheless, Henderson was a staunch supporter of Medina. He considered him to be an outstanding, aggressive commander and a hard taskmaster to whom he occasionally assigned officers he felt needed educating.

Henderson also maintained that there had never been any collusion between Lieutenant Colonel Barker and members of the task force or brigade staffs, and that there had positively been no collusion or conspiracy between himself and the division staff.

In his testimony to Colonel Wilson during the Inspector General's investigation, Henderson had said that in July 1968 one of his battalions had participated in a joint operation with ARVN troops and Regional Forces/Popular Forces to check into the VC propaganda. Under questioning before the Inquiry, however, he admitted that he had misled Colonel Wilson. They *had* conducted several joint operations with the 2nd ARVN Division, he said, but none for the specific purpose of going into My Lai.

At the end of his first appearance before the Inquiry Henderson was asked if he had anything he would like to add. He gave quite a long dissertation strongly supporting his men and their commanders. Although he acknowledged his responsibilities as commander, he pointed out that there had been many problems demanding his attention during and after the My Lai operation. Even so, he said, he was willing to accept the blame if anything had gone wrong.

---

6. A Vietnamese organization that gathered population data and reported grievances of the people to province headquarters. This will be discussed later in greater detail.

He also told us that he had found it easy to talk to General Young, the assistant deputy commander of the Americal Division, whom he saw nearly every day and whom he had kept fully informed as to the progress of all the investigations. He had, however, found it difficult to talk with General Koster, and although he did not want to be critical, Henderson said, the rule was that when Koster visited the brigade area Henderson was to ignore his presence and go about his business unless Koster specifically asked to see him.

Since Colonel Henderson was our first witness and we were still unfamiliar with the activities surrounding My Lai, we were ill equipped to question his version of what had happened. However, in questioning other witnesses, we realized there were gaps in his testimony; also, others remembered things differently and there were critical differences in the sequence of events. We recalled Henderson four more times, for a total of thirty hours of testimony, in an attempt to reconcile these contradictions. But it seemed to members of the Inquiry that on each subsequent appearance he would bring out something entirely new, which further complicated our efforts. Undoubtedly, much of this was due to the difficulty of remembering things clearly after twenty months, but there may have been other explanations, unknown to members of the Inquiry. Pertinent portions of Colonel Henderson's subsequent testimony will be covered in Chapter II.

chapter 8

Warrant Officer Thompson's Testimony

Our next witness was Warrant Officer Hugh C. Thompson, who had been assigned to B Company, an aero scout unit of the 123rd Aviation Battalion, known as the Warlords. On the morning of March 16, 1968, he was the pilot of the observation helicopter that was part of a three-helicopter aero scout team whose mission was to fly over and around the battle area, often at treetop level, to locate enemy forces, defensive positions, weapons, supply dumps, and the like, and to relay this information to the ground forces. As protection against enemy ground fire, there were two M-60 machine guns on either side of the aircraft, which that day were manned by Thompson's crew chief, Specialist-4 Glenn W. Andreotta, and his gunner, Specialist-4 Lawrence M. Colburn. The other components of the aero scout team were two helicopter gunships—often referred to simply as "guns"—that orbited over and around Thompson to provide additional protection.

I was surprised to learn that Thompson had been piloting an OH-23 observation helicopter, a small aircraft similar to those used to monitor highway traffic in the United States. Although the OH-23 was capable of doing the job, it was considered obsolete, and there were improved observation helicopters that could perform the task much better. In the central highlands we had replaced all OH-23s well over a year earlier. The principal drawback in the case of Thompson's helicopter was its primitive radio communications capability. He could speak directly to his unit operations center, located near the helipad at LZ Dottie, but he could not reach the ground commander he was supporting, the task force commander's helicopter, or his top supporting gunship. Thus in order to pass information to the ground commander (or to any other command network) he had to transmit it to his low gunship, which relayed it to the top gunship, which—finally —could pass it on to the proper party. This baroque process worked in reverse if one of the commanders wanted to contact Thompson. This of course not only delayed the transmission of information but also led to errors and omissions, and certainly eliminated any personal involvement. I have often thought that if Thompson had been able to communicate directly with Captain Medina and Lieutenant Colonel Barker, the course of events in My Lai-4 might have been changed somewhat—not drastically, perhaps, since most of the action in My Lai-4 had occurred before the aero scout team got there, but at least Thompson would have been able to notify the troop commanders, in his own words, of the large groups of dead noncombatants he was seeing in the area.

The supporting gunships were B model UH-1 helicopters, commonly referred to as Hueys, which were still being used extensively throughout South Vietnam. Their principal limitation was their low power and lift capability. Since they were armed with M-60 fixed machine guns and carried a large supply of ammunition as well as pods of 2.75-inch rockets, they were so heavy that they could not take on a full load of fuel, which restricted their flying time to a little over an hour. They could barely lift off the ground —they sort of staggered into the air—and in flight had to maintain a fairly fast air speed in order to remain airborne. Thompson's helicopter could hop from one place to another, but his supporting gunships had to fly about him in circles, generally at low altitudes. And because they had to refuel every hour while Thompson's observation helicopter could fly in excess of two hours, there seemed to be continual changes of gunships. Thompson said he was never sure which gunships were on station with him at any given time.

The initial mission of the aero scout team was to reconnoiter the area south of Highway 521, running generally east-west from the China Sea to Quang Ngai City. (In order to better follow Thompson's testimony, please refer to the accompanying aerial photo of the My Lai-4 area.) They arrived in time to see the artillery preparation—intended to suppress enemy defenses on the landing zone and detonate any mines or booby traps—which started at 7:24 A.M. and ended at 7:29. Within a minute the first of nine helicopters carrying Charlie Company arrived. Thompson remembered the artillery preparation and the helicopter landing zone as being just west of My Lai-4, and he said some of the artillery rounds landed on the western edge of the village. Two helicopter gunships (Sharks) from the 174th Aviation Company supported Charlie Company's landing and placed some suppressive fire on the western side of My Lai-4. The lift helicopters then returned to LZ Dottie to bring the remainder of Charlie Company to My Lai-4.

Shortly after 7:30 Thompson spotted an armed VC running toward a

AERIAL PHOTOGRAPH OF MY LAI-4 AREA

hedgerow just south of Highway 521, and had his door gunners take him under fire. He did not think they hit the VC, however, so he did not report it as an enemy KIA (killed in action).

The aero scout team then flew about two miles to the east, where they observed the landing of Bravo Company, which appeared to be going well. Thompson's team moved farther to the south and then, finding no indication of enemy activity, returned to the My Lai-4 area. On Hill 85, about a mile south of the settlement, Thompson spotted what he thought was a VC mortar position and, through his gunships, reported it to Barker and to his operations center at LZ Dottie. An infantry reaction platoon from the Aero Scout Company located at LZ Dottie was sent to check it out; they did not find the mortar position, but did turn up about forty rounds of 60-mm. mortar ammunition.

Since Charlie Company's landing had been completed, Thompson was given authority to reconnoiter north of Highway 521, where he noted several wounded civilians in the rice fields south of My Lai-4. He had his gunship notify Lieutenant Colonel Barker, expecting that medics from Charlie Company would be sent to give medical assistance. His door gunners dropped a gray-colored smoke grenade near each of the wounded to mark their positions.

Then Thompson was informed that three black-pajama-clad VC had broken from the column of civilians moving west along Highway 521 toward Quang Ngai City, and was directed to intercept them. By maneuvering low and to the front of these men, Thompson was able to stop two of them, who stood with their hands in the air. Soon another helicopter landed nearby to apprehend the suspects. (This, of course, was Colonel Henderson's command helicopter but Thompson did not know it at the time.) Thompson then flew to the helipad at LZ Dottie to refuel.

By nine o'clock he was back in the My Lai-4 area, and saw that all the wounded civilians he had marked with smoke grenades were now dead. This upset him because he was sure he had passed on a request for medical assistance. (Later testimony revealed that, in relaying the information to Barker, Thompson's gunships had referred to the wounded as VC, some of them armed. Although communications problems may have contributed to a misunderstanding, there was no justification for killing these people, whether or not they were Viet Cong.)

Thompson and others of the aero scout team saw one of the Shark gunships making east-west passes, or gun runs, seemingly directed at the people moving along Highway 521. Thompson spotted five to ten dead civilians and a couple of dead water buffalo on the road and in the ditches alongside. He particularly noted that a wounded woman who had been lying in the ditch just south of the road was dead by the time they returned from refueling. (Thompson later identified her in a photograph taken by an Army photographer.) All of this disturbed him greatly. He could not understand why the Sharks were killing innocent civilians.[1]

Thompson then flew to an area about two hundred yeards south of My Lai-4, where he saw a captain (Medina, but Thompson did not know his name) approaching a wounded woman whom the aero scouts had previously marked with a smoke grenade. Thompson said he put his helicopter into a stand-still hover close to the ground, about fifteen to twenty feet away, where he had a clear view of all that went on. According to Thompson and Colburn, one of his door gunners,[2] the captain prodded the young woman a couple of times with his foot and then stepped back and put a burst of M-16 rifle fire into her. This, of course, is quite different from the version of this incident given by Captain Medina to Colonel Henderson, who said that Medina had shot the woman when she made a move as if she were going to throw a grenade. Which account is the true one is impossible to say; the Inquiry did not make a judgment on this issue. In his subsequent court martial, however, Medina was charged with the murder of this woman.

As the aero scout team continued its observation around My Lai-4, the men saw a pile of bodies on the trail leading south out of the hamlet but weren't able to tell exactly how many there were. Not far from there they saw three to five other bodies in a courtyard. In Thompson's judgment, all these dead were civilian noncombatants.

Then, about seventy-five to a hundred yards east of My Lai-4, Thompson noticed an old irrigation ditch in which there were a large number of bodies. He landed nearby to talk with a sergeant who was in charge of a group setting up a defense line east of the ditch, and then walked to the ditch and noted that some of the people, although wounded, were still alive. He asked the sergeant if something couldn't be done for the wounded and was told that the only way to help them was to put them out of their misery. Thompson thought the man must have been joking, but suggested that he do what he could to help them. Thompson himself was not sure, but some of the later witnesses thought he had also talked with a lieutenant at the ditch site. (If so, it would have been Lieutenant Calley. If Thompson did talk to Calley, he couldn't remember what they said. As has already been noted, Calley refused to testify before the Inquiry, so we were unable to determine if in fact he had talked with Thompson.)

Thompson said the ditch was V-shaped, five or six feet across at the top

1. The aero scout team's assumption that these civilians had been killed by the Sharks caused considerable animosity between the two units, and it took some time for the wounds to heal. Actually, while it is true that the Sharks were making east-west firing runs, they were shooting fifty to a hundred yards south of the road at an armed VC, probably the same one Thompson's crew had seen earlier. The VC was killed and his weapon later recovered, accounting for the third and final weapon captured in the operation. As for the dead civilians, they had been killed by an element of Charlie Company while Thompson was refueling. This will be discussed later.
2. Specialist-4 Andreotta, the crew chief and other door gunner on Thompson's helicopter, was killed in a later action in Vietnam.

and three or four feet deep. Bodies were spread along it for fifty to seventy-five feet, and in some places filled the ditch almost to the top. He had no idea as to the number of bodies there were—it could have been fifty, a hundred, a hundred and fifty, or more. All he knew for sure was that a lot of people had been killed.

Thompson returned to his helicopter, and as they lifted off Andreotta reported over the intercom that a sergeant—but not the one to whom Thompson had spoken—was firing into the ditch. Thompson glanced back from the cockpit and saw a soldier with his weapon pointing into the ditch, but he did not see any firing nor could he identify the person or his rank.

The aero scout team could clearly see that a large part of My Lai-4 was burning and being systematically destroyed. Thompson, in particular, was greatly disturbed because of the large number of dead civilians (between one and two hundred by this time) and because his efforts to see that medical aid was given to the wounded were totally ineffective. His emotions, he said, could best be described as a combination of frustration and anger. In this frame of mind, he continued his observation mission.

Some time shortly after ten, he told us, he spotted a group of eight to twelve women and children running toward a bunker about two hundred yards northeast of My Lai-4, followed closely by a group of U.S. soldiers. With the scene at the ditch in mind, Thompson decided to land his helicopter between the advancing troops and the women and children, who by this time had crawled into the bunker. As he left the helicopter to talk to the lieutenant leading the Americans, Thompson told Andreotta and Colburn to cover him "real close." (Thompson testified that he thought the man leading this group was Lieutenant Calley, commander of the 1st Platoon, but in all probability he was confusing this lieutenant with the lieutenant he might have spoken to at the ditch. From subsequent testimony by members of Charlie Company and work by the panel staff in plotting the locations of groups and individuals at specific times, we concluded that it was Lieutenant Steven K. Brooks, commander of the 2nd Platoon, at the bunker site. Since Lieutenant Brooks was later killed in action in Vietnam, we were not able to confirm this.)

Thompson said that when he asked the lieutenant for assistance in getting the women and children to safety, the response had been, "The only way to get them out is with a hand grenade." So, after telling the lieutenant to keep his men where they were, Thompson himself went to the bunker and motioned for the Vietnamese to come out. When they had done so, he radioed for one of his gunships to land nearby. The low gunship, piloted by Warrant Officer Dan R. Millians, picked up about half of the women and children and flew them to safety near Highway 521, south of My Lai-4. The remainder of the group was taken out in a second trip.

Thompson's decision to use one of his gunships to evacuate the civilians is questionable. In that location and landing attitude, if the gunship had been subjected to enemy ground fire it would have had little defense. Also, as has already been noted, it was carrying a heavy load of fixed armament and ammunition, although much of its fuel had been used by that time, which lightened the weight. In all events, it was an extremely dangerous mission, and the crew of the gunship carried it out very skillfully.

Once in the air again, Thompson talked with his door gunners about returning to the ditch to see if anyone there was still alive, and both agreed it would be a good idea. This time Thompson landed somewhat closer to the ditch and removed one of the M-60 machine guns to provide cover for Andreotta and Colburn while they searched for survivors. Walking through, and often on, the bloody and mangled bodies, they found a child of about two who had been shot in the arm but was otherwise in good condition. They removed the child, becoming quite bloodied in the process. There were also some adults who were still alive, but because of the limited space and lift capability of the small observation helicopter, Thompson felt they simply could not take them out. One of the gunners held the child while they flew to the civilian hospital in Quang Ngai City. After leaving the child with the hospital attendants, Thompson returned to LZ Dottie at about 11:00 A.M.

Thompson was reported to have thrown down his helmet in anger and disgust as he got out of the helicopter, and some of the gunship crews were also greatly upset by what they termed "unnecessary killing." Thompson, along with a few gunship crew members, went to see their section leader, Captain Barry C. Lloyd, to whom Thompson expressed his deep concern over what he had seen that morning, as did the others, although perhaps not in such strong terms. Then Thompson, Lloyd, and some of the others went to see Major Fredric Watke, commanding officer of Company B, 123rd Aviation Battalion. Thompson testified that he believed he told Major Watke about everything—the scene at the ditch, the captain killing the young woman, the action at the bunker, and the larger number of dead civilians he had seen—but Watke later testified that he did not recall Thompson mentioning the ditch or the captain shooting the woman. He did remember the other parts of Thompson's statement and his reference to the "needless killing of women, children, and old men." Captain Lloyd and Sergeant Lawrence Kubert, the operations sergeant, generally agreed with Major Watke as to what Thompson had told him, but when they heard such terms as "murder" and "unnecessary killing," they knew that Thompson was very angry and upset. More importantly, whether he had mentioned everything or not, Thompson had leveled serious charges against Charlie Company's operation in My Lai-4, and other crew members had also reported what they had seen to Major Watke. In his testimony, however, Watke said he had felt that they, along with Thompson, had been "over-dramatizing" the situation, and that only about thirty noncombatants had been killed.

For all practical purposes, Thompson's involvement with the My Lai operation ended with his report to Major Watke. That evening after he returned to Chu Lai, the base camp of the Americal Division, Thompson said he filled in his personal flight log indicating his hours of flight and other details, and completed the aircraft log book. He then went to his unit's operations office and wrote out a report of his flight activities, including the details of his observations. This report was never located by the Inquiry, although considerable effort was made to find it.

That evening (March 16), still very depressed and despondent over the events of the day, Thompson went to see the division artillery chaplain, Captain Carl E. Creswell, to unload his grief. Thompson knew Creswell because he was interested in the Episcopal faith and had been receiving instruction for confirmation from the chaplain. After telling him everything he had seen and done during the entire day, Thompson felt greatly relieved. Creswell said he would do what he could and would make a report through chaplains' channels, and suggested that Thompson should take it up through command channels. Actually, Thompson had already done about everything he could do within the bounds of his authority: he had reported verbally to both his section leader and his company commander and had filed a written operational report; it would have been inappropriate for him to take further action at that time. The only other thing he could have done would be to bypass his immediate commanders and report directly to one of the division senior officers or to the division Inspector General.

Thompson said that a day or so later he was at the helipad at LZ Dottie when he was told by Major Watke to report to the Task Force Barker operations center to be questioned by a colonel. He was not certain of the exact day or date, but remembered that it was in the morning. (The Inquiry panel was later able to pin it down to Monday morning, March 18—a day later than Colonel Henderson had recalled.) Thompson did not remember the colonel's name but assumed it was the brigade commander, Colonel Henderson. He was not placed under oath or in any way advised of his rights.

There is considerable divergence between what Thompson testified he told Henderson and what Henderson recalled having heard. Thompson said he related the entire series of events of the morning of March 16. Henderson, however, recalled hearing that a captain had shot a Vietnamese woman and some general statements about wild shooting and unnecessary killing by the troops and helicopter crews. Also, Henderson said the meeting lasted for only a few minutes, while Thompson stated that it had lasted for at least twenty and possibly up to thirty minutes. Thompson remembered that Henderson took notes during the conversation but thought he had used a writing pad rather than a notebook. Moreover, while Henderson's impression of Thompson had been that he was inexperienced in combat and emotionally upset, Thompson felt that by that time he had been quite calm and collected and had given a logical, coherent account. No written statement was prepared and Thompson was not asked to sign anything. He said that in addition to himself and Specialist-4 Colburn, one of the gunship pilots, whose name he could not recall, was also interviewed by Colonel Henderson that day.[3]

When asked if he had ever been interviewed by Lieutenant Colonel Barker or if he had prepared or signed any written statement relating to the events of March 16, Thompson replied that he had not. The interview with Henderson was the last time he was questioned about the My Lai-4 incident, he said, until he was interrogated under oath by Colonel Wilson of the Inspector General's office in mid-1969, over a year later. Thompson remained in Vietnam with the Americal Division until August 1968, when his aircraft crashed as a result of engine failure and he suffered compression fractures of the back. He was evacuated to the U.S. Army hospital in Japan and was later moved to Fort Benning, Georgia, where he stayed until November 1968.

In my view, Warrant Officer Thompson reacted in about the way I would have expected any decent young man caught up in the midst of the My Lai madness to react. He had done everything he felt he could to report what he had seen, and during the operation itself had tried to intercede to stop the indiscriminate killing and help the civilians. During his appearances before the Inquiry he spoke softly but surely, was alert, and showed a keen knowledge of and interest in aviation. He appeared before us three different times, and on each occasion was cooperative in every respect.

Specialist-4 Lawrence M. Colburn, one of Thompson's door gunners, told the panel of essentially the same series of events on the morning of March 16 as related by Thompson, with one important difference. Thompson had said that when he left the helicopter to talk to the lieutenant and get the people out of the bunker he had told his door gunners to cover him. Colburn was a bit more specific: he said Thompson had told them to fire back if the infantry troops fired on the Vietnamese while he was trying to get them out of the bunker. Colburn did not elaborate on this, so it is a matter of conjecture as to what would have happened if the infantry had taken either the people in the bunker or Thompson under fire. Fortunately, this did not happen.

After they had evacuated the child from the ditch and returned to LZ Dottie, Colburn said, Thompson told his crew he was going to see Major Watke. It was obvious to Colburn that he was angry and upset. Colburn did not go with him, but Thompson later told him about the meeting.

Colburn said he and Thompson had gone to the airfield at LZ Dottie to

---

3. It was later determined that the gunship pilot was Warrant Officer Jerry R. Culverhouse. After testifying before the Inquiry, Culverhouse annotated a map showing the locations of between 175 and 230 dead civilians he had seen in the My Lai-4 area.

see Colonel Henderson on the same day, although they were interrogated separately. He thought it had been on the 16th, as he recalled having on the same set of bloodied fatigues. His session was only five to ten minutes long; he was not sworn in, did not make a written statement, and they did not go into much detail. He testified that he had told Henderson of placing smoke grenades near the wounded (a signal that medical help was needed) and later seeing them dead, of the captain shooting the young woman, of evacuating the people from the bunker, of sixty to seventy dead civilians in the ditch, and of taking the child to the hospital. The only thing he didn't tell Henderson, he said, was of the confrontation between Thompson's crew and the ground forces. He said Henderson had seemed interested and had taken notes during the meeting.

Colburn said there had been considerable discussion within the aero scout unit about the My Lai action for a few days, and then it stopped. Nobody had ever told him to keep quiet about the incident, but he knew of no investigation. He was later presented with a decoration for his part in the My Lai operation.

Warrant Officer Dan R. Millians' testimony concerning the incident also closely paralleled Thompson's. Millians, a gunship pilot, had flown in support of Thompson's observation helicopter twice on the 16th—once near the end of the artillery preparation and again beginning at about 10:30 A.M. He saw only one Viet Cong during that time—the one Thompson had ordered him to take under fire; but Millians did not think he had hit the man.

The number of dead civilians he saw had shocked him, he said, as had the number of buildings being burned. He had a good view of it because he and his co-pilot alternated flying, which had given him a chance to observe the ground action. He was certain he had seen at least seventy-five to a hundred bodies, and he identified their locations in about the same areas as had Thompson. While they were flying at an elevation of between 150 and 200 feet he saw an American firing into a ditch that contained, he estimated, fifty to seventy-five bodies. He could see the rounds impacting and someone's head being blown apart. At one point, he said, he told his co-pilot he wished he has his camera with him so he could get a record of some of the things he was seeing. Also, on several occasions he asked the high gunship flying with Thompson to contact the ground forces in an effort to put a stop to the unnecessary killing, but he didn't know if his requests had been transmitted.

It was Millians' gunship that landed to evacuate the Vietnamese at the bunker. He told us how he had landed and, in two flights, lifted these people to safety near Highway 521. He was not sure how many he had taken out —maybe twelve to fourteen. When asked if he thought it had been wise to land a gunship in enemy territory, he could offer no opinion as to whether or not it was a normal procedure. But, as already noted, under the circumstances it was probably the only course of action that could have been taken.

Millians did not go with Thompson when he reported to Major Watke; he could only say he was certain that Thompson had talked with someone but he was not sure of his identity. Millians had never been asked for a statement about the incident nor had he ever been aware that an investigation was being made.

The members of the Inquiry were most favorably impressed with Warrant Officers Thompson and Millians. With few exceptions, this could be said for all the other helicopter pilots we interrogated, officers and warrant officers alike; they were of an extremely high caliber, and the warrant officers in particular were a young, eager, straightforward group. Most of them were only about twenty years old and just out of high school when they entered the Army. They had been put through an intensive course of instruction to qualify as helicopter pilots and then sent off to South Vietnam. They did not know much about the Army, but they were excellent pilots and, above all else, they told it as it was.

chapter 9

Captain Medina's Testimony

Captain Ernest L. Medina, Charlie Company's commander during the My Lai operation, had attracted considerable publicity and had engaged F. Lee Bailey as his lawyer. We had no idea what to expect.

They arrived at the Inquiry with considerable fanfare, meeting with the newspaper and television reporters on their way in. In addition to Bailey, Captain Medina was accompanied by one other civilian lawyer and a military lawyer. Some members of the panel were amused by the fact that Bailey and his assistant were dressed almost identically, almost as though they had decided to wear their uniforms since they were going to a military outing.

Within the Inquiry we always advised the witness if we had any reason to think he might have committed an offense chargeable under military law. Medina was the first such witness, so after he was sworn in and informed of the purpose of the Inquiry and his rights as a witness, Colonel Miller advised him that he was suspected of murdering Vietnamese civilians, disobeying orders and regulations, and misprision (withholding information) of felonies, specifically of murder.

Bailey asked several questions concerning the form of Medina's testimony, his right to confer with counsel, and the availability of a verbatim record. After some sparring he was told he would have the opportunity to review Medina's testimony but that its release would be at the discretion of the Secretary of the Army, and that whenever Medina wished to confer with his counsel he could. He did so often. Aside from the initial questioning, Bailey had only a few interjections, but there was no question as to who was controlling Medina's testimony. It was apparent throughout his appearance that Medina had been well rehearsed.

The questioning started with the orders and instructions Medina had received for the operation. He said the brigade commander had told them that previous failures of Task Force Barker had been due to lack of aggressiveness, not closing rapidly with the enemy, and not securing enemy weapons. The task force commander had informed them that intelligence reports indicated the 48th Local Force Battalion was located in My Lai-4. They were also told that by 7:20 A.M., when the artillery preparation was to start on the proposed landing zone and My Lai-4, all the women and children would have left the village to go to the market in Quang Ngai City or Son Tinh. In addition, the operations officer had gone over the scheme of operation for the various elements of the task force.

Following the briefing, Medina accompanied Barker on a reconnaissance flight by helicopter. They did not fly over My Lai-4 but well to the north of it. Barker pointed out where the artillery preparation was to be placed on the landing zone west of the hamlet and told him what he wanted Charlie Company to do in My Lai-4, which was essentially to burn the village, destroy the livestock, and close the wells. Medina got the impression that the task force had been given permission to do so by either the senior district or senior province U.S. advisor.

After returning to LZ Dottie, Medina assembled all the men of the company and issued his instructions for the operation. Basically, he said, he had given them the same information and instructions he had been given at the briefing and during the aerial reconnaissance. He told them the 48th Local Force Battalion was in My Lai-4, with an estimated strength of 240 to 280; Charlie Company would be outnumbered two to one and should expect heavy contact with the enemy. He emphasized that they should be aggressive and should check all bunkers and positions to prevent any attacks from the rear.

The 1st Platoon, under Lieutenant Calley, would be responsible for the southern part of My Lai-4; Medina told them to move rapidly from the landing zone through the hamlet to drive the VC eastward into the rice paddies. The 2nd Platoon, under Lieutenant Brooks, would conduct a similar operation in the northern portion of the hamlet. Lieutenant La Cross' 3rd Platoon would be held in reserve, to be used as might be needed, and would follow behind the other platoons to complete the destruction of My Lai-4.

The following morning, the first lift, comprised of the 1st Platoon, Medina's command group, and parts of the 2nd Platoon, was picked up by eight or nine helicopters at LZ Dottie. In order to stay out of the line of artillery fire and to deceive the enemy, they flew in a wide sweeping arc to the southwest and then turned east and landed from the south. As they approached My Lai-4, Medina said, he had clearly seen the artillery landing on the hamlet. Later, the gunships accompanying the flight placed suppressive fire on the LZ and the western edge of the My Lai-4. Since he did not hear any enemy fire as the first lift was landing he reported that the LZ was cold, but one of the helicopter pilots broke in and said, "Negative, the LZ is hot. You are receiving fire." This testimony was at variance with the operations log of the Americal Division, which indicated that the landing zone had been cold during the first lift and hot on the second. Medina could not explain this discrepancy; he merely restated that he had reported the LZ cold and a helicopter pilot had reported it hot.

At about this point in the testimony there was a most interesting discussion. When Medina was asked if he had received any instructions as to what to do with the civilian population when the hamlet was burned, he replied, "No sir." He had been told only that there would be no civilians in the hamlet because they would be at the market, and no plans had been made to care for the women and children if they returned. He said, however, that it was normal procedure in such situations to instruct civilians to move directly to the district headquarters. (In this instance it would have been Son Tinh District.)

Medina was asked whether telling his company that the civilians were to be away from the hamlet could have been interpreted by the men to mean that everyone remaining would belong to the 48th Local Force Battalion. Bailey objected strenuously on the ground that this was speculation, so after some discussion and a short recess the question was rephrased and answered as follows:

QUESTION: Captain Medina, in your instructions to your unit and with the circumstances that existed, was there anything which was said which might have incited the members . . . to, say, extra-aggressive actions when they entered the village to the point of committing atrocities?
(The witness conferred with his counsel.)
ANSWER: No, sir. I did not say anything that would indicate to an individual in a proper state of mind . . . that he was to go in and slaughter women and children. Any reference made as to what we might find in My Lai-4 was that of the 48th VC Battalion. The women and children would be gone to the market at 0700 in the morning. I was trying to prepare them mentally and physically to meet a VC main force battalion that outnumbered my people approximately two to one. Now my recollection was of a VC battalion being approximately 250 to 280 men. And I was trying to build their morale up, get them psychologically prepared to go in and do battle with the 48th VC Battalion.

Medina's version of killing the woman in the rice paddy, and the events leading up to it, closely paralleled that given by Colonel Henderson, except that Medina described it in more detail. He said that while they were landing at My Lai-4 and setting up the company command post on the western edge of the hamlet he heard lots of firing and assumed that the first and second platoons were quite heavily engaged with the enemy. Shortly thereafter, he was informed that the gunships had killed a couple of VC whose bodies were lying in the rice paddy north of My Lai-4. He debated with himself whether to send a squad or the entire platoon to recover the weapons; he finally decided that a squad might be pinned down by enemy fire so he sent the 2nd Platoon.

Later he received a radio message from Major Charles C. Calhoun, the task force operations officer, who said there were several VC lying in the rice paddies south of the hamlet and told him in rather strong terms to get somebody down there to recover their weapons. First Medina dispatched an element from the 3rd Platoon, and then decided to check into it himself. He moved his command post to the southwest corner of the hamlet and, accompanied by his radio operator and a couple of other men, moved into the rice paddies. After proceeding about two hundred yards he found the body of a woman, but as he was walking away he caught a movement out of the corner of his eye. He thought the woman was going to throw a hand grenade, and by natural instinct, he said, he whirled and put a burst of M-16 rifle fire into her, killing her instantly.

Then he moved to a point near the trail leading out of the south-central part of the My Lai-4, where he was joined by the remainder of his command group and the mortar platoon. During this move he saw a few bodies lying in the rice paddies. He was told that Private First Class Herbert L. Carter had accidentally shot himself in the foot, so he called in a medical evacuation helicopter to fly Carter to the hospital. Medina saw some more bodies lying on the trail; he estimated that there were about twenty to twenty-four of them and assumed they had been killed in crossfires between U.S. and VC forces. Even though these bodies had been only about twenty-five yards down the trail and in clear view, he had not gone to inspect them and offered no explanation as to why he had not. It was at about this time that Major Calhoun told him a helicopter pilot had reported that innocent civilians were being shot and directed him to make sure this was not being done. Medina sent word to his platoon leaders to instruct their men not to shoot or harm any unarmed civilians.

Eventually the command group entered My Lai-4, moving along a northeast track that left the hamlet on the mideastern edge. Medina said he had seen no bodies during the move. At about 10:30 A.M. a security perimeter was set up to the east and the remainder of Charlie Company had lunch, during which Medina asked his platoon leaders for a report on how many VC had been killed thus far. The reports totaled ninety—the number of enemy killed in action Medina relayed to Task Force Barker. He did not report any civilian casulaties at that time.

During the lunch break Medina was only fifty to seventy-five yards from the ditch containing the large number of dead civilians, and when the company moved to the east he passed even closer to it, but he steadfastly insisted he had no knowledge whatsoever of either the ditch or its contents.

That afternoon, as Charlie Company moved to the east, the 2nd Platoon rounded up about eighty-five civilians. Medina had an interpreter tell the women and children to go to Quang Ngai City, and apprehended the military-age males as VC suspects. Later these men, along with some others who had been taken by Bravo Company, were turned over to a Vietnamese National Police interrogation team that had been flown in from Son Tinh District headquarters. Captain Eugene M. Kotouc, the task force intelligence officer, had come with them to assist in the questioning. While Captain Medina and Captain Michles of Bravo Company were making arrangements for the night defensive positions, they noticed that the National Police were harassing some of the VC suspects. They told the police to stop it, that they did not want any harm done to the prisoners.

While they were at the night bivouac area that afternoon, Major Calhoun radioed to ask Medina how many civilians had been killed. When Medina said he did not know exactly, Calhoun told him to go back to My Lai-4 and get a count—he wanted to know how many women and children had been killed. (Actually, Calhoun was relaying a directive from Colonel Henderson that was somewhat more specific; Henderson wanted to know not only how many had been killed, but also their sex, ages, and how they had died.) Medina said he had objected because of the time—about 3:30 or 4:00 P.M. —and distance involved, and because they were trying to prepare their night defensive position. Major General Koster broke into the radio transmission and, according to Medina, said, "Negative, there is no need to send them back to go through that mess," or words to that effect. Medina said he told Koster that he had seen twenty to twenty-eight dead civilians and had received a reply of "That sounds about right." Medina said he had reported only those he himself had seen since he had received no reports of dead noncombatants from his platoon leaders. In any case, neither then nor at any other time did Charlie Company or any other U.S. unit return to My Lai-4 to make a physical body count.

The night in the bivouac area with Bravo Company was uneventful. Early the next morning Major Calhoun ordered Charlie Company to conduct a sweep operation about four kilometers southward to the Song Tra Khuc River and Bravo Company to conduct a parallel operation along the coast. During Charlie Company's movement south two men of the 1st Platoon were wounded by a mine or booby trap while setting up an observation post on Hill 85 and had to be taken out by helicopter. Charlie Company burned My Khe-3 and My Khe-1, which Medina described as deserted villages. Although they had received a caution from task force headquarters about killing or harming civilians, no one had told them to stop burning dwellings or villages.

Upon reaching the river, Charlie Company conducted a search of My Khe-2, which netted them three VC suspects, one woman and two men. The woman, who was wearing only pajama bottoms, was faking insanity, but when she was given some whiffs from an ammonia capsule she snapped out of it, Medina said. She later proved to be a VC nurse. One more male suspect was captured in a cave, but he refused to talk. Medina seemed to take considerable delight in telling us how he finally made him talk. He put the man against a tree and, with his M-16 rifle, placed a shot about a foot above his head. The suspect still would not talk, so the next round was placed about three inches lower. When he still wouldn't talk, successive shots were lowered until the next round would go through his forehead. As Medina was lining up his sights (he said he would not have shot him—he had the safety on), the suspect decided to talk. He was the VC equivalent of the Quang Ngai Province chief and gave them considerable information, including the fact that the 48th Local Force Battalion was located west of Highway 1. (If true, this would have placed the 48th Battalion quite a distance from My Lai-4 on the day of the incident.)

The following day—March 18—Charlie Company was to return north so that they could be helicoptered back to LZ Dottie. When they reached a point just north of My Lai-1, or Pinkville, Colonel Henderson called Medina to tell him to secure a landing zone so that they could talk in person. This was done. Lieutenant Colonels Blackledge and Luper were with Henderson, Medina said. His report to the panel as to what happened and and what was said on the ground was almost identical to the version given by Henderson.

Later in the afternoon Charlie Company moved to a pick-up zone in the vicinity of My Lai-3 and were returned by helicopter to LZ Dottie. Medina remained until all the men had been taken out. When he arrived at LZ Dottie, Lieutenant Colonel Barker told him that Colonel Henderson had questioned some men from Charlie Company and that a helicopter pilot had made some accusations. At Barker's request, Medina conducted an informal investigation, talking to his platoon leaders and some of the participants, but all denied any wrongdoing. In reporting his findings to Barker he also told him he still thought something might have happened because of the allegations of the helicopter pilot, and suggested that an investigation should be conducted by someone other than himself.

Barker told Medina that he should advise his men not to discuss the My Lai operation since it was being investigated. Medina said that he had done so, but not in a way that implied they should not talk to any investigating officers. Even so, intentionally or not, right there within Charlie Company a form of coverup was initiated.

About this time Lieutenant Brooks told Medina that one of the men in his platoon, Private First Class Michael A. Bernhardt, might be writing to his congressman about the operation, as Bernhardt had done before on rather minor matters. Medina stopped and talked with Bernhardt one evening on the way to the mess hall and suggested it would be best if he did not write his congressman since the matter was being investigated. Medina did not actually say Bernhardt could not but only that it would be best not to.

In concluding his testimony, Captain Medina said:

- He had never made a written, signed statement about the My Lai incident until he was questioned by Colonel Wilson in May 1969.
- He had never been aware that Barker was conducting an investigation.
- He had not prepared an After Action Report and had not been aware of the one prepared by Barker.
- They had received no training in Hawaii on the Geneva Convention, only on how to handle prisoners of war.
- About 60 to 70 percent of the men in Charlie Company were new when the unit was sent to South Vietnam, and their indoctrination after arrival had been minimal.
- He had been aware of the contents of some of the pocket cards issued by MACV headquarters, but copies had not been provided to the men in his company.

Throughout the questioning Medina was adamant in his assertion that he had seen only twenty to twenty-eight noncombatant casualties, which he had reported to Colonel Henderson. At that point in the investigation we had no basis upon which to discredit his testimony, but it did not seem to ring true. When we were able to pinpoint the location of many of the civilian casualties and to question some of the members of the command group as to what they had seen, we became convinced that he had not told us the whole story. As it turned out, what Medina told the Inquiry on this matter was an out-and-out lie, as is revealed in these extracts from his testimony during Colonel Henderson's trial.

QUESTION: Did you, at any time, tell Colonel Henderson that you saw bodies in a group?
ANSWER: No, sir, I did not. I told Colonel Henderson that I saw approximately 20 to 28 bodies. I did not tell him, and I kept the information from him, that the bodies I did see, 25 to 28 were on the northsouth trail, in a group.
QUESTION: Did you at any time tell Colonel Henderson that you saw bodies in a ditch?
ANSWER: No, sir. I did not.
QUESTION: What did you fail or omit to tell Colonel Henderson?
ANSWER: When Colonel Henderson questioned me as to the number of bodies that I saw, I told him 20 to 28. I did not indicate to him that they were in one particular location. When he questioned me about how these bodies may have been killed, I gave him the information as to artillery, gun ship, and small arms fire. At the same time, not wanting to believe myself that my people would have done this, I was trying to convey the same conception to Colonel Henderson, that my people would not do this. I did not tell him of the conversation that I had with my platoon leaders on the evening of the 16th at the night defensive position. I was being questioned by the task force, about approximately how many non-

combatants had been killed, and I was trying to get my platoon leaders. I could not get an answer from them, so I gave Major Calhoun a figure of 20 to 28, at which time the division commander had also monitored the transmission over the radio, and I gave him the same information. So I continued to use this figure that I had seen, the information to give to Colonel Henderson. I did not tell him that in questioning my platoon, my first platoon leader, Lieutenant Calley, would not give me a correct answer. He hemmed and hawed, and failed to give a direct answer. I asked Lieutenant Calley, "Did you see 100, 150, or what?" And he gave me a figure of approximately 50. I did not tell Colonel Henderson that. I questioned the second platoon leader, Lieutenant Brooks, and he gave me a like number, 100 to 150, and I did not give that to Colonel Henderson. And the third platoon leader, La Cross, gave me a figure of 6, and I did not give that figure to Colonel Henderson.

* * *

QUESTION: Did you testify falsely before General Peers as to the number of civilian casualties that you saw?
ANSWER: I was not completely candid with General Peers.
QUESTION: Did you testify falsely?
ANSWER: I answered all his questions. I did not give him all the information I had, sir.

* * *

QUESTION: You deliberately lied to General Peers, when you knew what he was asking for, didn't you?
ANSWER: I wasn't completely candid with him, sir.
QUESTION: And General Peers was asking you questions: "Question: You were in the area, and the men were dispersed, and in your judgment, was it possible that this could have happened, and you would not have known about it at that time? Answer: It is possible that this could happen. I did not see it, but I did hear about it." That is an outright lie, is it not?
ANSWER: I did not see it, but I did hear about it.
QUESTION: Now, you were charged with failure . . . to report it?
ANSWER: Suppression of a felony, I believe.
QUESTION: And that charge was dismissed, was it not?
ANSWER: Yes, sir.
QUESTION: Before Calley's trial?
ANSWER: Yes, sir.
QUESTION: And at the time you came forward and stated that you knew about 106 civilians being killed?
ANSWER: Yes, sir.

chapter 10

More Testimony

Early in the Inquiry we continued to question officers whom we considered to be key witnesses. For the most part, these sessions were exploratory; we were trying to gather as much information as possible about the planning and conduct of the Task Force Barker operation and the subsequent reports or investigations.

Lieutenant Colonel Richard K. Blackledge was the intelligence officer with the 11th Infantry Brigade at the time of the My Lai incident. He told us he did not know much about what was happening on March 16 except for the operational reports citing enemy killed and weapons captured, which were received at the brigade tactical operations center throughout the day. When the figures were added up that night to be sent to division headquarters, they totaled 128 VC killed in action and six weapons captured. Later information from Task Force Barker reduced the number of weapons to three. Blackledge agreed that this was a very small number in relation to the number of enemy reported killed.

As the brigade intelligence officer, Blackledge made frequent visits to Quang Ngai Province headquarters and the 2nd ARVN Division to confer with his counterparts and exchange information about enemy activity; occasionally he was able to pick up some intelligence documents. On one of these visits he received a copy of the translation of a VC radio broadcast and gave it to Colonel Henderson, the brigade commander; he identified it as one of the enclosures to Henderson's April 24 Report of Investigation. Blackledge said he had recognized the magnitude of the accusations made in the VC broadcast, but from what he knew of the My Lai action had had no reason to believe them.

Another document that came to his attention at about the same time was a printed VC propaganda leaflet accusing U.S. troops of atrocities in the My Lai area. A group of children had come to the gate in the barbed-wire fence at Landing Zone Uptight and pushed it through to one of the sentries on duty. Blackledge had not believed its accusations, either, and had processed it as a routine bit of information.

He said he had been greatly pleased and somewhat surprised when, one day during the operation, Colonel Henderson invited him to accompany him on his command visits aboard his helicopter, which had never happened before. He remembered most vividly the visit to Charlie Company and Henderson's talk with Captain Medina. However, even though he was only a few feet from Henderson and Medina, the helicopter orbiting overhead was making so much noise he could hardly hear anything, and the few words he did catch were so garbled he couldn't understand them. At one point both men became most emphatic in their conversation, raising their voices and gesturing with their hands, and later in the helicopter Henderson said he had straightened out Medina, although he did not tell Blackledge what they had been talking about.

As the operations officer of the 11th Brigade, Major Robert W. McKnight accompanied Colonel Henderson in the command helicopter on the morning of March 16, but he said he had been so busy operating the radio to relay Henderson's instructions to Lieutenant Colonel Barker and the aero scout team that he hadn't seen much of what was happening on the ground. He saw the bodies of only five noncombatants but noted that several houses were burning in My Lai-4 and that considerable smoke was billowing up. Although he was aware that it was against division policy to burn dwellings, he said, he had not called it to the Henderson's attention or done anything to have it stopped. Later, while Henderson was conferring with General Koster at LZ Dottie, McKnight talked with Major Calhoun, his counterpart at Task Force Barker, and was given the impression that the operation was going well.

He was familiar with the Lieutenant Colonel Barker's Combat Action Report, but did not know why it had been prepared. He thought it might have been the result of a directive from division headquarters.

He said it was normal practice within the Americal Division for the division commander to be briefed on and personally approve all operations of battalion size or larger, but he was not sure whether General Koster had given his approval to the March 16 operation. He felt sure, however, that Brigadier General Lipscomb and his successor, Colonel Henderson, had been familiar with the plans. He hadn't been present when Henderson talked to the commanders and staff of Task Force Barker at LZ Dottie on the afternoon of the 15th, McKnight said, nor at the briefings given to the unit commanders by Barker and his staff.

McKnight said the brigade had formulated a Standing Operating Procedure while still in Hawaii, and he felt it was adequate and consistent with that of Task Force Oregon, which the Americal Division was using until it could develop its own. Ironically, the Americal Division SOP was published on the very day of the My Lai operation, but McKnight had seen a draft copy before the operation and was familiar with its contents. It specifically prohibited burning dwellings, killing livestock, and using artillery against suspected enemy locations when noncombatants would be endangered.

After the My Lai operation, McKnight had been aware that some kind of investigation was being conducted, but he had not been brought into it, he said, and did not know the details.

Lieutenant Colonel Robert B. Luper commanded the artillery batallion that supported the operations of the 11th Brigade, and one of its batteries provided direct support to Task Force Barker. This battery, commanded by Captain Stephen J. Gamble and located at LZ Uptight, fired the artillery preparation for the combat assualts of both Charlie and Bravo companies on the morning of March 16. Luper testified that he was with Colonel Henderson and Lieutenant Colonel Barker while planning the operation, although he had not been present when Barker issued the orders to his commanders. The artillery preparation for Charlie Company had been planned to impact on the southwest corner of My Lai-4, and the landing zone was to be about a thousand meters southwest of the hamlet. This did not jibe with what Henderson had told us; he had said that Luper had not participated in the planning although, he said, Luper had known the landing zone was to be located immediately west of the hamlet and the artillery preparation was to impact upon the landing zone. When we asked about the advisability of firing artillery into the hamlet, Luper said he had seen no objection since it had been directed by the ground commander and there were to be no civilians in the impact area.

On the morning of the 16th Luper flew with Henderson in the command helicopter. By the time they arrived over the area the artillery preparation had been completed, and he assumed it had landed where planned. When we told him that the artillery preparation had impacted in the landing-zone area, he said that if the location of the artillery preparation had been shifted it would have been done by the ground commander and adjusted by the artillery liaison officer with Task Force Barker. In flying over the My Lai-4 area Luper saw a group of about fifty or more civilians streaming southward out of the hamlet toward Highway 521 and, at about 8:00 A.M., a group of twelve to twenty civilian bodies on the road just south of the hamlet. He heard the report that sixty-nine VC had been killed by artillery, which pleased but did not overly impress him. When asked about such a large number of enemy being killed by artillery, he replied that perhaps the battery had been lucky to have caught them in the open. Since he had received no reports of civilians being killed by artillery even though some of the bodies he had seen were within the area where he thought the artillery was to impact, he decided that these deaths had been caused by other means —possibly by firing from gunships. In any case, from the facts as he had known them at the time, he had not felt that an Artillery Incident Report was necessary.[1] Later, however, he did recall a report at the evening staff briefing that ten to fifteen civilians had been killed by artillery. (No such report was ever submitted to higher headquarters.)

There was a major discrepancy between Henderson and Luper concerning the possibility that civilians had been killed by artillery fire during the incident. Henderson had thought that about 50 percent of the twenty to twenty-eight civilian deaths had been caused by artillery, and he told the Inquiry that he had asked Luper to check into it. Luper emphatically denied that he had received such a request and appeared to be irritated with the Inquiry for even bringing it up. According to him, he and Henderson had never discussed artillery and, more specifically, Henderson had never suggested filing an Artillery Incident Report.

Thus even though there was ample evidence that as many as fifteen civilians had been killed by artillery, no report was ever submitted, and the failure to do so was one of the most glaring examples of command failure following the My Lai operation. Either Colonel Henderson or Lieutenant Colonel Luper could have initiated such a report; if either man had done so, it would have triggered an immediate and proper investigation. Further, since the report would have been submitted through the chain of command to USARV, in all likelihood the true facts of the incident would have been uncovered, and MACV and USARV headquarters, being aware of these facts, would then have been able to take proper disciplinary action at that time.

Luper had not been aware that Henderson had conducted an investigation of the incident. He, along with Blackledge, had been with Henderson when he talked with Medina in the field, and he thought they were discussing the young woman whom Medina had reportedly killed. He did not know Henderson had reported to General Koster that twenty civilians had been killed, nor was he aware of any VC propaganda about the My Lai incident. On the other hand, he said he had not been instructed to suppress information about it.

From the testimony of the senior commanders and staff officers of the 11th Brigade it appeared that they rarely talked with one another, which I found difficult to believe or accept. The 11th Brigade had been taken over from the

---

1. USARV Regulation 525–7 outlines the procedures to be followed when U.S. artillery causes death or injury to friendly military or civilian personnel: Immediately submit an initial report, followed by telephone spot reports; an investigation under the provisions of Army Regulation 15–6; and a final report to be submitted to USARV within fifteen days giving time, place, units involved, casualties, disciplinary action taken, and solatium payments made if Vietnamese were involved.

3rd Brigade, 4th Infantry Division, and I was well familiar with their headquarters; the offices were in a small area, and the officers also lived quite close to each other. In addition, they ate together and probably had a drink together before dinner. Certainly under those circumstances, and with the My Lai operation being reported as the biggest success of the brigade to that date, one would have thought it would have been the central topic of discussion, but everyone claimed they had not talked about it.

During the next few days we questioned several witnesses from Task Force Barker who provided us with considerable information as to how the operation had been planned and some of the details of its execution. We continued to be confronted with numerous contradictions in testimony. Some of these were minor, but others had serious implications and might have been part of an overall effort to suppress information.

One of the most serious problems we encountered was the loss of memory on the part of many witnesses. This was understandable, because it had been over twenty months since the operation had taken place and many of the events had become confused with other operations. In a short while, however, the panel knew so much about the My Lai incident that an interrogator could remind a witness of what he had been doing—without, of course, trying to put words into anyone's mouth. Even so, when a witness said "I just don't remember" it effectively served to terminate that portion of his testimony.

Aside from Lieutenant Colonel Barker (who, as has already been noted, was killed in action not long after the My Lai operation), the person who knew most about Task Force Barker activities was Major Charles C. Calhoun, who had served in the dual capacity of task force operations officer and executive officer, the number-two man. We talked with him three times, and he was able to fill in some of the gaps in the testimony of previous witnesses.

Calhoun explained that he did not know too much about the planning for the operation because he had been in Saigon for a week on in-country leave and did not return until two or three days before it was to start. He told us that Lieutenant Colonel Barker and Captain Eugene M. Kotouc, the task force intelligence officer, had picked up information from several places that the 48th Local Force Battalion had returned from the mountains to the west and was now in the My Lai area. He was not sure if the Americal Division headquarters had been aware of the plans for the operation, but he felt certain that the 11th Brigade had been familiar with them. He assumed that the brigade had obtained approval of the extension of the area of operations into the 2nd ARVN Division area, as they had done in previous operations.

When the company commanders and the task force staff were assembled on the afternoon of March 15, Colonel Henderson gave them a brief talk about what to expect of the operation. This was followed by Kotouc's intelligence briefing, during which he said that the 48th Local Force Battalion was probably back in the My Lai area and that all the women and children would have left My Lai-4 by 7:00 A.M. to go to the market in Quang Ngai City. Then Calhoun outlined the concept of operations, based upon the plan that had been developed by Barker, which called for the operation to last two or three days. Calhoun said he had been specific about the actions to be taken by each company on the first day, but subsequent activities had been left open so that they could be adjusted to the situation. During the briefings, he said, he neither gave nor heard any instructions to burn the hamlet or kill the livestock, and it was not called a search-and-destroy type of mission.

After his briefing, Calhoun said, Barker took the company commanders on a reconnaissance flight, but since Calhoun did not accompany them he did not know if Barker had given them any additional orders. Calhoun had agreed with Barker's decision to locate the landing zone three to five hundred meters west of My Lai-4 and to have the artillery preparation impact on the LZ as well as on the western edge of the hamlet. The gunships accompanying the lift helicopters were also to place suppressive fire on the western part of the hamlet, which Calhoun had felt was necessary because of the presence of the 48th Local Force Battalion and was permissible because there would be no civilians in the village.

Calhoun was in the task force tactical operations center during the initial part of the operation directing activities there while Barker controlled the operation from his command helicopter. The operations sergeant handled most of the radio traffic but Calhoun heard some of the reports coming in from the field units and had been aware of reports of enemy casualties from both ground and helicopter units. The task force operations log had an 8:40 A.M. entry from Charlie Company that "elements counted 69 VC KIA as a result of artillery fire"; Calhoun did not recall receiving such a report so early in the day and could not explain the entry. He thought the total figure of ninety enemy killed had come from Charlie Company only after they had reached their night defensive position. He had also been told that throughout the morning there had been considerable radio traffic, particularly between helicopter units, indicating that civilians were being killed. He had not heard any of this himself, he said, because in his capacity as both executive and operations officer he had frequently been out of the operations center checking on the activities at LZ Dottie.

At about 11:30 A.M., Calhoun said, Barker returned to LZ Dottie and asked him if he would like to fly over the area. He did so, but since they were at an altitude of fifteen hundred feet most of the time he could not see much of the ground action in My Lai-4. He did not see any bodies but he did see some smoke coming from the hamlet. While airborne, Calhoun received a radio call from Barker, who told him to pass instructions on to Captain Medina to "get control of his unit" and to make sure that no civilians were being harmed and that the hamlet was not being burned. Calhoun said he did this and received a "roger" (transmission understood) from Medina. At the time he did not know the reason for this order, but after he returned to LZ Dottie Barker told him that Major Watke, commander of the Aero Scout Company had reported that some of his pilots had observed a woman being shot, other civilians being harmed, and some buildings being burned. Barker told Calhoun he suspected that some civilians had been killed by artillery.

At about 3:30 that afternoon Calhoun was in the task force operations center with Barker when they received a call from brigade directing Charlie Company to return to My Lai-4 to determine not only the number of civilians killed, but also their age, sex, and how they had died—whether by artillery, gunships, small arms, or other means. When Calhoun contacted Medina to give him these instructions Medina told him he knew twenty to thirty civilians had been killed, mostly by artillery fire,[2] and that he objected to returning to My Lai-4 because it was getting late and he would have to re-form his company and go back three or four thousand yards. Major General Koster, who was monitoring the conversation, broke in to say he did not want the company to return to the hamlet. That ended it, Calhoun said, and he notified brigade of Koster's action to countermand the order.

After the operation was completed Calhoun had not been aware of any investigation, he said, except the informal one that Barker told him was being conducted by Colonel Henderson. The only suspicious activity he knew about was the helicopter pilot's report that an American had shot a Vietnamese woman.

Although Major Calhoun was a useful witness and helped close many information gaps, he was also somewhat of an enigma. Every time he was asked to respond to a key question he would say that he had been flying too high to see anything, he had never heard of it, or he did not remember. This just did not ring true to us; he was too fine an officer not to have known what was going on within that small task force headquarters, and we could not understand it.

Captain Eugene M. Kotouc, Task Force Barker's intelligence officer, was accompanied by military legal counsel when he appeared before the Inquiry, which surprised us somewhat because at that time we had no reason to suspect him of any wrongdoing. He confirmed much of what Major Calhoun had said, but there was one important difference. Kotouc remembered clearly that Barker had issued instructions not only to burn the hamlet but also to destroy the defensive positions and kill or run off the livestock. He said there had been no mention of polluting the wells, nor of how to handle civilians, but he felt the task force policy for collecting and

---

2. This information was never entered into the task force log nor was it transmitted to the brigade tactical operations center.

moving civilians to safe areas had been understood by everyone.

He also provided us with some insight into some of the events at LZ Dottie. Kotouc assisted Barker in presenting the intelligence briefing to the commanders, during which he told them to expect strong enemy resistance —something like two hundred VC of the 48th Local Force Battalion. However, he said, he had been talking about the entire Pinkville area, not just My Lai-4. He also told them that the civilians would have left My Lai-4 by 7:00 A.M. to go to the market in Son Tinh. Even so, during the briefing on the artillery preparation some thought had been given to any Vietnamese who might remain in the village, because they had wanted to keep civilian casualties to a minimum.

Kotouc was present during Medina's briefing to the entire company. Medina reviewed past events and discussed the problems with minefields and the fact that they had not yet really engaged the enemy. He also told them about the presence of the Viet Cong battalion and the absence of civilians, and emphasized that they could expect to encounter strong enemy resistance immediately upon landing. He illustrated his talk by using the point of a shovel to outline the operation in the dirt and to mark important locations. Someone asked about the Rules of Land Warfare, Kotouc said, and Medina responded by telling the men to "do what was right." Although Medina had said nothing specific about how to deal with civilians, Kotouc told us, he had certainly not said anything about killing them. Kotouc noted that during and after the briefing the men seemed to be nervous, punching one another and shaking their heads; he felt they were definitely keyed up in anticipation of the coming action. He told us he thought it was possible that the men, being so worked up and thinking no civilians would be in the area, might kill anything in sight.

When Bravo and Charlie companies reached their night defensive position on the afternoon of March 16, Kotouc and his interpreter flew out to the area, along with some National Police who were going to question some VC suspects who had been apprehended. He said he talked with Medina about civilian casualties, because he had heard the conversation over the radio about Charlie Company returning to My Lai-4 to make a more precise body count. Medina explained that General Koster had told him not to do so. There were about twenty to twenty-five dead civilians, Medina said, but they were pretty badly shot up and he had not wanted to start picking them up and counting them. Medina had seemed quite distressed about shooting the woman, however, because he felt it had been a mistake.

Kotouc also told us that there were between thirty and fifty Vietnamese men, under guard, being questioned by the National Police who had come with him on his helicopter flight, and he said he talked to a few of them. When we asked him who controlled the National Police, he replied that normally they took their orders from senior ARVN officers, but he was not sure who controlled them when they were working with or under a U.S. unit.

In concluding his testimony Captain Kotouc said that Lieutenant Colonel Barker had been a strong leader and that the task force had been pretty much a one-man show. He had not been aware of any investigations and had not been asked by Barker to assist in preparing an After Action Report. He felt that Task Force Barker had been a fine outfit, and found it hard to believe the allegations being made against it; there was no coverup that he knew about, he said, but if there were one, it was probably in Saigon.

Captain Charles R. Lewellen, assistant operations officer for the task force, had been the night duty officer on March 15–16, and when he was relieved on the morning of the 16th he stayed in the operations center to tape-record the operation on the task force command radio net. He explained that he had been in Vietnam before with another combat infantry brigade and had taped some of the action. Upon returning to the United States he had found some of these combat tapes to be excellent training aids for others who were being sent to Vietnam, so he had continued the practice on his second tour of duty. He made the Task Force Barker tapes available to the Inquiry, but aside from confirming a few points in various witnesses' testimony and helping to establish the time sequence, they did not reveal any new information.

Lewellen was so busy listening to and taping the radio traffic that he actually knew very little about the operation as such. He did recall, however, the 8:29 A.M. report of eighty-four VC killed in action. He had not considered the ten or eleven civilians reportedly killed by Bravo Company to be unusual, which may be a reflection of Task Force Barker's somewhat callous attitude with respect to civilian casualties. Noncombatants, including women and children, were routinely included in body counts, since at times they fired back at the U.S. forces. Lewellen had heard nothing about any other civilian casualties, and had no knowledge of the rest of the operation or its aftermath.

Master Sergeant William J. Johnson was one of our strangest witnesses. As the operations sergeant for Task Force Barker, he was at the focal point for handling all the reports coming in from Lieutenant Colonel Barker's command helicopter and from the three rifle companies, and was also responsible for maintaining the operations log and relaying pertinent data to the 11th Brigade. He was assisted by an operations clerk, but it was he who was responsible. Of all the people in the task force operations center on March 16 he should have been the most knowledgeable, and we were eager to hear his testimony.

But it was for nought: he told us absolutely nothing during his appearance before the Inquiry. To every question on such matters as the task force briefing, the report of the sixty-nine VC killed by artillery, and the differences between the task force and 11th Brigade logs, he replied, "I just don't remember" or "I'm trying to run it back in my mind." I pointed out to him that he was a senior sergeant with extensive experience and holding down a highly responsible position as the operations sergeant of the School Brigade of the Infantry School at Fort Benning, Georgia, and might be expected to have a better memory than he was displaying at the Inquiry. His response was a classic: "I've tried, sir. I've put this thing over in my mind. In fact it is going around right now." He either had the worst of all memories or was covering up. His responses were so evasive that I began to wonder if he were pulling my leg.

We recalled him in early February 1970, hoping that his memory might have improved. It had not. Before his testimony, Lieutenant Colonel Fred Mahaffey of our staff went over with him, item by item, the entries in the Task Force Barker and 11th Brigade logs, as well as the transcript of the tape made by Captain Lewellen. It did not affect his memory one iota. Mr. MacCrate, Colonel Franklin, Lieutenant Colonel Bauer, and others questioned him, using varying approaches, but to no avail. In closing he thanked us for our hospitality and said, "I wish that God speeds you all."

Captain Dennis R. Vasquez, the task force artillery liaison officer, said he was with Lieutenant Colonel Barker in the command helicopter on the morning of March 16. He was in radio contact with the artillery firing battery at LZ Uptight and adjusted the original marking round from about a thousand meters northeast of My Lai-4 in one shift to the area of the LZ just west of the hamlet. (This was somewhat unusual, as it normally takes several rounds to adjust on the center of impact before firing for effect.) He recalled that the initial rounds were white phosphorus (smoke) rounds and the remainder were high explosives. About a hundred rounds were fired over a period of about ten minutes (actually it was five minutes), he said, with ten to twenty rounds landing along the western edge of My Lai-4.

The report of sixty-nine VC killed by artillery came in from the ground forward observer soon after the operation started, but Vasquez had seen no bodies in the area of the artillery preparation and doubted the report. However, he granted that since some of the rounds had landed in the hamlet, the VC casualties could have occurred there. No other artillery was fired into the area of My Lai-4 on the 16th and, to his knowledge, no artillery fire landed at the location where the sixty-nine VC were reported to have been killed.

Lieutenant Colonel Barker's helicopter normally flew at twelve to fifteen hundred feet,[3] so Vasquez hadn't been able to see much of what was happening on the ground. He had seen some bodies on the road south of My Lai-4, but hadn't been able to identify them. Oddly enough for an artillery officer, he had had no binoculars—because, he said, Task Force Barker was short of equipment. This bordered on the absurd.

Because there was no radio communication within the helicopter,

3. To have been flying at this altitude seems ludicrous when other helicopters working at treetop level and receiving no ground fire and the units on the ground had reported no hostile fire.

Vasquez and Barker had had to converse by shouting. Vasquez said he had expressed his doubts about the sixty-nine VC killed by artillery, and Barker had responded by reminding him that the report had come from the ground but said he would check it out anyway. Vasquez made no further inquiries, and as far as he had been concerned the matter was closed.

Captain Steven J. Gamble, the commander of the artillery battery that supported Task Force Barker, had attended the commanders' meeting at LZ Dottie on March 15 but had not heard the instructions Lieutenant Colonel Barker issued to the infantry company commanders because he had been conferring with Captain Vasquez at the time. Gamble thought the artillery preparations were to be fired on the landing zones, and did not know that part of the preparation for Charlie Company had landed on the western portion of the hamlet itself. Later that morning, he said, he received word that sixty-nine VC had been killed by the preparation in support of Charlie Company. He had never been aware that any civilians had been killed during the operation or that an investigation had been conducted, and he had never been questioned about his role in the action.

Of all the artillery personnel questioned by the Inquiry, Gamble was one of the most knowledgeable. He fully understood the meaning of no-fire, specified-strike, and free-fire zones. He also knew that, even though it was often perfunctory, clearance to fire into the My Lai area had to be obtained from Vietnamese authorities. Most importantly, he was fully familiar with the USARV regulation that, regardless of the type of zone being fired into, if any civilians were killed or wounded an Artillery Incident Report was to be initiated. Hence, it was most regrettable that he hadn't known civilian casualties were thought to have resulted from the artillery fire.

One thing had stuck in Captain Gamble's mind. He said that about a month after the My Lai incident he had had a visit from the division artillery commander, Colonel Mason J. Young Jr.,[4] and Lieutenant Colonel Luper. During their conversation, Gamble had mentioned something about the sixty-nine VC that had been credited to artillery and air strikes during the Task Force Barker operation and Luper had said, "We're not sure that those were all enemy." Gamble said they had not pursued the subject, however, and he had not had an opportunity to question Luper further about it.

Captain William C. Riggs, commander of Alpha Company at the time of the incident, gave us his version of the role played by Alpha Company. in the operation. During the night of March 15–16 the company moved from its night defensive position south of LZ Uptight to blocking positions along the Diem Diem River to prevent any VC from fleeing northward from the My Lai area. They encountered minor resistance and one man was

---

4. Gamble was mistaken either about the date of the visit or the name of the commander, because Colonel Young had been replaced by Colonel Lawrence M. Jones on March 31, 1968.

wounded, but all three platoons were in position by 7:25 A.M. They observed no other VC on the 16th but on the morning of the 17th saw what they thought were VC crossing a bridge to the south. Alpha Company took them under fire and they withdrew. Later that day, two platoons of Alpha Company moved across the river and set up night ambush positions while the remaining platoon set up an ambush north of the river. At about 9:15 P.M., the elements south of the river were hit by what they thought was a mortar attack but later proved to be hand grenades thrown by enemy sappers (demolitions experts); two men had been killed and five wounded. On the 18th the company withdrew northward to its positions near LZ Uptight.

Captain Riggs was not familiar with the operations of Charlie and Bravo companies. He never knew that an investigation was being conducted, nor had he ever been questioned about the operation.

Major Frederic W. Watke was one of the most complex witnesses we had during the entire course of the Inquiry. He had been the commander of Company B (Aero Scout Company), 123rd Aviation Battalion, which was an organic part of the Americal Division. His company had been formed only recently in South Vietnam from various bits and pieces and was still having growing pains. It was, in effect, a small air cavalry troop consisting of four aero scout teams and three infantry squads of ten men each—a total of about 110 officers and men.

Throughout his testimony Major Watke was quite uncertain about the sequence of events. He voluntarily made available to us the letters he had written to his wife during this period, and using these and various log entries we were finally able to clear up the confusion and be quite specific about the relevant dates.

Watke attended the Task Force Barker briefing on March 15 and his memory of the plan of operation was generally consistent with that of other witnesses. He had had the distinct impression that Charlie Company would encounter strong resistance in the My Lai-4 area the next day, and felt it was appropriate to locate the landing zone close to the hamlet in order to reduce the company's casualties as it moved over the open area. He also thought the plan to put an artillery preparation on the landing zone and western edge of the hamlet to destroy mines and booby traps and to pin down the enemy was appropriate. My Lai-4 had been described as hostile but he did not remember hearing anything about destroying the buildings or killing the livestock and the inhabitants. Nor did he recall hearing that the My Lai residents would be away at market or any instructions about how to handle noncombatants. It had appeared to him to be a normal, straightforward operational plan and order.

When the operation began on the morning of the 16th Watke was with the aero scout team as co-pilot of the low gunship, flying at elevations of two to three hundred feet. He observed the artillery preparation, which lasted for about five minutes, and then he saw hundreds of people from all the nearby settlements fleeing south to Highway 521 and then toward Quang Ngai City. After about an hour and a half, when the gunship became low on fuel, he returned to the tactical operations center at LZ Dottie. He said he had not seen any bodies or any buildings being burned. They had fired at an armed VC south of Highway 521, but Watke did not think they had hit him.

After returning to LZ Dottie he was busy for about two hours placing his infantry-reaction platoon so that it could destroy the mortar rounds Warrant Officer Thompson had spotted on Hill 85. During the morning Watke heard that the artillery preparation had caused some civilian casualties and that a problem had developed between his aero scout team and the ground unit.

At about 11:00 A.M. Thompson and a couple of other command pilots came into the operations center to complain about the ground troops indiscriminately shooting civilians, principally women, children, and old men. Thompson, the spokesman for the group, told Watke about the group of women and children fleeing from advancing U.S. troops and seeking refuge in a bunker, and about his confrontation with the officer in charge, who had a "distinctive marking" on his helmet. When the officer had refused to stop the firing, Thompson had told him he was going to get the civilians out, and if he were fired upon his crew would return the fire. Thompson did get the people safely out; his low gunship, piloted by Warrant Officer Millians, landed and then flew the civilians out of the area. Watke thought Thompson had said that Millians had landed once to lift out nine women and children, but Millians had actually landed twice and had removed twelve to sixteen. Watke remembered that a child from this group had been wounded and Thompson had taken him to the hospital in Quang Ngai City. (This too was in error; as already noted, Thompson took the child from the ditch later, not from the bunker.) Watke had been concerned about using a gunship for the evacuation, which he felt was dangerous in hostile territory because the gunship, with its small lift capability, was not designed for that type of operation.

As previously mentioned in the discussion of Thompson's testimony, there were considerable differences between what Thompson thought he had reported to Watke and what Wake recalled hearing. For example, Watke thought Thompson had said about thirty civilians had been killed but Sergeant Kubert, the operations sergeant, thought the pilot group had said it was more on the order of 150. Watke had been bothered more about the confrontation between Thompson and the ground unit than he had been about civilian casualties; he had felt his pilots were overdramatizing the situation and had not been convinced that many civilians had been killed.

A little later, Watke walked up the hill from the heliport at LZ Dottie to see Lieutenant Colonel Barker at the operations center and tell him about the pilots' report of indiscriminate firing and the confrontation. Barker had been quite concerned, Watke said, and had radioed Major Calhoun, who was then in a helicopter near My Lai-4, to instruct him to find out if anything unusual was going on and, if so, to see that it was stopped.

Watke said he talked with some of the helicopter crewmen, who told him, in effect, that "there were some dead civilians out there." During the afternoon Barker reported that they had been unable to locate any officer in Charlie Company with a distinctive marking on his helmet (the one with whom Thompson had had the confrontation at the bunker). Barker also said a few noncombatants had been killed, but only during the course of a justifiable combat operation, and there were no indications that a large number had been killed. Watke was satisfied that he had done his duty by reporting the situation to Barker, and did nothing further to check the report of civilian casualties because he felt that was Barker's responsibility. He told us, however, that he had not believed what Barker had told him.

After returning to his base at Chu Lai, Watke said, he gave considerable thought as to what he ought to do. He was worried about the confrontation between Thompson and the Task Force Barker ground troops, and was especially apprehensive that Barker would report it through command channels to division and to his commander, Lieutenant Colonel John L. Holladay. Finally, at about 10:00 P.M., he decided to go see Holladay himself and, he said, he told Holladay about Thompson's allegations—essentially the same report he had given to Barker.

The day after Major Watke's appearance before the Inquiry, we questioned Lieutenant Colonel Holladay. There were several highly critical differences between what he said Watke had told him and what Watke thought he had told him. He testified that Watke had mentioned the bodies in the ditch, a sergeant shooting into it, and a captain shooting a woman, which Watke had not remembered Thompson telling him. Whereas Watke primarily recalled the confrontation, Holladay had been concerned about the needless killing of noncombatants, which he had thought was about 125. They had discussed the confrontation, which they agreed was the result of the use of excessive firepower, and the discrepancies between the reported number of enemy killed and the small number of weapons captured. As Watke put it, they had "agonized over it for some time" but felt it was too late to awaken the division commander to report it to him, so waited until the next morning. (One might wonder why, instead of agonizing over it, they had not called in Thompson, Millians, Culverhouse, and the other crewmen on Thompson's helicopter who had had a firsthand view of the activity in order to get a complete story.)

At about 11:00 A.M. the next day, Sunday, March 17, Holladay and Watke reported to division headquarters to see General Koster, and checked in with Colonel Parson, the Chief of Staff. General Koster was not there, so they saw Brigadier General George W. Young instead. Here again we found the same differences in their testimony: Watke contended his report had covered only the confrontation and some "indiscriminate shooting" while Holladay thought they had told Young that a large number of civilians had been killed. General Young's recollection of the report was somewhat closer to Watke's version—the confrontation and some civilians being killed as a result of being caught in crossfire.

That afternoon Watke and Holladay went to a meeting at 11th Brigade headquarters at Duc Pho to discuss coordination between Watke's aero scout unit and the ground units—but what had impressed Watke most about this meeting was that the Task Force Barker operation of the previous day had not even been mentioned, much less discussed or analyzed.

Then he told us about the meeting on the 18th in Lieutenant Colonel Barker's van at LZ Dottie; in addition to himself, Henderson, and Barker, General Young and Lieutenant Colonel Holladay had been present. Watke recalled General Young saying "Only the five of us here know about this," but he hadn't taken this as directing a coverup, only as advice to keep it quiet until the allegations could be checked into. At the meeting Watke was asked to tell what had happened. He said he told them about the confrontation and the excessive use of firepower—essentially the same report he had already given to Barker, Holladay, and Young; if it had been different, he said, they would have questioned or interrupted him but they didn't. As could be expected, Holladay's testimony on this point was quite different. Watke remembered that Barker had also given a brief account of what he had discovered, but had not referred to any of the allegations Watke had mentioned. Then, Watke said, Young directed Henderson to investigate the incident to find out if there had been any unnecessary killings, and he felt it was meant to be an in-depth investigation, although no deadline was set for its completion.

After the meeting Henderson and Watke talked briefly—but Watke could not remember what about—and then Henderson said he wanted to talk to Thompson and some of the other pilots who had been on duty on March 16. Watke sent Thompson, Culverhouse, and Colburn to see him. Afterward Thompson told Watke that he had told Henderson the same things he had already reported to Watke.

A few days later, Watke told us, there was an argument about the incident in the mess hall, and he had intervened to tell the men it was being investigated and to calm down. And, although Watke didn't mention this, Sergeant Kubert and others testified about another occasion when Watke assembled the company to hear a briefing by an intelligence officer from the division staff, who said, among other things, that 120 civilians had been killed at My Lai. One of the men said, "You mean those women and children," and then things had gotten out of hand—some witnesses said the situation had nearly turned into a riot. Once again, Major Watke had intervened to quiet things down.

Some time later, Watke told us, Barker informed him that they were still unable to locate the officer to whom Thompson had spoken at the bunker. Also, in mid-April, Holladay advised him that a report of investigation of the incident had been submitted, and that although it was inconclusive nobody was found to have committed a crime.

Watke's helicopter was shot down on April 17, 1968, and he was seriously injured. After a few days in the hospital at Chu Lai he was evacuated to an Army hospital in Japan and then to the United States. Thus his knowledge of any investigations or reports ended at that time.

In reviewing Major Watke's testimony, it seemed to the panel that he knew much more than he was telling us. He appeared to have a mental block —or perhaps a lapse of memory—and always stopped just short of relating the full story. The possibility also existed that he was purposefully withholding information. And, because his testimony was at such variance with that of Warrant Officer Thompson and Lieutenant Colonel Holladay, when he was recalled to testify he was advised of the thinking of the Inquiry and given time to consider seeking legal counsel. He had military counsel with him during his next appearance, but this did not seem to have much effect. He still seemed restrained and withdrawn.

Because of the differences between Major Watke's and Lieutenant Colonel Holladay's testimony, we decided to recall them together. Watke stuck to his story that a relatively small number of civilians had been wounded —he always found it difficult to say "killed"—and Holladay was still positive that he had heard that more than a hundred had been killed. Watke made no attempt to refute any of Holladay's statements, but he made no attempt to bridge the gap, either.

As we were nearing the end of the Inquiry we recalled several of the key witnesses, including Major Watke. He was again advised of his rights and of the Inquiry's suspicions as to the offenses he might have committed. He could have chosen to remain silent but decided not to. His lawyer had left the service and was no longer available, and although Watke could have had other counsel he elected to proceed without any.

His testimony at this session was much more direct and filled in many of the gaps. He explained that the incident had made such an impression on him that he had been unable to tell all about it—it simply would not come out. In the back of his mind he had also been concerned about the effect the actions of the aero scouts, especially their confrontation with the ground unit, could have upon his military career. Although he insisted he still could not recall having heard about the bodies in the ditch and a captain shooting a woman, he admitted that he *had* had the impression that a large number of civilians had been killed (not wounded). Most importantly, he told us that toward the end of March 1968, when no Report of Investigation had been made and he had not been questioned further, he had become convinced that a definite coverup was underway. In this regard, he and Holladay were of the same opinion. Major Watke had thought about getting documentation from his men and submitting it to higher authority, but said he hadn't had the heart to do it.

First Lieutenant Dennis Johnson, of the 52nd Military Intelligence Detachment, and Sergeant Doung Minh, an interpreter, had accompanied Charlie Company in its combat assault at My Lai-4 for what Johnson had understood was to be an interrogation mission that would last three or four days. Johnson appeared before the Inquiry with military counsel.

On March 16 he landed with the second lift into My Lai-4 and joined Captain Medina's command group. He said that he and Sergeant Minh skirted the western edge of the hamlet and then moved eastward along the southern edge. At that time he saw only one body, that of a boy about six years old. This had greatly affected him, he told us, because he had a son about the same age.

Later we talked with Sergeant Minh, who said they had not skirted the hamlet but had cut through it at a southeast angle. He had seen more than a few bodies of women and children—he said it was more like fifteen to twenty—as well as some dead animals, and had asked Johnson why there was so much killing. Johnson said he had tried to pacify Minh by saying that sometimes such things happen in combat—sometimes innocent people were killed. Minh said he had also talked to Captain Medina about the dead civilians, and Medina had told him that they had been ordered to shoot anyone they saw in the area.

Johnson and Minh interrogated an old man who told them that a large group of VC had left the hamlet early that morning; they passed that information along to Medina. They observed the medical evacuation of Carter, and in this vicinity Johnson saw ten to thirteen dead civilians in a rice paddy; he assumed they had been killed by artillery or gunships but did not inspect them. When he was later shown pictures of twenty to twenty-five dead women and children on the road just south of My Lai-4, Johnson was certain he had not seen those bodies because he had not been there. He thought the helicopter that had flown him to the Bravo Company area at about 11:30 A.M. had landed well to the west of the road. (Actually, it had put down about fifty yards east of the road, and Johnson had had to pass near the pile of bodies to get to the helicopter. Thus unless he had steadfastly been looking in the other direction he must have seen these bodies, because they were in plain view less than fifty feet from him.)

When asked why he had not told Medina about the dead noncombatants he had seen, Johnson said he had assumed that Medina had also seen them. Further, he felt his sole responsibility was to interrogate VC prisoners and suspects, and it was Medina's and Barker's job to report casualties. He was most emphatic that he had not seen anyone shoot, kill, or touch anyone while he was in My Lai-4. Even so, he implied that he had been appalled at all the bodies he had seen and had been glad to leave the Charlie Company area.

When Johnson and Minh arrived in the Bravo Company area they screened the twenty-five or so suspects the company had rounded up. Many of these men and women had South Vietnamese ID cards, and no one was detained. Johnson stayed in the area until Charlie Company joined Bravo Company and Captain Kotouc arrived with the National Police to interrogate the Charlie Company suspects. He heard none of the questioning and saw nothing unusual while with Bravo Company. A short while later he and Minh returned to LZ Dottie even though the operation continued for two or three more days. He was sure he would not have left the field without permission, but he couldn't recall who had given it to him.

At LZ Dottie, Johnson did not report what he had observed to Lieutenant Colonel Barker, Major Calhoun, or Captain Kotouc. Sergeant Minh told us he had urged Johnson to do so, or to let him do so, but had been told that Johnson would do it. When they returned to Duc Pho, Johnson reported to his immediate superior, Captain Albert C. Labriola, commander of the 52nd Military Intelligence Detachment, but did not mention having seen dead civilians in the My Lai-4 area. Again, Minh said, he had suggested that Johnson report what they had seen, but again Johnson told him he would take care of it.

Lieutenant Johnson had received training in Officer Candidate School and had attended an intelligence course as well as participating in the training in Hawaii and the 11th Brigade indoctrination in South Vietnam. Although MACV Directive 20–4 specifically instructed intelligence officers to report any suspected war crimes or atrocities, Johnson said he did not remember hearing about this directive and had not been aware that he had any responsibility in this area.

When he was recalled in February 1970, Lieutenant Johnson was advised of several acts of commission and omission of which he was suspected by the Inquiry. He elected to continue testifying, with counsel, but his responses were essentially the same as those he had given earlier.

Another team of specialists also accompanied the second helicopter lift into My Lai-4: Specialist-5 Jay Roberts and Sergeant Ronald L. Haeberle of the 11th Brigade public information detachment. Roberts was a staff writer and Haeberle a photographer.

Haeberle had had two cameras with him, one a government issue loaded with black-and-white film and another, his own, loaded with color film. Generally, he had used the government camera to take pictures of rather routine combat scenes, although he did include a few pictures of houses burning and crops being destroyed. He had photographed the results of several atrocities with his own camera. He turned in the black-and-white film to the public information office but kept the color film. When he returned to the States he sold the pictures to *Life* magazine and other publications for a great deal of money. It was his My Lai photographs that were published in the December 5, 1969, issue of *Life* just as the Inquiry was getting under way.

Roberts and Haeberle accompanied Charlie Company's 3rd Platoon, under Lieutenant La Cross, on its movement south to the vicinity of Highway 521, where Haeberle photographed soldiers firing into rice paddies, several bodies on the road, and a dead woman just south of the highway. Upon returning to My Lai-4, they accompanied the 3rd Platoon through the western portion of the hamlet. Haeberle took a color photo of a group of eight or nine women, children, and babies that had been rounded up. He told us that he and Roberts had turned away from the group for a moment, and when they heard M-16 rifle fire they turned around, to see that all these people had been killed. Whether they actually saw these murders is inconsequential; there is no doubt they knew an atrocity had been committed.

Later they moved to the southern edge of the hamlet to join Captain Medina and his command group. They saw the pile of bodies on the road outside the hamlet and Haeberle took a color photo of it. They also saw a toddler literally being blown apart by a burst of rifle fire. Haeberle took black-and-white pictures of an old man being led from a house for interrogation, of the command group resting along the edge of the village, and of the evacuation of Private First Class Carter.

Then they flew by helicopter to the Bravo Company area, accompanied by Lieutenant Johnson and Sergeant Minh. They remained there for a few hours talking with people, and Haeberle took a few pictures of some of the men in the unit. Later in the afternoon they returned to LZ Dottie. Roberts knew Lieutenant Colonel Barker, and he and Haeberle talked with Barker for some time at his command post but, they said, they had not told him of the many civilian bodies they had seen or of the atrocities they had witnessed. In fact, they said, Barker had done most of the talking, telling them about the success of the operation thus far. If at that time Barker knew only what Medina had officially reported to him—that ninety VC and ten or eleven civilians had been killed—an eyewitness account of the noncombatant casualties seen by Roberts and Haeberle could have had a profound influence upon him and his subsequent actions.

When they returned to 11th Brigade headquarters at Duc Pho, Haeberle turned in his black-and-white film to Sergeant John Stonich in the public information office, but neither he nor Roberts mentioned the atrocities they had seen. On the contrary, a few days later Roberts wrote a glowing account of the Task Force Barker operation for the brigade newspaper, *Trident:*

TF BARKER CRUSHES ENEMY STRONGHOLD

For the third time in recent weeks 11th Brigade infantrymen of Task Force Barker raided a Viet Cong stronghold known as "Pinkville," six miles northeast of Quang Ngai.

"Jungle Warriors," together with artillery and helicopter support hit the village of My Lai last Friday morning. Contacts throughout the morning and early afternoon resulted in 128 enemy killed, 13 suspects detained and three weapons captured.

A Task Force Barker company of the 1st Battalion, 20th Infantry conducted a combat assault west of My Lai and quickly killed one VC while moving away from the LZ. "Shark" gunships from the 174th Aviation Company killed four more enemy during the assault.

"Aero Scout" helicopters from the 123d Aviation Company were supporting the infantrymen and killed two enemy. The "War Lords" also located 40 60mm mortar rounds.

The infantry company, led by CPT Ernest Medina, engaged and killed 14 VC and captured three M1 rifles, a radio and enemy documents, while moving towards the village. One of the ten suspects apprehended by the company told an interpreter that 35 VC had moved into the village two hours earlier.

As the "Warriors" moved through the marshes a mile west of My Lai they counted 69 enemy bodies killed by ground troops and a battery of the 6th Battalion, 11th Artillery. CPT Steven Gambel, fired on the enemy from a location three miles to the north. A platoon of "Barker's Bastards" from the 4th Battalion, 3d Infantry was airlifted into a position south of My Lai. The unit, led by 2LT Tom Willingham, engaged an unknown number of enemy along the beach one half mile south of the village. When contact was broken 30 Viet Cong lay dead.

Early in the afternoon the platoon observed enemy soldiers escaping into a tunnel complex. Eight of the enemy were killed and web gear, hand grenades, and small arms ammunition was recovered.

The three recent engagements by the 11th Brigade in the My Lai-Pinkville area has cost enemy forces a total of 276 men.

If either Haeberle or Roberts had told their superiors what they had seen —and if Haeberle had turned in his color film to brigade headquarters— the tragic events of the Task Force Barker operation might have been uncovered at that time. Their rationalization for not doing so was that they thought what they had seen was just the way war was fought. But the fact that Haeberle kept and later sold those very incriminating color photos, and that Roberts neglected to mention civilian casualties or atrocities in his story, casts grave doubt on their role of objective observers or innocent bystanders.

To get some perspective on Charlie Company, we called Lieutenant Colonel Edwin D. Beers, commander of the 1st Battalion, 20th Infantry, as a witness, because Charlie Company had been detached from his battalion to become part of Task Force Barker. Beers felt that the men in the battalion had been well trained in Hawaii and were familiar with the Rules of Engagement being employed in Vietnam. In Hawaii he had heard Captain Medina referred to as "Mad Dog," but had not taken this to be derogatory, merely an indication that Medina was aggressive and always on the go.

Beers had been told to select his best company for Task Force Barker, and he had picked Charlie Company. As the parent commander, he had kept track of its activities, and on March 18, 1968, he flew out to Charlie

Company's field location. He noted that some of the men were drinking beer during the operation and that their appearance did not measure up to his standards. He spoke to Medina about maintaining those standards, he said, but when the task force was disbanded and Charlie Company returned to battalion control in April it was not the same top-notch company it had been before. There seemed to have been a breakdown in leadership, perhaps due to the lack of guidance from the top.

When Beers and Medina discussed the company's operation, there was no mention of civilian casualties. Later, Colonel Henderson told Beers that Medina might be "in trouble" about shooting a woman, but Henderson did not seem very concerned and Beers heard no more about it. No investigating officer ever came to his battalion to interrogate witnesses; if there was an investigation, he had not been aware of it.

The early portion of the Inquiry was like a nightmare to me. Initially, I had thought that perhaps a few civilians had been killed but I didn't think it was going to be such an extremely serious matter. However, when the facts started coming out and I became aware of the magnitude of the atrocity in terms of hundreds of civilians being killed, along with rape and the unwarranted destruction of property, I was stunned that these things could have been done at all, let alone by a U.S. Army unit. Once having recognized the extent of the tragedy, I became somewhat numb to the details given by subsequent witnesses. From that point on, the Inquiry was just plain hard work.

chapter 11

Colonel Henderson Recalled

Colonel Henderson was recalled to testify on December 11, 12, and 19, 1969. By this time, from testimony of others and from the logs and some letters, we had developed a sequence of events during and after the incident that was at considerable variance with the version he had given in his first appearance. Therefore I advised him:

> There is now some evidence tending to raise the suspicion that during and after the My Lai-4 incident, you were negligent or derelict, or even in direct violation in complying with orders and directives pertaining to the reporting and investigation of alleged mistreatment or wounding or killing of civilians, that is to say, war crimes, and that you may either have suppressed or contributed to the suppression of information pertaining to the unlawful killing of civilians at My Lai-4 on 16 March 1968. . . . There is some evidence which indicates that your prior testimony before this investigation may have been incomplete in part or in part intentionally false.

He was again advised of his rights with respect to giving testimony and having legal counsel. He said that he did not desire counsel, but I told him not to make the decision at that time, that I wanted him to think about it. What I was trying to tell him, without actually saying so, was that the members of the Inquiry panel felt he truly needed counsel. We recessed until the following day, but he again refused counsel.

Since some aspects of our information disagreed with his, I outlined the sequence of events as we understood them. Some of the more pertinent points were:

- Colonel Henderson's order (which was countermanded by General Koster) for Charlie Company to return to My Lai-4 was given on the afternoon of the 16th. Charlie Company was extracted from the field and Alpha Company withdrew to LZ Uptight on the afternoon of the 18th.
- Major Watke and Lieutenant Colonel Holladay reported to General Young regarding Warrant Officer Thompson's report on the morning of the 17th. Thereafter, they flew to Duc Pho to discuss coordination of helicopter operations with members of the 11th Brigade staff.
- Lieutenant General Edgar C. Doleman, a retired officer who was making a study of communications facilities in South Vietnam, visited the 11th Brigade and the Americal Division on March 16 and 17. General Koster picked him up at Duc Pho at about 4:00 P.M. on the afternoon of the 16th and they flew to LZ Dottie, arriving at 4:45. Lieutenant Colonel Barker briefed them on the My Lai operation and they left at 5:15. General Doleman spent the night of March 16–17 at Americal Division headquarters at Chu Lai. The following morning General Koster flew with him to Duc Pho, where they spent the remainder of the day with Henderson visiting units in the field.
- The meeting at LZ Dottie of General Young, Colonel Henderson, Lieutenant Colonels Holladay and Barker, and Major Watke took place shortly after 9:00 A.M. on March 18. After this meeting Watke arranged for Warrant Officers Thompson and Culverhouse and Specialist-4 Colburn to report to Henderson for questioning.
- At about noon on the 18th Henderson flew to Charlie Company's field location and conferred with Captain Medina.

In his initial testimony, Henderson said he had directed the resweep of My Lai-4 on the morning of the 17th while Charlie and Bravo companies were still in their night bivouac area. In his later testimony he changed it to the afternoon of the 17th or 18th after his talk with Medina. He recalled that both Barker and Medina had objected because it would mean that their men would miss the helicopter extraction and would have to walk through mine-infested areas. We discussed the timing at some length. He remained steadfast in his insistence that his order to resweep My Lai-4 had been countermanded on the 17th or 18th even though the evidence that it took place on the afternoon of the 16th was conclusive.

Henderson also said that on March 18 Barker told him he had landed at My Lai-4 on the 16th and, since he had not seen anything unusual, had been sure that Thompson's allegations were unfounded. (There was no other testimony or evidence to indicate that Barker or anybody else in authority had landed at My Lai-4 during the operation. Barker's command helicopter had landed just south of My Lai-4 to evacuate Private First Class Carter, but Barker had not been aboard. That Barker did not personally check on the operation was another aspect of the tragedy. Surely, at a minimum, he would have seen the stack of civilian bodies on the road immediately south of the hamlet if he had been present when they picked up Carter.)

During the morning of the 16th while he was flying over My Lai-4 Henderson saw a hootch burning. He thought Barker had told him the burning was being done by the ARVN or National Police, and told Barker to get them under control or get them out. (Henderson apparently did not know that there were no National Police or ARVN in the area at that time; they joined the operation to interrogate suspects only after Charlie and Bravo companies had reached their night bivouac positions.) Later, Henderson said he saw several buildings burning in My Lai-4, but he was not aware that on the 17th several villages were put to torch by Bravo and Charlie companies.

He had originally testified that when he arrived at LZ Dottie on the morning of the 17th, or possibly the 18th, Watke had met him and told him about Thompson's observations, and he had interviewed Thompson and then had flown out to talk to Medina. In his later testimony he said he had been wrong; it was not Watke who had met him but Watke's executive officer, Captain Clyde P. Wilson. (Wilson later vehemently denied that he had met Henderson or talked to Thompson.) As for the date, Colonel Henderson did not recall that on Sunday, the 17th, Lieutenant Colonel Holladay and Major Watke, after reporting to General Young, had flown to Duc Pho to confer with Henderson and some members of his staff about aero scout helicopter operations. And although Henderson maintained that he had questioned Thompson and conferred with Medina before meeting with General Young and the others, all evidence—including his arrival time in the Task Force Barker log—indicated otherwise. The point here is that he maintained he had personally started the investigation, and the sequence of events he gave would tend to support this. All indications, however, were that he had been directed by General Young to "investigate it" and only then had he questioned Thompson, Culverhouse, and Colburn and flown out to Medina's field location.

In his recall testimony Henderson dropped a small bombshell by telling us of still another report he had submitted to division on about April 4–6, 1968. He said General Young had told him, a few days earlier, that General Koster wanted Henderson to put his oral report of March 20 into written form, but not as a formal report. The completed report was three or four pages long, he said, addressed the allegations made by Thompson, and made certain recommendations concerning the handling of civilians. He said he had showed it to Lieutenant Colonel Barker and Major McKnight and believed he had filed a copy in the safe in the operations office, although he did not recall logging it in. He thought he had taken it to division headquarters himself and had discussed it with the Chief of Staff, Colonel Parson. Two or three days later, General Young told him that General Koster was satisfied with it.

The most interesting aspect of this report, however, is that neither General Young, General Koster, nor Colonel Parson recalled ever seeing or being aware of such a document when they were asked about it during the Inquiry. It had not been entered into the division log nor was a copy of it ever found in any of the headquarters. It appeared to the Inquiry to be a figment of Henderson's imagination or that, if he really had prepared such a report, he kept it to himself.

Henderson also elaborated upon his mid-April meetings with Colonel Toan and Lieutenant Colonel Khien after he received a copy of the VC propaganda and the unsigned statement. As Henderson remembered it, Toan told him about the letter he had received from either the village or district chief, accusing U.S. forces of killing five hundred Vietnamese civilians in two separate incidents, and Khien showed him a copy of it. When Henderson asked them what they thought about it, they both gave him the impression that it was VC propaganda. According to Henderson, Toan had reported the information to Lieutenant General Lam, who had directed him to investigate it. Toan had then directed Khien to look into the matter, but Khien told Henderson he did not intend to do so—that he planned only to conduct a counterpropaganda campaign. Henderson said he offered troops of the 11th Brigade to form a joint task force with the ARVN 2nd Division or Regional Forces/Popular Forces of the province to conduct an operation into the area, but they did not seem interested. When questioned by the Inquiry as to why he, with all of the assets available to him, had not initiated his own operation, he offered no explanation except that all his battalions were engaged elsewhere.

It was after his discussion with Colonel Toan and Lieutenant Colonel Khien, he said, that he initiated his report of April 24, 1968. This contradicted his previous testimony in which he had said that General Koster had directed the investigation after receiving the VC propaganda Henderson had sent to him. It also contradicted the testimony of General Koster, who later told us that he had visited Colonel Toan and Lieutenant Colonel Khien at about that same time and had been given generally the same information, after which, through either General Young or Colonel Parson, he had ordered Colonel Henderson to put his oral report of March 20 into writing.

Then we got down to the question of whom Henderson had talked with prior to his appearance before the Inquiry. He said he had seen Lieutenant Colonel Blackledge, but they had not discussed My Lai. Also, about a year earlier he had gone to a conference at Fort Benning, Georgia, where he had seen Captain Medina and thirty to forty junior officers who had served in the brigade, but they did not discuss My Lai either. On December 1, the day before his first appearance at the Inquiry, he had attended a party in Washington with some of his former commanders and staff officers, but, again, he said the subject of My Lai had not come up. This seemed incredible to us, since the incident was much in the news by this time, but we did not press the issue. I was a little perturbed, however, when I found that he had talked with Warrant Officer Thompson at a session of the House My Lai subcommittee after I had instructed him not to talk with anyone concerning the incident, but it turned out that Henderson had only wanted to know if Thompson had been the pilot of the observation helicopter.

This led to a more pertinent discussion concerning his telephone conversations with General Koster, of which there had been a total of five. We wanted to know the specifics of each conversation. Henderson said that Koster had called him in mid-November 1969, after the My Lai incident had broken in the news media, wanting to know the details of the operation and particularly about the reports. Henderson gave him the information and reminded him that he had countermanded Henderson's order for Charlie Company to return to My Lai-4, which, he said, Koster only vaguely remembered. There were three other calls between then and November 29, of which Koster had initiated two. These were not short calls, some of them lasting as long as twenty minutes, during which they discussed various aspects of the My Lai operation. In addition, after his initial appearance on at the Inquiry and despite the fact that he had been directed not to talk with anybody concerning the incident or his testimony, there was still another call on December 5 in which they had discussed Henderson's testimony. Thereafter he had talked briefly with Koster at the House of Representatives, but this had primarily been to identify Warrant Officer Thompson. These discussions greatly concerned the panel members. General Koster had not yet appeared before the Inquiry and we had no idea how he would testify, but some of us felt these conversations might have given Henderson an opportunity to create impressions in Koster's mind that would influence his recall of what had happened. Some members of the Inquiry felt even more strongly, and saw these conversations as being very suspicious, even conspiratorial, since both men knew they would be called as witnesses.

We also found that on November 27, 1969, at about the time the Inquiry was initiated by Secretary Resor and General Westmoreland, Henderson had prepared a fourteen-page statement and eleven pages of questions and answers in case he was called before one of the congressional committees. He told us that in preparing this material he had given considerable thought to his role in the incident and what he would say if called to testify, and agreed to release it to the Inquiry as a matter of record. It was fairly consistent with his initial testimony, although it did contain several additions and some differences from his testimony up to that time. For example, in his written statement he said:

- He discussed the twenty-four civilian deaths that had occurred during the My Lai operation with his staff. (When questioned by the Inquiry, none of these men indicated that they had any knowledge of any civilians being killed.)

- After he received the directive to conduct a formal investigation, he telephoned the requirement to Lieutenant Colonel Barker. (Why, when at the time Barker was his executive officer and worked within a few feet of him? And what happened to all the detailed instructions he told us he had given to Barker?)
- He advised General Young that as a result of his discussion with Warrant Officer Thompson he had started a commander's type of investigation. (No mention was made of the meeting with Young, Barker, Holladay, and Watke, at which he was told to investigate the incident.)
- In May 1969 he called Colonel Donaldson, then the Chief of Staff of the Americal Division, and requested a copy of his report of April 24, 1968. (Why hadn't he also requested copies of his report of April 4–6 and Barker's formal report, which he had endorsed—especially since he had repeatedly testified that the April 24 report was not really a Report of Investigation and that the others had been much more complete?)

There was no mention at all in his written statement of the April 4–6 report. A few things in the statement, however, were consistent with his testimony, even though they were at variance with the testimony of other witnesses: that he had taken the lead in initiating an investigation; that all the information concerning the acceptance of his reports and directions for follow-up action had come from General Young; and that the incident had resulted from the action of one of his units and he would accept all responsibility. In sum, his written statement was helpful in giving us some idea as to Henderson's line of thinking, but it did not add much to what we already knew.

On December 11, 1969, General Westmoreland showed me the following letter he had received from Colonel Henderson.

10 December 1969

The Chief of Staff
United States Army
Washington, D. C. 20310

Dear General Westmoreland:

1. Following the My Lai operation 16 March 1968, I conducted a command inquiry based upon an eyewitness report which suggested that noncombatants had possibly been killed by "wild shooting" of ground troops and gunships and by command channel reports that twenty noncombatants had been killed by artillery and gunship fire. This inquiry was initiated by me without guidance or knowledge of any higher headquarters. Consequently, the depth of the inquiry was based solely upon my judgment. I did not treat it lightly; however, I was

unable to produce a single additional witness or a thread of evidence to substantiate the eyewitnesses report. An effort to conduct a sweep in the objective area on 17 March 1968, which could possibly have more positively identified cause of noncombatant deaths and shed additional light on the subject was aborted. Following the initial inquiry and again as a part of the formal report of investigation, I advised my Division Commander that irresponsible acts of killing noncombatants did not occur. I currently maintain that conviction. This judgment was mine alone, and I am unwilling to share the responsibility with anyone. I informed the Board of Investigation, headed by Lieutenant General Peers, of this position at the conclusion of my testimony on 2 December 1969.

2. I continue to maintain the highest admiration, confidence, and faith in the integrity, fighting qualities and courage of the officers and men, 11th LIB, present during the alleged incident.

3. In the interest of strengthening the American people's confidence in its Army, and to halt a growing disenchantment within the Army junior officer corps, a speedy decision is urgently needed. Consequently, I urge that the Army announce its findings even though the current investigation proceeds and that the responsibility without qualification be assigned solely to me. I, of course, defer to the Army the manner and substance of such announcement.

Respectfully,

Oran K. Henderson
Colonel, Infantry

General Westmoreland asked me what I thought of it and what he ought to do about it. I told him I thought it was a magnanimous position for Colonel Henderson to take but somewhat ludicrous in light of the exploratory status of the Inquiry. In any event, we had no findings at that time and all I could suggest was that he file it and acknowledge its receipt.

When asked about this letter, Henderson acknowledged that he had written it and that it had been delivered through the Office of Legislative Liaison. He said he had heard from several people that they were disturbed by the investigation, that some young officers were considering resigning, and that others were reluctant to go to South Vietnam. He felt the image of the Army was being damaged, and that if he were to assume full responsibility for the My Lai incident it would counteract the impression the public was getting. With some reluctance he agreed to have the letter entered into the record.

I have often thought about what might have happened had General Westmoreland acted on Colonel Henderson's suggestion. Obviously, he could not have done so because at that time there was no basis upon which to act, but let us suppose that something like that had been done at that point. Given the mood of the American people and of Congress, they would have been up in arms and the Army would have been accused of a whitewash, a result totally at odds with what Colonel Henderson had hoped to achieve by his letter.

chapter 12

Division Higher Echelon Testimony

The most difficult period for me during the Inquiry was when Major General Samuel W. Koster, commander of the Americal Division, and Brigadier General George H. Young, assistant division commander for maneuver elements, appeared. Both were friends of many years' standing; we had served together in the plans and operations section of the Army General Staff from 1953 to 1956, when we had been in almost daily contact. Both were outstanding officers, and had been well liked and respected throughout the staff. I considered them to be close friends, had great admiration for them, and had enjoyed our working relationships.

Since they were at the very hub of the investigation and I would have to submit my judgment of their activities in the final report of the Inquiry, I suffered more than a bit of mental anxiety. However, my job was to uncover the facts and to report them, and I was determined to do so fairly and objectively. It was not a very pleasant position to be in, but that is the way it had to be.

Before we questioned Generals Koster and Young in December 1969, we reviewed their testimony to the CID and the Inspector General and interrogated some of the men directly connected with their activities, specifically Colonel Henderson, Lieutenant Colonel Holladay, and Major Watke. Thus by the time they were to appear before the Inquiry several doubts had been raised in our minds about their role in the events surrounding the My Lai incident. Accordingly, they were advised of these suspicions, dealing primarily with possible acts of dereliction of duty and negligence. They could have chosen to remain silent, but neither of them did so and neither appeared with legal counsel.

As the assistant division commander for maneuver elements, General

Young assisted the division commander in monitoring the operations of the combat units. He had taken over the job only the day before the My Lai operation but before that he had served for over four months as the ADC for logistic support. At the time of the Inquiry he was stationed in Europe.

General Young had not been aware of the plans for the March 16 operation into the My Lai area and did not think the plan had been approved by the division headquarters. The first news he had of the operation, he said, was at the division staff briefing on the evening of the 16th reviewing the results to that point. He remembered it well, as it was the largest body count reported so far by the 11th Brigade. The ratio of 128 VC to two Americans killed seemed extremely high, and he had also been upset at the low weapons count (three). There was no report of sixty-nine VC having been killed by artillery or of civilian casualties. Moreover, General Koster never mentioned to him that he knew twenty to twenty-eight civilians had been killed in the operation.

His version of what had been reported to him by Holladay and Watke, and the events following, contradicted the testimony of Holladay, Watke, and Henderson. He recalled that Holladay, and perhaps Watke, came to see him after the staff briefing on the 16th, while both of them said they had seen him early the next morning. Young remembered their telling him about a gunship pilot who had charged that U.S. forces had fired into a group of civilians. Also, this pilot had landed and moved some civilians to the protection of a cave, after which he had had a confrontation with an American officer or senior NCO. Young remembered nothing else about Thompson's allegations; this, of course, was almost totally inconsistent with what Holladay and to a considerable degree with what Watke had testified they told Young.

Immediately after Holladay's visit on the evening of the 16th, General Young went to see General Koster.[1] After telling Koster of his conversation with Holladay and mentally combining this news with the disparity between the number of weapons captured and the enemy body count, he recommended that the matter be investigated. He was thinking in terms of a full and proper investigation under Army Regulation 15–6, he said, but Koster directed him to have Colonel Henderson investigate it and report as soon as possible. Even though he had been directed to so inform Henderson, Young had not felt that he himself was supposed to supervise the investigation. Koster did not tell him that civilians had been killed or that he had countermanded an order for Charlie Company to return to My Lai-4 to make a body count.

The following morning, the 17th, he held a short meeting with Colonel

---

1. All other evidence indicated that General Young's recollection of subsequent events was about a day ahead—that is, what he thought took place on the 16th actually happened on the 17th, etc.

Henderson and others—he didn't remember exactly who was present—in Barker's van at LZ Dottie, during which he had done most of the talking. Specifically, he directed Henderson to conduct an investigation that he thought would focus on the shooting toward civilians and the confrontation. He also thought it would be a full-fledged investigation, including signed statements from witnesses, to determine whether the pilot's allegations were true or false.

On the morning of the 18th Henderson informed him of the progress of his investigation. Young had been somewhat surprised to learn that Henderson was actually doing the questioning himself but had not told him to get someone else to do it. Henderson said he had talked with Captain Medina and other officers and men associated with the operation, and he planned to talk with others before submitting his report. However, he did not mention that Medina had shot and killed a young woman. From what Henderson told him, Young assumed he had taken written statements and was conducting a thorough investigation.

General Young was not present on March 20 when Henderson gave his oral report to General Koster, but Koster told him about it later. Koster also said he had directed Henderson to put the report into writing, which surprised Young as he thought his original instructions had implied a written report.

When we showed General Young a copy of Colonel Henderson's written report of April 24, 1968, he said this was the first time he had ever seen it, although he knew it had been submitted, because General Koster had told him about it. Koster had said the investigation had turned up no evidence that civilians had been indiscriminately killed or that houses had been burned. Apparently he had been satisfied with the report. Henderson had also told Young of his findings. General Young thought the written report had followed the oral report by only a few days—not as late as April 24— but he was fairly certain there had not been two written reports. Young considered the report we showed him to be totally inadequate, and had he seen it at the time, he said, he would have recommended that it not be accepted.

Young had never seen the unsigned statement appended to Henderson's written report, but said that Lieutenant Colonel Guinn, who was then acting Quang Ngai Province senior advisor, had told him about it. As he recalled, it involved two hamlets and charged that a sizable number of civilians had been killed by U.S. forces, but he did not remember that the hamlets were Tu Cung and Co Luy. He relayed this information to General Koster, he said, in late April or early May.

As for the so-called formal report of May 1968 that Henderson had told the Inquiry about in his testimony, General Young had had no knowledge of it. As far as he was concerned, General Koster had never told him to direct Henderson to prepare it and he had never issued such instructions.

Henderson, of course, had told us that General Young had not only told him to make this investigation but had tacitly approved Barker as the investigating officer. None of this jibed with Young's recollection.

We recalled General Young later to review with him the sequence of events on March 16–18 as we knew it, because what we knew was different from what he had told us. He still felt his meeting with Lieutenant Colonel Holladay had been on the 16th but conceded that it could have been the 17th. When shown the Task Force Barker log, which indicated the time of his arrival and departure on the 18th, he allowed that perhaps that too was correct. Colonel Henderson had testified that at the meeting in Lieutenant Colonel Barker's van General Young had been disturbed about the pilot marking the wounded with smoke grenades and his confrontation with a ground commander, and had asked why charges had not been filed against the pilot. Also, Major Watke had stated that at the beginning of the meeting in the van General Young had said "Only five of us here in this van know about this." Young did not recall any of this. When questioned concerning his instructions to Henderson to "investigate this," however, he conceded that he had given no specific instructions as to the kind of investigation it was to be.

There was one entry in the task force log that concerned me very much. Recalling that Holladay and Watke had reported Thompson's allegations to Young early on the morning of the 17th and that he had informed Koster of the allegations about noon on the same day, why had Young visited LZ Dottie that afternoon as shown in the log, and what had transpired there? It seemed a strange time for him to go to the task force unless he was checking some aspect of Thompson's allegations, but Young said he did not recall the visit at all.

Lieutenant Colonel Tommy P. Trexler's testimony may have shed some light on this visit, but we could not be sure because he could not remember the date. Trexler, the division intelligence officer, periodically flew with Young on his visits to the various units, and recalled that they had gone to Task Force Barker a day or two after the My Lai-4 operation. Shortly after takeoff in the helicopter, Young told him he wanted to discuss the operation. "I don't specifically remember just what he said, but he did talk to me about five to ten minutes," Trexler told the Inquiry. "I really thought they had burned houses which they should not have done. Certainly, from what I remember General Young had told me, I did not get an indication that there had been really any extensive killing of civilians, although it was enough that it disturbed him. . . . General Young, I felt, was following up on it quite aggressively." Young told us he did not recall having made such statements, and again denied any knowledge of civilians having been killed or houses burned, but if Trexler's recollection was accurate, it was another indication that perhaps Young had in fact been aware of these things.

The most striking difference between General Young and General Koster was their understanding of who had been responsible for what. We questioned each man on this point for several hours, but were as confused at the end as we had been at the beginning. Koster's interpretation is summarized in the following statement, which was read to Young at his recall appearance on December 23, 1969:

> I believe I [said], with words along the line, you [referring to General Young] will ride herd on this thing, something on the order of that, not to the extent that he conduct the operation himself, much as you conduct the inquiry or you do this and so on, but I always looked to one of the assistant division commanders to look after the southern area, primarily, as I was concerned to a greater extent with the north. I'm sure I gave him the message that I felt he would supervise this and check it.

Further, Koster felt that Young had kept him informed as to the progress of the various reports of the My Lai incident.

General Young, however, did not agree with General Koster's interpretation. For one thing, he said, as the assistant division commander for maneuver elements he worked as much in the north as he did in the south. As he saw it, after he relayed Koster's instructions for an investigation of Thompson's allegations to Colonel Henderson, he had been involved only peripherally. As far as he knew, Henderson had dealt directly with Koster and he, Young, had neither issued further instructions nor checked into subsequent developments. He did recall discussing the inadequacy of a report with Koster at some point, but he did not think it related to Henderson's report of April 24. From his knowledge of the operation, Young told us, he had always thought Thompson's allegations were unfounded; if he had thought otherwise, he would have recommended that they be investigated by an officer outside the 11th Brigade.

Personally, I found the statements of both men concerning their command relationships to be almost unbelievable; as general officers they were too competent for this sort of mishmash. One would have thought they lived worlds apart and hardly ever spoke to each other. In fact, they lived next to one another, their offices were a few feet apart, they had many of their meals together in the commanding general's mess, and they sometimes joined the staff for a drink or so before the evening meal. In a typical division in South Vietnam a great deal of day-to-day business was carried on as a result of this kind of proximity. If the relationship between Koster and Young was as distant and uncommunicative as they indicated to the Inquiry, it was quite apparent that there were serious personnel problems within the division command and staff.

When it came to questioning General Koster, the Inquiry knew there was considerable discrepancy between what he had told the CID investigators and the course of events as we understood them, so we were well aware of the difficulties we faced in trying to resolve these matters.

First we discussed some of the general's policies regarding the operation of the American Division. In regard to the destruction of houses, Koster said that the burning of even a single dwelling required approval by a general officer, which we confirmed by checking published directives of the division. But not only had Task Force Barker burned or destroyed a large number of houses in My Lai-4, on the following day they had burned out at least five other small settlements, possibly uninhabited—and yet nobody had done anything to stop it. General Koster said he had not been aware that any dwellings had been burned.

He told us that it was normal within the division to use artillery preparation on a landing zone for a combat assault, but not on inhabited areas, and that this policy applied whether the area was controlled by the government of South Vietnam or by the Viet Cong. Further, gunships could take armed VC under fire but were prohibited from firing at unarmed civilians. VC field fortifications, tunnels, and military supplies could be destroyed. From my knowledge, the policies of the American Division were comparable with those of other U.S. divisions in South Vietnam; the difference was in their enforcement.

Koster said he had placed great emphasis on the indoctrination of incoming personnel. First he talked to each incoming group for about half an hour, stressing the importance of supporting the people and government of South Vietnam, and then the Staff Judge Advocate would usually give a half-hour briefing in which he covered the handling of noncombatants and prisoners of war and reviewed the contents of the pocket cards issued by the Military Assistance Command, Vietnam. Koster felt that this and the other indoctrination given to incoming personnel, as well as the training the 11th Brigade had undergone in Hawaii and South Vietnam, had given the task force units a thorough familiarity with the Rules of Land Warfare.

In regard to civilian casualties in the Task Force Barker operation, he recalled that Henderson had told him at LZ Dottie on the 16th that he had observed six to eight civilian casualties, but did not remember telling Henderson to stop any "unnecessary killing." Some time later that day he became aware that twenty to thirty civilians had been killed, but wasn't sure whether Henderson had called him that evening to give him this information or had done so at some other time. He was sure he had expressed concern over the killing of civilians in both cases, and this had prompted him to send a letter to all his subordinate commanders on March 24, 1968, emphasizing the safeguarding of noncombatants.

It is ironic that on March 16, 1968, the day of the My Lai operation, the American Division published "Combat Operation, Rules of Engagement." It was a fine document. Although it addressed the application of firepower, it was clear that civilians were to be protected from death or injury. Since a preliminary draft had been circulated throughout the division, General

Koster felt that all his commanders had been well aware of its intent.

When asked why the twenty to thirty civilian casualties had not been reported to higher headquarters, Koster replied that no official report of such casualties had been received from the 11th Brigade. Then he told us that Lieutenant Colonel Jesmond D. Balmer Jr., the division operations officer, had advised him that it was not necessary to report civilian casualties. Koster said he had thought this was somewhat unusual, but had not questioned it.

When we questioned Balmer and several others in the operations section, none of them recalled ever being told about civilian casualties during the My Lai operation, or discussing the requirement to report civilian casualties with General Koster, much less advising him that there was no such requirement.[2] We could only conclude that either somebody was not telling the truth or there had been a tragic, and inexplicable, loss of memory.

The fact is that no report of any kind, other than the operational report of 128 VC killed in action, was ever sent to higher headquarters. This greatly puzzled members of the Inquiry. Even though General Koster had not been thoroughly familiar with MACV Regulation 20–4, he was certainly aware of its existence and intent. Also, at that time the division had been operating under the Task Force Oregon SOP, which required the reporting of civilian casualties, and on previous occasions the Americal Division *had* reported noncombatant deaths—generally few in number, but they had been reported. And, if true, we found it hard to understand how Koster would accept the word of any subordinate officer on such a critical matter without checking it against appropriate regulations. The fact that the 11th Brigade had not officially reported the casualties was a serious matter but, even so, General Koster had been informed on at least two occasions of twenty to thirty noncombatant deaths, whether "officially" or not, and he wasn't even sure if he had passed this information on to his staff. It seemed to the panel that Colonel Henderson's reports, both oral and written, however informal and inadequate they might have been, should have been relayed to higher headquarters.

This failure of the division to report the civilian casualties as they were known by the commanding general, and possibly others within the division headquarters, was one of the critical findings of the Inquiry. Knowing how sensitive both MACV and USARV headquarters were about civilian casualties, had these been reported, it seems almost certain that an official investigation would have been initiated.

General Koster thought he had discussed the allegations in the VC propaganda and the subsequent Report of Investigation with his immediate superior, Lieutenant General Robert E. Cushman, commander of the Third

2. It turned out, however, that Balmer had told General Koster this, but not while they were in Vietnam. It was later, in Washington, over the telephone.

Marine Amphibious Force (III MAF), or possibly with some other officer in that headquarters. However, when we questioned General Cushman, he told us he could recall no such discussion, nor could the III MAF deputy commander, Major General William J. Van Ryzin; the operations officer, Brigadier General Carl H. Hoffman; or another officer in the operations section. Koster said he had also informed Lieutenant General Lam, commander of the Vietnamese I Corps, of the report of investigation but, when we questioned General Lam, he could not remember it.

When asked about the operation of Task Force Barker, Koster said he did not remember flying over the area that morning, although he conceded that he could have done so. His version of the meeting with Colonel Henderson at LZ Dottie was generally consistent with that given by Henderson.

He was not sure how he had heard that Henderson had ordered Charlie Company to return to My Lai-4 to make a body count on the afternoon of the 16th, but he knew he had talked on the radio in his helicopter with the company commander (Captain Medina) and somebody in task force headquarters about it. After listening to their reasoning, he gave careful consideration before countermanding Henderson's order, he said. His rationale had been that it was too late in the day and would unnecessarily subject the company to enemy mines and booby traps. He did not think, however, that his countermanding of this order on the 16th should have precluded Henderson from sending troops back to My Lai-4 at some later time, and he thought the aero scouts would have been a good unit for such a mission. The members of the Inquiry agreed with him on that score, but had some reservations concerning his judgment in countermanding the order in the first place. There were still about four hours of daylight, and the unit would have had to travel only a little more than a mile over ground they had already covered. In any case, we felt that Koster should have located Henderson and discussed the decision with him personally. Henderson had been informed of Koster's action soon thereafter by Task Force Barker, but as far as we were able to ascertain it was never mentioned again. As it was, this decision contributed, either wittingly or unwittingly, to the suppression of information about the My Lai incident.

General Young reported Warrant Officer Thompson's allegations to General Koster on the 17th. Koster's understanding of the report was that the pilot had had a confrontation with a ground commander and that U.S. forces had been shooting more than was necessary. It had seemed strange to him that a helicopter pilot could make such a determination, but he had not realized that at times Thompson had been hovering only a few feet off the ground.

Koster had assumed that the investigation he ordered would be an in-depth one (although, he said, he had not asked for written statements), primarily to determine whether there had been excessive use of firepower and to clarify the circumstances surrounding the confrontation. He said the

B-E.—
U.S. Army Photographs

THE INVESTIGATORS

A. Lieutenant General William R. Peers.—*Wide World Photos.*

The legal members of the inquiry: B. Robert MacCrate, civilian legal counsel; C. Bland West, general counsel and deputy to General Peers; D. Colonel Robert W. Miller and E. Jerome Walsh.

On-scene investigation in the My Lai area—Walsh, MacCrate, and General Peers.—*U.S. Army Photo*

Pentagon news conference, March 17, 1970. *Left to right,* General Peers, Secretary of the Army Stanley Resor, Army Chief of Staff William C. Westmoreland.—*United Press International Photo*

THE "INCIDENT"

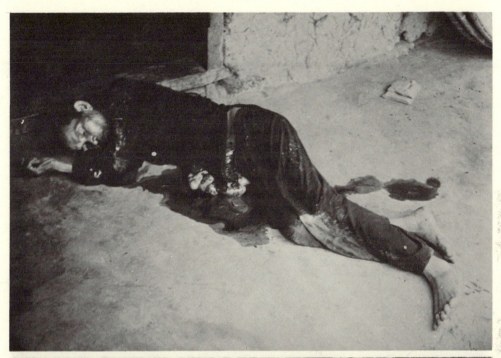

THE PRINCIPALS

Ronald L. Ridenhour. His letter to General Westmoreland triggered the My Lai Inquiry.—*Wide World Photos.*

First Lieutenant William L. Calley, Jr. Charges were prepared against fourteen men. Four were actually tried. Calley was the only one convicted. He was sentenced to life imprisonment. His sentence was reduced to twenty years by the reviewing authority, then to ten years by the Secretary of the Army. Later he was released on parole.—*United Press International Photo.*

Major General Samuel W. Koster. The charges against him were dismissed on January 29, 1971. He received a letter of censure. Later, the Secretary of the Army vacated his rank of temporary major general, reducing him to his permanent rank of brigadier general, and withdrew his Distinguished Service Medal. He retired from the Army on January 1, 1973.—*Wide World Photos*

Captain Ernest Medina. He was command of Charlie Company, which included Lieutenant Calley's platoon. He was court-martialed and found not Guilty. —*Wide World Photos.*

In action at My Lai-Son My. *Left to right,* Lieutenant Colonel Francis Lewis, division chaplain; Lieutenant Colonel Patrick Dionne, public information officer; Brigadier General George H. Young, Assistant Division Commander of the American Division; Lieutenant Colonel Frank Barker, Commanding Officer of Task Force Barker. Charges were prepared against all except Dionne. Barker, an aggressive participant in the body-count competition between unit commanders, was killed before the inquiry was completed. The charges against Chaplain Lewis were withdrawn by the Secretary of the Army. Although the charges against General Young were dismissed, the Secretary of the Army issued a letter of censure and withdrew his Distinguished Service Medal.—*U.S. Army Photo.*

Colonel Oran K. Henderson. The charges against him resulted in a court-martial. He was aquitted.—*Wide World Photo.*

Charges dismissed
A. First Lieutenant (a captain when the picture was taken)
   Thomas K. Willingham.—*United Press International Photo*
B. Major David C. Galvin.—*United Press International Photo*
C. Major William D. Guinn.—*United Press International Photo*
D. First Lieutenant (later Captain) Kenneth W. Boatman.—
   United Press International Photo

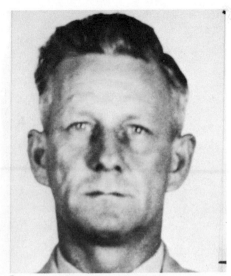

Charges dismissed

A. Major Fredric W. Watke. Letter of administrative admonition.—*Wide World Photos*

B. Lieutenant Colonel Robert B. Luper.—*United Press International Photo.*

C. Major Charles C. Calhoun. Letter of reprimand.—*United Press International Photo.*

D. First Lieutenant Dennis H. Johnson. Letter of reprimand.—*U.S. Army Photo.*

E. Captain Eugene M. Kotouc.—*United Press International Photo.*

My Lai-4, burning.—*U.S. Army Photo.*

results of Colonel Henderson's investigation had come to him piecemeal from Young and Henderson, and he could not recall having received a comprehensive oral report from Henderson. (This was in direct contradiction to what Young had told us—that he had heard about this report from Koster—and to Henderson, who said he had made an oral report to Koster on March 20.) However, Koster said, from the interim reports he had gotten the impression that Henderson had talked with everyone responsible for the operation as well as with a cross section of the personnel in both ground and air units. He thought Henderson had indeed made an in-depth investigation, which had found no evidence of excessive use of firepower. This greatly relieved him, as he had thought that perhaps indiscriminate firing by ground troops, gunships, and artillery had caused the civilian casualties.

We asked General Koster if he had ever been aware of a written report dated April 4–6 that Henderson claimed to have prepared based on his oral report. Koster said no, he did not recall it, and in fact, he said, he had not requested a written report until after he had seen the allegations in the Viet Cong propaganda and the Son Tinh District chief's letter. Then, he said, he had directed Henderson to put his oral report into writing and also to include an investigation of the VC charges. The result, however—Henderson's report of April 24, 1968—responded only to the propaganda and did not cover his former investigation; Koster had considered it to be inadequate. Normally, such a report would have been logged in and filed within the division, he said; if it had not been, he could offer no explanation.

Some time after his return from leave in Hawaii on May 8, 1968, through either General Young or Colonel Parson, the division Chief of Staff, General Koster ordered Henderson to prepare a formal report. However, in their testimony both Young and Parson said they had neither received such a directive nor passed it on to Henderson. An order should have been published directing the investigation, but Koster could not recall this having been done. He thought Colonel Henderson would be conducting the investigation, since he was one echelon above the task force level, and was quite surprised when he heard that Lieutenant Colonel Barker was conducting it. The Report of Investigation was submitted a week or so later, about May 15–16, and Koster's description of its format and conclusions was very similar to Henderson's testimony in this regard. Koster said he discussed the report with Young and Parson, but, again, neither had any knowledge of such a discussion or of seeing the report.

Master Sergeant Gerberding, the brigade intelligence sergeant, vaguely recalled seeing a letter from Koster to Henderson concerning the VC propaganda and the district chief's report and directing Henderson to investigate them, but he was far from certain about this, and did not recall ever seeing the report itself. All of this, combined with the lack of any notations in logs or journals concerning such a report and the fact that we could find no one who had made a sworn, written statement, made it appear highly questionable to me and other Inquiry members that this report had ever existed.

It should be noted that later, during testimony for General Koster's Article 32 investigation, Lieutenant Colonel Barney Brennan Jr. claimed that in May 1969 Lieutenant Colonel Harry Lowder (both men were in the Americal Division at the time) had showed him a copy of Barker's Report of Investigation after the then division Chief of Staff, Colonel John W. Donaldson, had asked them to search their files for documents relevant to the My Lai incident. Lowder denied having seen such a report, as did Donaldson, but Donaldson did say, during his testimony for the Article 32 investigation, that he had heard about Brennan's story during his home leave in November-December 1969.

Regarding the testimony in the Article 32 investigation, as a result of the Army's query to USARV in April 1969 pertaining to the allegations in the Ridenhour letter, Colonel Whitaker, USARV Inspector General, visited headquarters of the Americal Division in search of information and documents. He spent two days there and talked with Major General Gettys, then the commanding general, and Colonel Donaldson; both stated they had no knowledge of any investigation of the My Lai incident. He also had discussions with members of pertinent staff sections with similar results. Searches were made throughout the headquarters for documents, but the only one that was found was Barker's Combat Action Report, *not* his Report of Investigation. It would seem that if Lowder, who was then the personnel officer, did in fact have a copy of Barker's Report of Investigation he would have had no reason for not making it known to Colonel Whitaker.

During the course of the Inquiry we made a diligent effort to locate the document or any information concerning its existence and contents, but Henderson and Koster were the only ones who knew anything about it.

(As for Donaldson having heard Brennan's story during his home leave, it appears to me that he should have made this fact known to the Inquiry when we talked with him during our visit to South Vietnam—he was then a brigadier general and an assistant division commander—or in a written statement he later was requested to provide to the Inquiry. Also, although the Inquiry did not call Brennan to testify, had he volunteered his information to the Inquiry we would have welcomed him with open arms.)

In concluding General Koster's testimony, we discussed the telephone calls between him and Colonel Henderson shortly before the Inquiry got under way. He recalled three such calls, the first after his testimony to the CID in order to clarify some of the dates and events, after which, interestingly, he submitted an addendum to the CID modifying somewhat his answers to their specific questions. The last of the three calls had been made a few days after Henderson's initial appearances before the Inquiry. In his testimony, Henderson had said there was a total of five calls, the first one in mid-November, which would have been about ten days *before* Koster was questioned by the CID. We were never able to clarify completely the number and dates of all the calls. Koster and Henderson agreed, however, that their conversations had covered Thompson's allegations, the countermanding of Henderson's order for Charlie Company to return to My Lai-4, and the investigations and reports of the incident. These telephone calls, I felt, had greatly conditioned General Koster's thinking and his recollection of events, investigations, and reports.

During the next few days we interrogated several key members of the division staff. Since many of the critical issues in their testimony have already have been discussed, only the highlights will be given.

For a person in such a key position, the division Chief of Staff, Colonel Nels A. Parson, surprised us by apparently knowing so little. He recalled that a helicopter pilot had reported "the killing of civilians, probably unnecessary killing of civilians," and that one of the assistant division commanders (specifically who, he wasn't sure) was to look into it. He believed Colonel Henderson had written a report, but did not remember ever having seen it.

When confronted with some statements of witnesses who said they had dealt with him, he said he could not recall them specifically, but if they said they had spoken with him it must be true. He did not recall Major Watke and Lieutenant Colonel Holladay reporting to General Young on the morning of March 17 or Colonel Henderson delivering his report of April 24.

Parson seemed quite amazed that something of the magnitude being reported in the news media could have happened without his knowledge. From the information of the incident available to him at the time, he had not thought it was of major importance or that the initial allegations had been borne out by follow-up information, so he had dismissed it from his mind. He explained this lack of knowledge in part by saying that he was not operationally oriented and had had major administrative problems within the headquarters, particularly in regard to the reorganization of the division.

Personally, I found his attitude toward his position as division Chief of Staff to be astounding. A Chief of Staff serves as the right hand of the commander and helps coordinate and supervise the activities of the entire staff. He must have the complete confidence of the commander and be intimately familiar with everything that takes place within the division. This certainly did not seem to be have been true in this case.

Lieutenant Colonel Jesmond D. Balmer Jr., the division operations officer, had been on R&R leave in Hong Kong until March 17 or 18, but he nevertheless was relatively well informed about the Task Force Barker operation. This, he explained, was the result of a detailed briefing of all the division's operations held during his absence, which his assistant, Lieutenant Colonel Kelley, and others in the operations section had given him when he returned. The only major discrepancy in his testimony was that he thought Bravo and Charlie companies had been lifted out of their night bivouac area on the 17th, whereas both companies had continued the operation for a day or two longer. He had not been aware of any civilian casualties or that General Koster had countermanded an order for Charlie Company to return to My Lai-4. He had thought there was a plan for both Bravo and Charlie companies to sweep back through the area on their return to LZ Dottie but that it had been scrapped due to the heavy minefields in the area.

He did not recall ever talking to General Koster about the reporting of civilian casualties while he was in South Vietnam. However, after the incident was brought to light in the news media, Koster had called him to discuss that matter as well as to clarify some of the abbreviations used in the daily situation reports to higher headquarters. He said he had told the general there was no requirement to report civilian casualties within the division or to higher headquarters, but if any had been reported, they should have been forwarded as part of the operational report.

As has already been noted, Balmer was grossly in error in this regard. Specifically, MACV Directive 335–12 of November 1967 clearly established such a reporting requirement in "incidents which could be detrimental to US/GVN relationship. Such incidents include, but are not limited to, the following when caused by Americans: Injury, death or mistreatment of noncombatants or significant damage to Vietnamese property in the course of tactical operations." Similar requirements were included in USARV and III MAF directives and regulations. In addition, there were numerous other documents issued by higher headquarters that clearly established the intent of minimizing civilian casualties. The division SOP was so strong in this regard, in fact, that it should have triggered automatic reporting.

Balmer concluded his testimony by discussing the functioning of the division and some of its operations during his tenure as operations officer, which provided the Inquiry with valuable insight into the inner workings of the division and its relations with other organizations.

Lieutenant Colonel William D. Kelley had been acting operations officer, during Lieutenant Colonel Balmer's R&R leave, and generally confirmed Balmer's testimony. On occasion he had served as special projects officer for the chief of staff and had assisted in preparing the division Regulation 525–4 "Combat Operations: Rules of Engagement," issued on March 16, 1968. His impression was that all commanders within the division had been familiar with this regulation well before its publication, and he felt that the noncombatant casualties in the My Lai operation should have been reported to the division. Although he had not seen Lieutenant Colonel Barker's Combat Action Report before, when we showed him a copy he said he thought it should have included a report of civilian casualties, livestock destroyed, and dwellings burned.

As a matter of interest, he told us that in April 1968 he had taken command of the 1st Battalion, 6th Infantry, and in September Lieutenant

Calley had been assigned to his battalion as the civil affairs officer. Kelley thought Calley had done a remarkable job, considering his lack of experience, that he had been aggressive and hard working, and that he had established good working relations with his Vietnamese counterparts.

Lieutenant Colonel Tommy P. Trexler, division intelligence officer, appeared only briefly before the Inquiry but gave us an excellent account of how his intelligence staff functioned and his role in it. It seemed obvious that he was a good intelligence officer, not the desk-sitting variety but someone who made frequent visits to field units and other ARVN and U.S. headquarters to obtain firsthand information.

He knew there were strong division policies regarding the reporting of civilian casualties and the burning of houses, and could offer no explanation for the 11th Brigade's failure to report them. Like many others of the division staff, he had not known that anything had gone wrong during the My Lai operation nor had he heard about any investigation or reports. He had been somewhat suspicious of the ratio of weapons captured and friendly forces killed in comparison to the number of enemy killed—normally they would have captured about thirty weapons—but a smaller count was not too unusual, as the VC were often armed only with hand grenades.

He believed the helicopter flight when General Young told him about the My Lai operation was the same one during which he had seen the billowing smoke from several large fires along the coastline. The time and circumstances would indicate that this was on March 17, when General Young visited LZ Dottie—the day Bravo and Charlie companies burned five hamlets.

Major John D. Beasley III, special assistant to the Chief of Staff, had no knowledge of the My Lai incident, did not recall attending the evening briefing, and had not been aware of Colonel Henderson's report of April 24. He had, however, seen one of the attachments, the VC propaganda titled "The American Devils Devulge Their True Form." Beasley was in a fine position to know what was going on in the division because he kept all the papers for the general officers and the Chief of Staff in his safe and had access to them unless they were marked personal.

If a report had come into the headquarters for any of these men, Beasley would have seen it unless it were hand-carried by a colonel or higher grade. He described the normal procedure for handling a report. After receiving it, it would be logged in and routed to the staff. In some urgent cases, he would send papers directly to the Inspector General or Judge Advocate General for immediate action. If any formal investigation had been directed and orders cut, he would have known about it, but he could not recall any such orders or any Report of Investigation, including the one Colonel Henderson said he had submitted in early April or the so-called formal report of about May 20. Moreover, Colonel Parson had never mentioned an investigation or report of the incident to him.

Lieutenant Colonel John T. Jones, Staff Judge Advocate, had absolutely no knowledge of the My Lai incident, not even from rumors. Normally, he attended the evening staff briefing, and if twenty to twenty-five civilians had been reported killed, he said, he would have noted it because of the possibility that claims or solatiums (payments to the families of civilians killed by friendly forces) would be involved. If there had been an official investigation and orders prepared designating an investigating officer, he said, he would surely have known about it. And if the investigation had been of a war crime, he would have had primary responsibility for it. He said there would be no difference in the type of investigation whether an incident occurred in a VC-controlled or a government-controlled area.

Jones had served with the Americal Division until April 2, 1968; he was to be replaced by Lieutenant Colonel Melville A. Wilson, but Major Robert F. Cameau served as Staff Judge Advocate for a few days until Wilson could take over. Major Cameau had not seen Colonel Henderson's April 24 report while he was in Vietnam, but when he returned to the United States and was assigned to the Judge Advocate General's office at the Pentagon it came to his attention during the Inspector General's investigation. His first reaction was: Why didn't I know about this at the time? He felt that the report and its attachments, which cited criminal acts, were of such significance that they should have been reported to MACV. He would have recommended this action if he had seen them in Vietnam, he said, but would have done considerable checking with Vietnamese authorities to clarify some of the details first.

Cameau also told us of a reunion of 11th Brigade officers at Cameron Station in Alexandria, Virginia, in November 1969, which the battalion commanders and other officers in the Washington area had attended. He said their discussion of My Lai had been limited to their reactions to the reports of the incident then in the news.

Later we talked with Lieutenant Colonel Wilson, who became the division Judge Advocate General on April 7, 1968, but his knowledge of the investigations and reports was as limited as that of Jones and Cameau.

If anyone in the division should have known about an investigation—and particularly a formal one—it should have been the Judge Advocate General, the senior legal officer in the headquarters. But these men knew nothing, and could only express dismay that they had not been informed or brought into the case.

Lieutenant Colonel James H. Hetherly, the Inspector General, did not recall the briefing the evening of March 16 at which 128 were reported killed. Similarly, he had never heard that any civilians were killed, or of any kind of investigation being conducted or of any reports. Here again was an officer in a critical position with respect to inspections and investigations, but he was completely in the dark.

Lieutenant Colonel Charles Anistranski, division civil affairs officer, was responsible for developing plans and supervising projects in support of the Vietnamese civilian population. Whenever a Vietnamese civilian was killed or injured it was he who arranged for a solatium payment to be made to the family, which General Koster insisted be done in VC-controlled areas as well as in government areas. Anistranski had made several investigations of this kind for Koster and felt that if twenty or thirty civilians had been killed at My Lai, he would have been asked to look into it. At the evening briefing on the 16th Koster questioned the ratio of VC killed in action to weapons captured. The briefer said he would check, but that was the last Anistranski ever heard about it.

For approximately a week, the My Lai operation was discussed around the headquarters and in the mess halls by enlisted personnel, Anistranski said—including comments about committing atrocities and shooting up a village; in one instance, Lieutenant Calley's and Sergeant Mitchell's names were mentioned in regard to an investigation being conducted "down south" (that is, 11th Brigade headquarters). Anistranski said he had not tried to find out who made this statement because there were always rumors and a lot of hearsay talk about different operations. After a while the My Lai rumors stopped and nothing more was said about it, which he felt was the result of the division policy of squelching rumors.

Lieutenant Colonel Francis Lewis, the division chaplain, frequently needled Anistranski about civilian casualties, sometimes at the evening staff briefings, when he would imply that not all the reported Vietnamese casualties during operations were combatants. He also occasionally came to Anistranski's office to talk about civilians or livestock being killed. Anistranski had paid attention to Lewis because he sometimes received valuable information from him; as chaplain, Lewis talked with the troops a good deal. He had, in fact, told Anistranski that he had heard that some women and children had been killed during the time of the My Lai operation, although Lewis hadn't told him where he had obtained the information and had not actually mentioned My Lai.

As a result of this conversation with Lewis, Anistranski went to see Colonel Henderson at Duc Pho. Without mentioning anybody's name, he asked Henderson if he needed any help in regard to civilian deaths—in making payments to families of victims or anything like that—to which Henderson had replied, "No, I don't. And if we need any assistance from you I'll contact my S-5 [brigade civil affairs officer], and you and the S-5 will work it out." Anistranski said he had waited for this contact but never heard anything. However, he felt he had carried out his responsibilities by going to see Henderson about it.

When Anistranski saw Captain Donald J. Keshel, the 11th Brigade civil affairs officer, he asked him about the My Lai operation and was told to talk to the brigade commander. Since he had already spoken to Henderson, Anistranski "dropped out of the picture," as he put it. It seemed to us that he had been getting the well-known run around, but he felt he had had no right to question a full colonel about his operations, so he had dropped the matter.

Later, from the U.S. advisory group with the 2nd ARVN Division, Anistranski obtained a copy of a letter to Colonel Toan from the Quang Ngai Province chief criticizing the Americal Division for not providing enough support to protect against VC concentrations. Anistranski showed the letter to Colonel Parson, who in turn took it to General Koster. Koster called Anistranski in and asked him where he had gotten the letter; Anistranski told him, and that was the last he had heard of it. He also told us he was certain the letter had been signed by the province chief and had not been written by the district chief to the province chief.

It seemed clear to us that Anistranski—through Chaplain Lewis, rumors, hearsay, and other sources—had obtained a considerable amount of information about the incident. We put some straightforward questions to him while taking his testimony but he told us no more than has been reported here; he felt he had executed his responsibilities and did not want to become further involved.

Colonel Mason J. Young Jr., division artillery commander, had extensive knowledge of the regulations and directives concerning artillery fire control: no artillery was to be fired on populated centers in either VC- or ARVN-controlled areas unless it was specifically requested by the infantry unit being supported; the infantry commander must accept responsibility for such firing; and if any civilians were killed as a result, an Artillery Incident Report must be filed.

He recalled having been briefed on the results of the My Lai operation by Lieutenant Colonel Barker and Major Calhoun, but some time earlier he had heard that some noncombatants had been caught in crossfires. Thus he had been aware that civilians had been killed but wasn't sure where he had heard it—perhaps at the evening briefing. When the sixty-nine VC killed by artillery were called to his attention by the Inquiry he replied that he had never been informed of this, which certainly would have required a report. He said, however, that Lieutenant Colonel Luper, the artillery battalion commander, had seen what appeared to be civilian bodies on the ground, although Young did not feel an Artillery Incident Report had been necessary in that case because Luper had not known how these people had been killed.

Captain Creswell, the division artillery chaplain to whom Warrant Officer Thompson had told his story on the evening of the 16th, had never mentioned anything to Colonel Young about it. As the division artillery commander, Young felt he should have been informed of such a report. He said he vaguely recalled hearing something about an investigation, but all he knew was that Henderson was checking into something through infantry channels.

Finally, Colonel Young told us that while he was stationed at Fort

Leavenworth, Kansas, General Koster had visited and had dinner with him in early December 1969. They had acknowledged, as a result of the news reports, that something must have happened at My Lai, but Koster had not seemed to know much about it.

Captain Creswell told us that Thompson was very upset on the evening of the 16th while he related what he had seen and experienced that day. Thompson said he had seen an "awful lot of bodies"; had landed his helicopter to evacuate some civilians and had threatened an American officer in the process; had seen many bodies in a ditch; and had taken out a small child and flown it to a hospital. Creswell had been convinced Thompson was not talking about just a few civilians being killed, but a large number. He suggested that Thompson file a protest in command channels, and he would do so in chaplains' channels. (Chaplains' channels are for technical chaplains' matters; a report of the killing of a large number of women and children is not such a matter and should have been reported through Creswell's command channels. The result of his not doing so was that the division artillery commander was never made aware of Thompson's charges. If he had been, he would have been obliged to discuss them with the division commanding general and to have initiated an Artillery Incident Report if the information so dictated.)

When Creswell related Thompson's story to the division chaplain, Lieutenant Colonel Lewis, recommending that an investigation be conducted, Lewis had seemed sympathetic and said he would take it up at the command briefing. Three or four days later Lewis told him that the machinery was being geared up and that Thompson was not the only one complaining. About two weeks later Lewis informed him the investigation was progressing, and Creswell said he had felt relieved because he believed in the investigative process, especially since the incident had been reported through command channels. In all events, he did not pursue the matter.

He neither saw nor heard of a Report of Investigation, but was sure that if Thompson's allegations had been given more than a cursory examination they would have been substantiated. He expressed utter disbelief when he was told by the Inquiry that sixty-nine VC had been reported killed by artillery, and was positive that if such a number had been cited at the division artillery briefing he would have remembered it.

Chaplain Creswell said he had never discussed the My Lai operation or Thompson's story with the division artillery commander, but nobody had ever told him to keep quiet about it.

Lieutenant Colonel Francis Lewis, division chaplain, remembered that at the briefing on the evening of the 16th when the results of the My Lai operation were given (he recalled 124 VC killed) Lieutenant Colonel Anistranski had laughingly said under his breath, "They were all women and children." When only three weapons were reported captured, there had been considerable murmuring and buzzing among the staff members. Generals Koster and Young were at the briefing but Lewis was not sure if they could have heard what was going on. The thing that stuck in his mind was that 124 people—women and children—had been killed and only three weapons captured. In his opinion it was common knowledge within the division that something had gone wrong in the operation.

On the 17th Captain Creswell came to tell Lewis of Thompson's allegations. Creswell was very upset and gave Lewis the impression that many innocent women and children had been killed through the use of unnecessary firepower. Lewis recalled Creswell telling him about a sergeant firing on civilians, but couldn't remember anything about bodies in a ditch, the evacuation of women and children from a bunker, or taking a wounded child to a hospital.

When he talked to Lieutenant Colonel Barker about the operation he was told that it had been investigated but Barker hadn't seemed overly concerned about women and children being killed by artillery, gunships, and ground fire. As Lewis remembered it, Barker had said, "Well, Colonel Lewis, as far as I'm concerned it was combat. These occurred. It was tragic that we killed these women and children, but it was in combat operation. That is what I will report back to Colonel Henderson." Although this had not entirely settled his qualms, Lewis had great confidence in Barker's integrity, so he accepted this explanation.

Even so, Lewis told us, Chaplain Creswell was more incensed over Thompson's allegations than he, and continued to question him about them. As a result, Lewis talked with several members of the division staff, including Lieutenant Colonel Balmer and his replacement, Lieutenant Colonel Baxley, and Lieutenant Colonels Trexler, Anistranski, and Qualls. He said he had asked them "What about the 124 women and children we killed? What are we going to do about this?" He was not sure, but thought it was Balmer who assured him that the incident was being investigated and told him to keep quiet about it. Informally, he informed Colonel Parson of Thompson's report, and was told that it was common knowledge that an investigation was being conducted. When he asked how it was coming, Parson replied, "It is not to be talked about; we're not saying anything about this." Lewis said he had wanted to talk to General Koster, but Parson would not let him do so. Finally, he got the impression that the matter was being taken care of, and that satisfied him. Lewis said he also talked with some of the U.S. advisory staff at Quang Ngai Province, who told him they knew nothing about an atrocity having been committed. Lewis had never heard of orders being published for an investigation, and had never seen a report or heard the outcome of any investigation.

Lieutenant Colonel Orbun Qualls, division personnel officer, had been aware that Task Force Barker had been in heavy contact but could not recall the details. He had not known that an investigation was being conducted and emphatically denied talking to Lieutenant Colonel Lewis about the My Lai operation.

It was quite apparent that the Americal Division had been put on notice from several quarters that a major tragedy had occurred during the My Lai operation. For one reason or another, however, the incident had never been properly investigated and had remained unknown to higher military authority and the American people until Ron Ridenhour sent his letter about a year later.

chapter 13

Trip to South Vietnam

Our visit to Vietnam was scheduled for late December. The paramount purpose of the trip, as I saw it, was to locate pertinent documents; in addition, we wanted to visit the scene of the Task Force Barker operation, and we also hoped to find and question some Vietnamese who were familiar with the incident. Finally, the trip had a psychological aspect—we wanted to satisfy some members of Congress and the American public that we were willing to investigate in South Vietnam itself.

For my part, I was not optimistic about what we would accomplish, especially in regard to locating documents. In April 1969, when USARV headquarters had conducted a preliminary search for documents at the Americal Division, the only document of any relevance that had been located was Lieutenant Colonel Barker's Combat Action Report covering the March 16 operation. The 11th Infantry Brigade had also conducted a document search and found nothing. Later, as a result of Colonel Henderson's request to the Americal Division Chief of Staff, a copy of his Report of Investigation was found in the 11th Brigade files and a copy was sent to USARV. The inability to find pertinent documents can be explained at least in part by the fact that unless one understood the details of the operation and its subsequent reports and investigations it would be difficult to determine whether a document was relevant or not. Another possibility, of course, was that such documents had been destroyed.

In organizing for the trip we divided the Inquiry staff about in half. One part was to remain in Washington, under the direction of Bland West, to continue interrogating witnesses and conduct other essential functions. Bob MacCrate, Jerry Walsh, and I—along with Major Clyde Lynn (recorder);

Specialist-7 Milton Brown and Private James Holland (reporters); Specialist-6 James R. Thomas (stenographer); Major William F. Gabella (information officer); Major David D. Dantzacher (interpreter); and Specialist-5 Robert Fromme (photographer)—were to go to Vietnam. We also wanted another combat-experienced officer to accompany us, and from the Army staff we selected Lieutenant Colonel John E. Rogers, who was a great help. Finally, we arranged for Warrant Officer Thompson to join us in Vietnam. Colonel Thomas F. Whalen, who had been in charge of our search for documents, and Lieutenant Colonel Leo Brandt had gone ahead earlier to make arrangements for us and establish liaison with staff elements of MACV and USARV and with headquarters down the chain of command —the Third Marine Amphibious Force (III MAF) and the Americal Division (and their Vietnamese counterparts), Quang Ngai Province and Son Tinh District, and the 11th Infantry Brigade.

We arrived at Saigon's Tan Son Nhut airport about 9:00 A.M. on December 26. Unexpectedly, quite a large group of reporters was there to meet us. Bob McCrate and I held a planeside press conference in which we explained the purpose of the trip and what we hoped to accomplish.

We went directly to MACV headquarters to discuss the details of our visit with Colonel Whalen and Lieutenant Colonel Brandt. Colonel Whalen had located a few soldiers connected with the My Lai incident who had returned to South Vietnam for a second tour. We questioned a couple of them that afternoon, and a total of nine while we were in South Vietnam, but none of them had anything of significance to offer.

Our first day there I paid a visit to the MACV commander, General Creighton Abrams, but he had been ill and was away, so I talked to his deputy, General William B. Rosson. We discussed our plans in some detail, and he offered no objections. He said that if we ran into any problems or needed additional assistance to let him know.

We knew we were short-handed, and requested some assistance from MACV. They made available to us Lieutenant Colonel Billy J. Stansberry, an interpreter; Navy Commander William J. Davis, as the Judge Advocate General's representative; Captain Werner Unzelmann from MACV intelligence; and Chief Warrant Officer Andre C. Feher, as the CID representative. Feher, an old hand in the investigation business, had been in South Vietnam for a considerable time, spoke some Vietnamese, and was well informed about the My Lai incident. In this regard, he had not only interrogated several Vietnamese but had also visited My Lai-4 and had taken photographs. He strongly suspected that more had taken place in the Bravo Company area than had thus far been brought to light. This opinion, as well as our own growing concern, prompted us to delve into Bravo Company's activities on March 16–18.

Like all large military headquarters, MACV had so many document files that it would have been physically impossible for us to conduct a complete search on our own. Accordingly, we told them what type of documents we were looking for and asked them to have each staff section search their files, give us the original or a true copy of anything they found, and then to certify that the search had been completed. We also arranged to make spot checks of certain files ourselves.

The following day Bob MacCrate, Jerry Walsh, and I flew to Long Binh to confer with Lieutenant General Frank T. Mildren, USARV deputy commanding general, and members of his staff. We had a good exchange of thoughts and reviewed the procedures they had employed in searching for documents within the Americal Division. Just to make sure they had not missed anything, we established the same procedures for searching their files as we had with MACV.

Soon thereafter we flew by to I Corps Tactical Zone (I CTZ), the area in which the My Lai incident occurred. We checked with III MAF headquarters, the senior U.S. military command in that zone at the time of the incident. They knew only of the operational report of the incident, so all we could do was to arrange for a search of their files.

Lieutenant General Hoang Xuan Lam was the commanding general of I CTZ. Since General Koster had testified that he thought he had mentioned the Task Force Barker operation and the investigation of civilian casualties to General Lam, Bob MacCrate, and I arranged to talk with him. General Lam said he had no recollection of General Koster or any other American ever mentioning My Lai or the Task Force Barker operation to him. Colonel Toan had told him of a village chief's report that U.S. troops had killed some civilians in Son Tinh District, but Toan had been assured by the U.S. commanders that they had checked into it and found it to be untrue. He was sure that he and his headquarters had received the official report of U.S. and VC casualties, but he could not recall having actually seen them. He had put the operation out of his mind until the Calley story broke in the U.S. press and was picked up by the Vietnamese news media. Then he had rechecked it with his subordinate commanders. Lam told us that Lieutenant Colonel Khien had conducted a form of investigation in November 1969 when he questioned several former My Lai-4 residents then living in a new refugee camp located a couple of miles to the west. Khien had concluded that about twenty-two civilians had been killed in the course of the operation on March 16, and that the VC leaflet claiming five hundred noncombatants had been killed was gossip. Lam said that his headquarters had been searched for documents, but nothing had been found.

When our meeting was breaking up General Lam asked if I would stay behind for a few minutes to talk with him in private. He told me he thought the American press was making too big a thing of My Lai. While it might be true that some civilians had been killed in VC territory, and he disliked seeing any civilians killed, that was the nature of the war and he could not be overly concerned by the reports of the incident. It seemed apparent to me that he was speaking not only for himself but for elements of his government as well, and his views were generally consistent with those being expressed by Vietnamese authorities to U.S. reporters throughout South Vietnam. Essentially, they wanted to play down the incident in order to minimize any disruptive effect it might have on U.S.-South Vietnamese relations.[1] I told the general that, although I appreciated his point of view, we had to obtain the facts of the incident so as to be able to refute or confirm whether or not atrocities had been committed. I had known General Lam for some time; I understood his position and felt he accepted mine.

Next we went to Chu Lai, Americal Division headquarters, where Major General Lloyd B. Ramsey, the commanding general, had made excellent arrangements for our visit. Warrant Officer Thompson joined us there.

On January 1, 1970, we made a low-level reconnaissance flight over the sites identified by Thompson. He flew as co-pilot in one helicopter, and I sat behind in the observer seat. Two gunships accompanied us to provide protection, and General Ramsey, in his command helicopter, directed the operation, with Bob MacCrate as a passenger.

We went directly to My Lai-4 and, flying at treetop level, Thompson pointed out where he had seen the bodies on Highway 521, where he had dropped smoke grenades to indicate wounded civilians, and the precise spot where he had seen the captain shoot a woman. We then went to the area where Thompson had seen the bodies in a ditch and had landed to talk to a sergeant. Finally, we flew to the area where he had seen the women and children running toward a bunker and had again landed and had had a verbal confrontation with an American lieutenant. This area was pock-marked with numerous mounds overgrown with grass, obviously some of the graves of the victims of the incident.

When we flew over the area again Thompson pointed out a courtyard within the hamlet where he had seen another group of bodies. We also flew to Hill 85 to the south to locate the site where he had spotted the rounds of 60-mm. mortar ammunition. Finally we flew to the coast and then south to the Song Tra Khuc River to observe the area where Charlie and Bravo companies had operated on March 17 and 18.

On January 3 we made a ground reconnaissance of My Lai-4. We flew to the hamlet by helicopter and upon arrival were given a briefing by Task Force Roman, which was to provide the security for our reconnaissance.

---

1. Most of the senior Vietnamese officers were unwilling to criticize U.S. forces. They did not want to "rock the boat" and jeopardize their relations with the U.S. government, which was furnishing them with weapons, material, money, and troops. In addition, as Asians they were undoubtedly reluctant to find fault or make disrespectful statements to anyone face to face. Instead, they played down charges against the Americans and couched their criticism in soft terms so as not to aggravate those hearing it. This should have been understood by the Americans dealing with Vietnamese in regard to the My Lai charges, but—either knowingly or unknowingly—they seemed to have missed the point and did not appreciate the enormity of the information being given to them.

Except for mines and booby traps the hamlet was considered secure, although subject to possible enemy sniper fire. Task Force Roman was built around C Company, 5th Battalion, 46th Infantry, augmented by scout, dog, and mine-detection teams. Helicopter gunship and artillery support were available on call. Before our arrival the security force had gone through the hamlet, cut the brush, and cleared the mines from the major trails, which they had marked with white tape. If we had to leave the main trails for any purpose, they would sweep the area with mine detectors first. Because of the remote possibility of enemy fire they asked us to wear steel helmets and armored vests. It was their show, so we did as requested.

We covered the hamlet quite thoroughly, identifying specific locations in some of the photographs, and places witnesses had mentioned. The hamlet area was almost entirely taken over by jungle undergrowth; visibility in most places was only five to twenty feet. The structures had further deteriorated in the intervening two years and were now almost completely destroyed. For all practical purposes, it was a dead village. After about two hours, we left My Lai-4 and walked southeast to the ditch. It too was overgrown so it was hard to estimate its size in width and depth, but it wasn't difficult to imagine what had taken place there on the morning of March 16, 1968.

We were accompanied by three Vietnamese who had been associated with the incident. Two of them had been interpreters with Charlie Company during the My Lai-4 operation—Sergeant Nguyen Donh Phu with Captain Medina and Sergeant Doung Minh with Lieutenant Johnson. They were most helpful in pointing out specific sites relating to the photographs. During later questioning, Phu generally corroborated Medina's testimony but recalled taking a different path through the eastern part of My Lai-4. More importantly, he said he had seen many more dead civilians than the twenty to twenty-eight reported by Medina. Sergeant Minh told us of his efforts to get the killing stopped and to have it reported to higher authority, to no avail. He too said they had taken a different path through the hamlet and had seen many more bodies than Johnson had testified to having seen.

The third Vietnamese was a civilian named Pham Chot, who had been a resident of My Lai-4 and an active VC. He had observed the Charlie Company operation from a hiding place on the north slope of Hill 85. Through Lieutenant Colonel Stansberry, Chot told us how had he returned to the hamlet the night of the 16th to find the body of his teen-aged daughter. He had buried her in a family plot a mile or so to the south and spent the rest of the night helping bury another hundred of the residents in hastily dug shallow graves. Another hundred or so were buried the following night. His wife and other child had fled the hamlet at the time of the attack, but returned in two days. Later, he said, he had decided there wasn't much hope in the VC cause, so he had surrendered to the province authorities through the amnesty program known as Chieu Hoi. Then he joined the Kit Carson scouts to serve as a guide for allied forces and to track down the VC. Whether he actively supported the government of South Vietnam or remained true to the Communist cause as a double agent may be debatable. However, his story was very touching and one could only feel a great deal of sympathy for him.

After seeing the ditch, we boarded armored personnel carriers and made a swing through the paddy fields around the southern and western portions of the hamlet to get a better look at its periphery. When we finally arrived back at our helicopters we had spent about three and a half hours in and around the hamlet and felt it had been most useful in giving us information with which to reconstruct some of the events that had taken place there.

Because of our increasing interest in Bravo Company's operation we decided to split the official party into two interrogation teams. Bob Mac-Crate and I would work down through the U.S. and Vietnamese headquarters, checking on reports and investigations of the overall My Lai incident, while Jerry Walsh and the others on his team would check into the activities of Bravo Company.

In Quang Ngai Province Bob and I visited the headquarters of the 2nd ARVN Division, Quang Ngai Province, Son Tinh District, and the office of the Census Grievance chief.[2] We also talked with some of the personnel then assigned to the various U.S. advisory groups. Following is the sequence of events subsequent to March 16, 1968, as we pieced it together from what they told us and from documents they made available to us.

The first information to come from the My Lai area was on March 18, two days after the incident, in a letter from one of the Census Grievance cadremen to his chief, Nguyen Duc Te.[3] It alleged that on March 15, 1968 (obviously an error since there was no operation on that date), there had been an allied operation in which 320 people had been killed in Thuan Yen (My Lai-4) and Binh Dong, 27 in My Lai, and 80 in Co Luy, a total of 427. Mr. Te did not recall forwarding the letter to the province chief (there was no indication that anyone else had, either), although he said he had probably discussed it with the province chief. We talked with him about the Census Grievance report alleging that one to two thousand civilians had been killed—the report Lieutenant Colonel Guinn said he had passed on to Colonel Henderson. Neither Mr. Te nor his deputy remembered anything about it.

Our documents team, aided by Lieutenant Colonel Stansberry, located some interesting documents in the files of the Son Tinh District headquarters. One was a report from Dinh Luyen Do, Son My Village chief, dated

2. In late 1967 Census Grievance teams had been formed in each province, to report to a province Census Grievance chief. As their name implies, these teams were to maintain population counts in the hamlets and villages, receive complaints from the people, take corrective action, if possible, and pass on information to their higher headquarters.
3. Document 13–1: Letter from Census Grievance Cadreman (March 18, 1968). See page 276.

March 22, 1968, which accused U.S. forces of killing 570 civilians—480 in Tu Cung and 90 in Co Luy.[4] Lieutenant Tran Ngoc Tan, formerly the Son Tinh District chief, recalled seeing such a report. He felt that much of it was VC propaganda, Mr. Do could not visit the village and got his information from Son My Village people who had come to Quang Ngai City. When we talked with Mr. Do, he first denied having written the report but later acknowledged it when he was shown a copy. He said it had been based on rumor and hearsay, and that only about thirty civilians had been killed—by artillery, gunships, and small arms during the firefight, in which hundreds of VC had been killed. He claimed that the information had been based mostly on VC propaganda; he hadn't been very disturbed by it. It seemed to us that somebody from ARVN or the South Vietnamese government had given him the party line because what he told us was at great variance with his report of March 22, 1968.

Lieutenant Tan said that on March 28 he sent a letter—titled "Confirmation of Allied Troops Shooting at Residents of Tu Cung Hamlet," based on Mr. Do's report—to the province chief.[5] It had not been a very strong letter and had prompted no action on the part of the province chief. According to Tan, a few days later Mr. Do gave him a more complete report, including a list of the civilian casualties by name. This had disturbed Tan very much, and on April 11 he sent a strong letter to the province chief, titled "Allied Operations at Son My Assembled and Killed Civilians,"[6] with copies to the 2nd ARVN Division, U.S. Quang Ngai Sector (Lieutenant Colonel Guinn's office) and to the U.S. advisor, Son Tinh (Major Gavin's office). A copy of this letter was located in the Son Tinh District files and given to us, but we were never able to find Mr. Do's letter with the list of civilian casualties. Tan was certain it was in the file, but although several searches were conducted it was never found.

To say that Lieutenant Tan's letter was strong is an understatement. It gives some detail of the operation, states that "only one American was killed by the VC, however, the allies killed nearly 500 civilians in retaliation," and closes with "Really an atrocious attitude if it cannot be called an act of insane violence. Request you intervene on behalf of the people." It was so pointed that anyone who saw it, Vietnamese or American, should have been alerted to the fact that a major atrocity had occurred and should have initiated a proper investigation at once. At a bare minimum the details should have been reported to higher headquarters.

Lieutenant Tan had been a totally cooperative witness, and he had a keen sense of loyalty and respect for all the Vietnamese people. He spoke practically no English, so Bob MacCrate and I told Stansberry what we wanted,

4. Document 13-2: Report from Son My Village Chief (March 22, 1968). See page 277.
5. Document 13-3: Lt. Tan's Letter to Province Chief (March 28, 1968).See page 278.
6. Document 13-4: Lt. Tan's Letter to Province Chief (April 11, 1968). See page 279.

and then he and Tan would talk, sometimes for ten or fifteen minutes, after which Stansberry gave us the details. (Much of the credit for the success of our trip belongs to Lieutenant Colonel Stansberry; not only was he able to speak several Vietnamese dialects, but he was obviously well liked by the Vietnamese.)

When we visited the 2nd ARVN Division, we talked with Colonel Toan, the division commander, and his intelligence officer, Major Pham Van Pho. The sequence of events in their headquarters was generally as follows. About the same time the 2nd ARVN Division received its copy of Lieutenant Tan's letter of April 11, Major Pho obtained a copy of a VC document.[7] in which American forces were accused of killing five hundred civilians in Tinh Khe (that would be either Son My or My Lai) on March 15, 1968 (apparently, again, an error in the date). On April 12 Pho forwarded these two documents[8] to Toan, who in turn sent a postal message to Lieutenant Colonel Khien referring to Tan's letter and directing Khien to conduct another investigation.[9] He concluded this message with, "In event report is not true, instruct Son Tinh District to rectify the above report. If correct, report to G-2 [intelligence office], 2nd Division; this headquarters will intervene." Toan said he had later discussed the report with General Lam, I-CTZ commander. This was probably the only report that was ever passed on to ARVN higher headquarters. Lam, however, took no action to insure that the incident was properly investigated within Vietnamese channels, nor did he pass the information on to his senior U.S. advisor, Lieutenant General Cushman.

Toan also told us that some time in mid-April General Koster and Colonel Henderson had visited him on separate occasions. Both men were familiar with the VC propaganda, Toan said, and he had given them the details of Lieutenant Tan's April 11 letter and told them of his decision to have Khien investigate it. He said they discussed it at some length. He had acknowledged that the village chief's report to Tan might have been based upon hearsay information received from visiting villagers. He had not, however, tried to play down Tan's letter; on the contrary, he said, he had called to their attention the similarity between it and the accusations in the VC propaganda. He said he had asked Koster to assist in any way he could to check into the incident.

Next we visited the Quang Ngai Province chief, Lieutenant Colonel Khien. It was fortunate that we saw him when we did, as it was his last day of duty in that assignment; he was being transferred to become the province chief of Quang Tri, the northernmost province of South Vietnam. He was most cordial and cooperative, and he was a great help in clarifying the

7. Document 13-5: VC Propaganda Broadcast, "American Evil Appears." See page 280.
8. Document 13-6: Maj. Pho's Memorandum to Col. Toan (April 12, 1968). See page 282.
9. Document 13-7: Col. Toan's Postal Message to Lt. Col. Khien (April 15, 1968). See page 283.

geographic terminology for us.

When we started discussing Lieutenant Tan's letters, Khien went to another room and came back with a sheaf of papers. They included Tan's letters of March 28 and April 11, Toan's directive to investigate further, and copies of the VC propaganda. One paper in particular caught our eye—the statement that had been one of the enclosures to Henderson's April 24 Report of Investigation. Up to this time, we had had no idea where this document had originated, who had prepared it, or whether it had been signed. Khien's copy, however, did have a signature—that of Captain Angel Rodriguez, who, it turned out, had been the deputy senior advisor to Major Gavin on the U.S. advisory team at Son Tinh District headquarters. At last we had found an original copy and knew the background of this important document.

We were never able to determine who had deleted Rodriguez' signature, or where this had been done. None of the witnesses testified to having seen a signed copy, and Lieutenant Colonel Guinn elected to remain silent when he was asked about it. Thus the author would never have been identified had not it been for Khien. Without the signature the statement appears to be of Vietnamese origin and tends to downgrade both the incident and the contents of Tan's letter. The signature could have been deleted only with malice aforethought.

As far as Khien could remember, the signed statement had been given to him by Guinn. He also recalled that he had discussed Tan's letter of April 11 with James May, the province senior advisor. When we talked with Lieutent Tan again, he recalled that Captain Rodriguez had come to him for information, and that he had seen Rodriguez' statement before it had been sent to the U.S. advisory staff at Quang Ngai.

We asked Lieutenant Colonel Khien about the investigation he had been directed to make by Colonel Toan. He explained that it could have been done only by conducting a ground operation into the area and all he had available to him were some Regional Forces units, which were not sufficiently trained for combat. When we asked him why he hadn't accepted Colonel Henderson's offer to provide some troops to assist or to conduct a joint operation, Khien just sort of shrugged it off. He did say that in June 1968, almost three months after the incident, they had started an operation to go into My Lai-4 but had encountered strong resistance. Almost simultaneously two allied aircraft had collided and the troops had been directed to secure the crash site. (By coincidence, one of the aircraft was the helicopter in which Lieutenant Colonel Barker and Captain Michles were killed.) Because of this they never reached My Lai-4, and the operation had been terminated. It seemed to us that Khien and other senior Vietnamese commanders had not been overly anxious to investigate the My Lai incident. They had probably been apprehensive about what they might find, and, above all, they had not wanted to report upon the actions of an American unit.

Khien evidently had made a personal effort during the summer of 1968 to check into the My Lai operation. He said that he had talked with twenty or more former residents of My Lai-4, but the information he received was sketchy. When Charlie Company's operation started on March 16 the people had fled the area and had not seen what happened. However, he had learned that the following day they had returned and buried over a hundred bodies. Both Robert T. Burke, who had replaced James May as province senior advisor, and Lieutenant Colonel John Green, Guinn's deputy, were with Khien when he made the interrogations and confirmed that he had talked with the people about a mile or so west of My Lai-4. Also, as Lieutenant General Lam had told us, Khien did go to the refugee camp in November 1969, after the incident had broken in both the U.S. and Vietnamese news, to interrogate several former residents of My Lai-4.

When Bob MacCrate and I visited the headquarters of the 11th Brigade at Duc Pho we asked them for the original of the file copy of Colonel Henderson's Report of Investigation. We noted some minor differences in typing between it and the copies that had been sent to Henderson, the American Division, and USARV headquarters. This was of no real significance, but it was interesting to know that the differences existed.

Meanwhile, Jerry Walsh and his group were interrogating Vietnamese from the Co Luy area in which Bravo Company had operated on March 16, 1968, and a couple of days thereafter. They talked to about twenty-five persons from the area and prepared transcripts of the interrogations; they also talked informally with others to obtain background information. A refugee camp had been set up by Quang Ngai Province headquarters on Highway 521 and many of the former residents of the My Lai-Co Luy areas had moved there. From the information they had gathered, Walsh felt certain that some atrocities had been committed by Bravo Company, but it was so jumbled and, at times, contradictory that it was difficult to piece together any kind of a picture. We knew we would have to probe much deeper into this area, and would have to question former members of Bravo Company when we returned to the United States.

Walsh and his group also uncovered some important information about My Lai-4. One of the Vietnamese they interrogated had survived the massacre in the ditch because he had been shielded by bodies and had been shot only once. He showed them the scars where the bullet had entered and left his calf and had quite a story to tell regarding the action at the ditch. Even more importantly, they questioned a young man from Binh Tay who had been hiding in the bushes and had seen his mother being raped and killed. This was the first indication we had that the 2nd Platoon of Charlie Company had gone into Binh Tay and committed additional atrocities there. As soon as Walsh told me about it, I sent the information to Bland West. When we returned to Washington, he told us that it had arrived at a most opportune time because they were just beginning to interrogate members of the 2nd Platoon, and they had quickly confirmed the events in Binh Tay.

Meanwhile, our document-collection team was methodically going through the files of each staff section of the Americal Division, 11th Brigade, and the U.S. advisory elements with the 2nd ARVN Division, Quang Ngai Province, and Son Tinh District. They were searching for any documents pertaining to the My Lai incident, and especially for:

- Colonel Henderson's Report of Investigation of April 4–6, 1968.
- Copies of Henderson's Report of Investigation of April 24, 1968. (Although we had a copy of this report, we were trying to find out who else might have known about it.)
- Lieutenant Colonel Barker's Report of Investigation of about mid-May 1968 endorsed by Colonel Henderson.
- Indications in the logs or journals that any of the above reports had been received.
- Orders appointing Barker as an investigating officer.

Except for Henderson's April 24 report, none of them was found.

For the most part, the documents found in the files by the collection team and those located by internal searches in the higher headquarters pertained to orders, regulations, directives, and the like—about six linear feet of them, in all. They were important to the Inquiry for background and reference purposes, but few of them related directly to the incident or subsequent reports or investigations. One reason we were given for the absence of crucial documents within the Americal Division was that in July 1968 USARV had conducted a routine command inspection of the division. In preparation the division and its subordinate commands had cleaned their files of any unnecessary documents. Even so, these documents should have been entered in the appropriate logs and journals and should have been sent to the U.S. Army Document Center in Suitland, Maryland, rather than being destroyed.

At the Americal Division headquarters, the collection team located a Viet Cong Notice dated March 28, 1968, entitled "Concerning the Crimes Committed by US Imperialists and Their Lackeys who Killed More Than 500 Civilians of Tinh Khe Village (Son My), Son Tinh District."[10] Its portrayal of the action was correct with respect to location and other details, but it was in error in citing the 82nd Airborne Division as the unit involved. Whether the document had been prepared in March 1968 or at a much later date—perhaps even after news of the incident had become public—we were never able to find out.

I visited the operations office of Company B, 123rd Aviation Battalion, in hopes of finding a copy of the operational reports that Warrant Officer

10. Document 13–8: VC Notice, "Concerning the Crimes Committed by US Imperialists and Their Lackeys" (March 28, 1968). See page 283.

Thompson and others said they had prepared on March 16 after they returned to Chu Lai. The requirement to make these reports had been established by the unit itself, rather than by higher headquarters. Some time after the My Lai operation, ostensibly to cut down on paperwork, the unit had decided to drop the requirement and all such reports had been destroyed. I was disappointed to learn this, but the action had been perfectly legal; I could find no indication of any intent to destory evidence relating to the incident.

The files of the U.S. advisory elements were likewise bereft of any significant documents, but in this case there was no satisfactory explanation for their absence. Certainly the advisory element at both province and district headquarters should at least have had copies of Lieutenant Tan's April 11 letter since we knew they had received it. And they should have had copies of Captain Rodriguez' statement, but none was found.

In assessing the overall document situation within the American Division, its subordinate units, and the advisory groups, we felt that some of the documents might have been selectively destroyed as a means of suppressing information of the incident. Some members of the Inquiry, in fact, felt there had been a concerted effort within the American Division to purge the files of relevant documents, but we we never able to find out when and by whom. We also felt that in some instances we might have been looking for fictitious documents—referred to in testimony but never actually existing.

Bob MacCrate was especially troubled by this lack of documents. Although he realized that some of them might have been removed to put the files in order for the Inspector General's inspection, the purging of division and U.S. advisory group files was so complete that he felt it was the result of a conspiracy. We explored every possible avenue in attempting to verify his suspicions, but in the end we could find no conclusive evidence. Still, it remained a distinct possibility.

When we returned to Saigon we made a courtesy call upon the deputy ambassador at the U.S. Embassy and informed him, in broad terms, of what we had accomplished in South Vietnam. I also had a short session with the CIA Vietnam station chief, but he said he had no information about the incident or reports and investigations. That evening Bob MacCrate, Jerry Walsh, and I had dinner with General Rosson, deputy MACV commander, and William E. Colby, deputy MACV commander for civil operations with ambassadorial status. In addition to discussing the results of our visit to South Vietnam, we talked about the American involvement in the war. It was most interesting to hear their viewpoints.

The following day we had a press conference at Ton Sun Nhut, and then returned to Washington and still another press conference at Andrews Air Force Base. Contrary to my rather pessimistic outlook at the beginning, we had achieved most of our objectives. On the whole, the trip had been most fruitful.

chapter 14

Continuing the Inquiry

While we were in South Vietnam, Bland West and his interrogation team had questioned forty-one additional witnesses from Charlie Company, which meant that we had the testimony of more than half the men in the company.

Before leaving for Vietnam we had set up a team to start preparing the final report. We had no idea when the Inquiry panel would complete its work but realized that we could not wait until the last minute to get going on the report. Colonel Franklin was selected to organize and head the group responsible for its preparation. I drew up a draft outline as a working document, but I also told Colonel Franklin to look at other reports from panels, study groups, and the like to determine the most applicable format for ours.

From within the Inquiry panel, Colonel Franklin put together a talented, combat-experienced group of writers—Lieutenant Colonels Charles J. Bauer, Fred Mahaffey, James H. Patterson, and Wallace W. Noll. Later Lieutenant Colonel John E. Rogers joined the group, and we also obtained two more operational analysts (Major George K. Garner and Captain Thomas Keenan), more secretaries, and larger office space. We requested assistance from the Army's Office of Military History, and they sent us Dr. Walter Hermes, whose writing abilities proved to be of great value to the Inquiry. The writing group began its work almost immediately by developing a preliminary format, assembling background materials, and preparing drafts of some of the introductory chapters.

While we were in Vietnam, Colonel Franklin and his group had participated in taking testimony during the day and at night had spent long hours putting together the bits and pieces of information and plotting the locations of men and units at specific times. They were able to follow the activities of some of the men throughout the entire Task Force Barker operation in My Lai-4. It was a tedious, time-consuming task that could only be done by persons who were thoroughly conversant with tactics, from the actions of a single soldier up to company and battalion levels. The job remaining was to reconstruct the operation of the entire company. Although all the writers participated in putting together the story of the tactical action, Lieutenant Colonel Mahaffey deserves special praise, as he served as the coordinator and did a great deal of the writing himself.

The morning after our return from Vietnam we had a long meeting with the Inquiry panel to bring everybody up to date, analyze our requirements, and assign specific tasks. As it worked out, some of the key decisions were:

- Bob MacCrate and I would focus our attention on investigations, reports, and possible suppression of information.
- Bland West would continue to direct the interrogation of Charlie Company personnel.
- Jerry Walsh and Colonel Wilson were to oversee the investigation of the Bravo Company operation, which had come to the forefront in South Vietnam. We had much work to do in that area.
- Colonel John W. Armstrong was assigned the task of checking into the activities of Alpha Company, as we had heard that at least one civilian had been wounded or killed in the Alpha Company area.
- Lieutenant Colonel Patterson was given the responsibility of checking into the aviation scene, to be assisted by Major Stanley Kraus, a well-qualified Army aviator. As more testimony was taken, this area was becoming cloudy, if not confused. We knew the air assault of Charlie and Bravo companies had been done with nine troop-carrying (slick) helicopters and two gunships. The 174th Aviation Company at Duc Pho had confirmed that number of slicks and guns, so we assumed they had conducted the lift—but it was not checking out. We were also having problems trying to identify the sequence of gunships flying in support of Warrant Officer Thompson.

Clearly, the four investigation teams had their work cut out for them. Some days we questioned as many as ten to twelve people, which added a huge burden to the witness section and to the workload of the reporters, reviewers, and lawyers who were putting the testimony in final form. In addition, each member of every team was expected to know not only what went on in his particular area but to be familiar with the testimony being taken by other teams. This could be done in two ways. First, any member of the Inquiry panel could sit in on, or even participate in, the interrogations being conducted by any of the teams. Sometimes there were as few as two persons conducting the questioning, while with some of the key witnesses as many as ten might participate. Second, panel members could read the testimony or listen to the tapes. This may seem to have been expecting too much, but in the final analysis I wanted to be able to rely on the judgment of each panel member in completing our report; if he were to provide an informed judgment each member would have to know the whole story, not just part of it.

We knew that each of the interrogation teams had many people to question and little time in which to do it. Accordingly, we asked each of them to draw up lists of the men they wanted to question in order of priority. To assist in this, Lieutenant Colonel Breen and his administrative group developed a "succession list" for each key position. Normally, a person would stay in command or staff position for about six months, but in some instances the turnover was more rapid. For example, we wanted to talk to all of those who had been operations officers with the American Division during the critical period before and after the My Lai operation. By using the various morning reports, logs, and personnel rosters, Breen was able to establish that from December 1967 to April 1968 three different persons had occupied that post in addition to another who was an acting operations officer, and that four other men had filled the position after the critical period. This was done for thirty positions within the American Division and the 11th Brigade and proved most helpful.

Colonel Whalen and Lieutenant Colonel Brandt finished their work in South Vietnam in late January 1970 and closed our liaison office with MACV headquarters. In order not to miss any possibility of locating documents relating to the incident, they conducted searches of the Records Holding Area in Okinawa and of the Overseas Record Center in Hawaii. They also screened the headquarters of U.S. Army Hawaii and U.S. Army Pacific. Several pertinent administrative documents were located, but nothing of any great impact.

The final repository for Army documents is the National Records Center at Suitland, Maryland, and many of the documents we used had come from there. However, we wanted to be sure we were not missing any relevant papers, so toward the end of January Patterson and eight other officers screened the appropriate files. During a weekend at the Suitland Records Center they reviewed the shipping papers of fourteen hundred shipping boxes and screened the documents in 275 of them. Out of these literally thousands of documents, they found only thirty-two that had not already been made available to the Inquiry. These included some directives, orders, logs, and miscellaneous documents from USARV, the American Division, Task Force Oregon, and the Quang Ngai Province advisory group. However, nowhere did they find any reference to a Report of Investigation of the My Lai incident in any form.

As we were nearing the end of the Inquiry we had accumulated twenty-five linear feet of documents. It would have beclouded the issue and made management of our report most difficult if all of them had been entered into the record, so only the most substantive were entered and the others were included in a twenty-five-page listing of titles.

Colonel Armstrong and his interrogation group were not long in checking into possible misconduct or war crimes within Alpha Company. We had already questioned Captain Riggs, and Colonel Anderson interrogated fifteen others from the company and several from supporting helicopter units. He could find no evidence to substantiate the allegation of misconduct within the company. Because Alpha Company had not become involved in any atrocities, the details of its operation were not included in our final report.

Lieutenant Colonel Patterson and Major Kraus continued to interrogate helicopter pilots and crewmen and check aviation log books. In the process, they had one fortunate break. We had thought all of the troop lift helicopters for the air assaults of Bravo and Charlie companies had come from the 174th Aviation Company at Duc Pho. However, one day Warrant Officer Thompson stopped by the Inquiry and was shown some photos of helicopters taken at LZ Dottie, My Lai-4, and in flight. Thompson noted that not all the lift helicopters were from the 174th Aviation Company. The photos were enlarged and checked with a magnifying glass. Sure enough, by checking the unit facsimile on the tail rudders they found that some of the helicopters were from other companies of the 123rd Aviation Battalion. Through the log books they found that of the nine lift helicopters, five were from the 174th and four were from other companies.

The pieces of the helicopter puzzle soon fell into place. All told, the Inquiry questioned thirty-five officers and men of the 123rd Aviation Battalion and seventeen from the 174th Aviation Company. By the time Patterson and Kraus were finished they had an almost complete crew listing as well as a time schedule covering the activities of each helicopter participating in the operation. They had done an excellent job of a meticulous and time-consuming project.

Time was getting very short, and so we had to focus on the primary functions of the Inquiry—the adequacy of reports, sufficiency of investigations, and possible suppression of information.

To tie up the loose ends, we drew up a tentative schedule of witnesses, including other officers at division and brigade headquarters, file clerks who received and filed papers within the headquarters, and various staff members of the U.S. advisory elements at the 2nd ARVN Division, Quang Ngai Province, and Son Tinh District. In addition, we planned to recall some witnesses to recheck their testimony against what we had uncovered during our trip to South Vietnam. In the process we uncovered numerous items of interest.

In early June 1968 General Koster had left the Americal Division to become the superintendent of the U.S. Military Academy and was replaced by Major General Charles M. Gettys. From his testimony, General Gettys seemed to be a no-nonsense commander who enforced compliance with regulations by all elements of the division. To illustrate, a rape of a Vietnamese nurse by American servicemen was alleged to have taken place northwest of Quang Ngai City. An investigating officer was appointed on written orders; a proper investigation was held; and the culprits were brought to justice. General Gettys was essentially a field soldier who felt that all other actions should support field operations. In that setting, Colonel Parson, the Chief of Staff, was not quite his kind of soldier, so in time Parson was replaced by the division support commander, Colonel Lewis R. Tixier.

From staff officers of the division operations section we finally got the background of Lieutenant Colonel Barker's March 28, 1968, Combat Action Report. It turned out to have been a rather routine procedure, which explained why the report covered only one day. In fulfilling a monthly USARV requirement of "Lessons Learned," the operations section periodically sent out requests to brigades for reports on specific operations. In this instance, they had requested the 11th Brigade to report on four actions, including "1st Battalion, 20th Infantry action vicinity BS7179 on 16 March 1968," which referred to Charlie Company. Hence, Barker was fully correct in responding to only one day of the operation, although the information in his report was at great variance with what had actually happened.

Other principals of the division staff whom we interrogated were Orbun F. Qualls, personnel officer; Frank P. Clarke, logistics officer; Patrick H. Dionne, public information officer; Stanley F. Holtom, psychological operations officer; William S. Augerson, surgeon; James H. Heatherly, Inspector General; Warren J. Lucas, provost marshal (all of the foregoing were lieutenant colonels); and Major George P. Keuchenmeister, Major James A. Logan, and Captain Seth R. Orell, briefing officers. Some of these men recalled that the results of the operation had been given at the command briefing on the 16th, but none was aware that any civilians had been killed or that any investigations had been conducted. In all, we questioned sixty officers and enlisted men from the Americal Division.

Lieutenant Colonel Holtom, the division psychological warfare officer, said that normally leaflets and loud speakers were used to warn the inhabitants of a village before it came under attack, but this had not been done during the My Lai operation. It was clear to the Inquiry that Barker had wanted to trap the 48th Local Force Battalion in My Lai, and alerting them to an attack would have defeated his purpose.

We talked with those responsible for handling papers for the command group. Aside from the Chief of Staff, they included officers serving as aides to the generals, secretary/stenographers, and administrative noncommissioned officers. The aides, who normally put the papers on the generals' desks in the morning and removed them at night to be placed in the security file cabinets, said they had seen nothing about the My Lai operation. When General Koster left he did not take any papers with him, but later he requested them. Lieutenant James A. Dickens, who had been Koster's junior aide, had reviewed them and noted that they were all personal. He had seen nothing relating to My Lai.

Both Bob MacCrate and I enjoyed questioning the administrative sergeants—Staff Sergeant Ritchie, Sergeant First Class Saimons, and Staff Sergeant Loftis. (Sergeant First Class Drosdick, who replaced Loftis in April 1969, was interrogated by Colonel Wilson in Vietnam.) They all appeared to be efficient and dedicated to their assignments, but each had a different operating method. It was their job to receive incoming documents, enter classified documents into the journal, and send them to the Chief of Staff or his assistant for routing. Since they logged only "secret" and "top secret" documents, they would not have handled Colonel Henderson's Report of Investigation, which he had classified "confidential." One of these men thought he had seen something on My Lai, but when he was shown the pertinent documents he could not recall having seen any of them.

It seemed that when each new man took over he would completely reorganize the filing system. One of the file cabinet drawers would not open, and it remained closed until Loftis was replaced by Drosdick, who had it opened by a safe specialist. We were hopeful that he might have found some useful documents, but the drawer contained only a flight helmet and an empty brief case.

General Koster's clerk/stenographer, Specialist-5 William P. Herris, said he had neither seen nor prepared any letters or memoranda relating to the My Lai incident.

We handled the 11th Brigade staff as we had of division staff, interviewing separate unit commanders, staff officers, NCOs, and clerks—a total of fifty-seven. Some of the more pertinent information obtained follows.

Sergeant Major Roy D. Kirkpatrick said he and others in 11th Brigade tactical operations center monitored some of the radio traffic during the operation. At one point he heard a helicopter pilot say that ground troops were shooting civilians, which made him think something unusual was going on. Captain James H. Henderson, the duty officer, called the Task Force Barker operations center to find out more about this, but no one he talked to knew anything about it.

Kirkpatrick was also quite certain that Lieutenant Colonel Luper, with assistance from Major McKnight, had been appointed to investigate the confrontation between the air and ground troops. He said the investigation had been kept "under wraps," so he did not know much about it except what McKnight had told him from time to time. He thought they talked with Warrant Officer Thompson (Thompson could not substantiate this). The report was typed in the operations office—he could not recall the name of the clerk—and McKnight had hand-carried it to division headquarters. We were never able to find anyone else who knew anything about this report. When Luper was recalled, he emphatically denied ever having conducted any kind of investigation. McKnight chose to remain silent when he was recalled, so we were never able to confirm or refute that such a report had been prepared.

When Master Sergeant Kenneth E. Camell replaced Master Sergeant Gerberding as brigade intelligence sergeant in October 1968, Gerberding turned Colonel Henderson's file, in a brown manila envelope, over to him. Camell reviewed the file in November or December 1968. He told us of two items in it that were never mentioned by any other witnesses, and we were never able to locate copies:

- A translation of a letter from the province chief that discounted the allegations of the district chief.
- A covering letter, for the translation, from an MACV advisor, whose name Camell could not recall.

Other pertinent documents in the file, he said, were Lieutenant Tan's letter of April 11, 1968; a copy of the statement of April 14, 1958, with Captain Rodriguez' signature; and a copy of Henderson's April 24 report. Camell did not recall seeing either a letter from General Koster to Henderson requesting a response to the allegations of the district chief or Henderson's reply. In January 1969 he had reorganized his files and placed the envelope in a secure file marked "Quang Ngai." He said he had not removed anything from the file, nor had Henderson when he left the brigade in November 1968. In April or May 1969 the personnel officer took the file to make copies of Henderson's report, and when the file was returned, Camel said, he noted that some of the documents were missing. In September he was again asked for that file, and it was never returned to him. We were never able to find out who had asked for the file or what happened to it.

Major McKnight, the operations officer, and his assistant, Captain Henderson, testified that Colonel Henderson had prepared and submitted a report of some kind in early April 1968. McKnight said Colonel Henderson showed it to him in late March or early April; however, when he was shown the April 24 Report of Investigation he thought that was the report he had seen. Captain Henderson, on the other hand, was positive that the report he had seen and which was in McKnight's possession was *not* the April 24 report. He remembered it as having been a one-page report about civilian casualties and the allegations by helicopter pilots, and he thought he had seen it about a week after the operation. (Colonel Henderson had said his report was three or four pages long and that he had submitted in on April 4–6.) We were never able to locate such a document, and no other witness was aware of it.

First Lieutenant John W. Moody, the brigade information officer, testified that neither Sergeant Haeberle nor Specialist-5 Roberts had reported to him what they had observed while with Charlie Company at My Lai-4, but he had read and approved Roberts' article on the Task Force Barker operation. Since it was consistent with the official operation report, he had seen nothing wrong with it. He had seen some of Haeberle's black-and-white photos, but said he had never been shown any color photos.

Sergeant First Class John Stonich, the NCO in charge of the information office, had also seen the black-and-white photos, which he had not considered unusual, even though some of them depicted actions in violation of division policy, such as setting fire to thatched roofs of houses, rice trays being thrown on the flames, and crops being destroyed by a soldier. Stonich was totally unaware that Haeberle had taken color photos with his own camera. He said there was no written directive, but it was the policy of the information office that any photos taken by anyone connected with that office were to be turned in and become government property.

Captain Albert C. Labriola, commander of the 52nd Military Intelligence Detachment, testified that Lieutenant Dennis Johnson, of his office, who had been with Task Force Barker on the 16th, had given him no indication that any atrocities or war crimes had been committed that day.

The actions of the 2nd ARVN Division, Quang Ngai Province headquarters, and Son Tinh District headquarters, along with their U.S. advisory staffs, were so interlocked that it is virtually impossible to consider them separately.

Until late 1967 the province chiefs had operated with considerable autonomy, reporting directly to Saigon. However, with the development of the U.S. CORDS (Civil Operations and Rural Development Support) organization, the Vietnamese corps commander and his U.S. advisory staff were given greater authority. In I Corps, Lieutenant General Cushman, commanding general of the Third Marine Amphibious Force, advised Lieutenant General Lam, I Corps commander, on military matters. Additionally, with the strengthening of the Regional Forces/Popular Forces program it was necessary for the province chiefs to have better liaison with ARVN operations; those provinces within an ARVN division's tactical area of operation were supposed to report to the division commander on military matters and to General Lam and Saigon on civil affairs. The shift was gradual because some of the Vietnamese were unwilling to accept the new structure. However, in Quang Ngai Province at the time of the incident, the commander of the 2nd ARVN Division could issue orders on military matters to the Quang Ngai Province chief, which in turn affected all the districts in the province.

James A. May, of the U.S. foreign service, was the Quang Ngai Province senior advisor and Major David C. Gavin was the Son Tinh District senior advisor, but they were away at the time of the My Lai incident. Lieutenant

Colonel William A. Guinn and Captain Angel Rodriguez had been acting in their stead.

Lieutenant Colonel Guinn was serving in the dual capacity of deputy senior advisor and senior sector (military) advisor, Quang Ngai Province, at the time of the My Lai incident. He worked closely with the province chief, Lieutenant Colonel Khien, who also wore two hats. As province chief Khien directed all Vietnamese civilian activities and as sector commander he commanded the province Regional Forces/Popular Forces.

In his testimony to Colonel Wilson during the Inspector General's investigation, Guinn had intimated that the Americal Division had attempted to conduct an investigation of the My Lai operation. He hadn't been aware of its progress but believed there had been nothing to it, and so he had not inquired into its details. When we queried him on this matter, he acknowledged he had said it, but he told us it was based only on Colonel Henderson's statement that he would investigate when Guinn gave him some information obtained from a Census Grievance report. Guinn had flown to Duc Pho and had seen Henderson as he was leaving his headquarters to board his helicopter. After giving Henderson a report of the Census Grievance data, which he had scribbled on a piece of paper, indicating that between one thousand and fifteen hundred civilians had been killed in the My Lai area, Henderson had told him he would investigate it. (As noted earlier, Henderson denied that this had happened.)

Guinn himself did not believe that an atrocity had been committed. If any civilians had been killed, he said, it would have been the result of bombing[1] and artillery. All clearances for the use of artillery by Task Force Barker in the Son My Village area would have come from Son Tinh District headquarters.

As he recalled, there was something going on between Quang Ngai Province, the 2nd ARVN Division, and the Americal Division but he could not remember the details. However, he was positive that by some means, verbal or written, information had come back to him concerning a Report of Investigation indicating that nothing had been found.

At the time of the operation into My Lai, Guinn thought the 48th Local Force Battalion was thirty or forty kilometers west of Quang Ngai City, which would have placed it forty or fifty kilometers west of My Lai. This opinion was later supported by other members of the advisory staff.

There was evidence that Guinn was very familiar with Lieutenant Tan's letter of April 11, 1968. General Young said that although he himself had not seen the document, Guinn had advised him of its contents; Young had passed the information on to General Koster, he said. Major Hancock, 2nd ARVN Division operations advisor, testified that some time in late March

---

1. There was no air support or bombing associated with the My Lai operation, but we did not know this at the time Guinn testified.

or early April Guinn had told him about a report given to the U.S. advisory element in Son Tinh District by Lieutenant Tan which claimed that U.S. forces had killed a large number of civilians. They had also talked about the VC propaganda. Major Thomas B. Earle Jr., 2nd ARVN Division intelligence advisor, said that Guinn had advised him of Tan's report and the VC propaganda and had said he was having the matter looked into and was passing the information upward through his channels. Lieutenant Colonel Khien, the province chief, was not one of the persons to whom Captain Rodriguez' "statement" was addressed; hence, it seems logical that one of the two copies forwarded to the province advisory staff must have been given to him by someone with authority to do so. The same applies to the (signed or unsigned) copy that eventually came into the possession of Colonel Henderson.

Despite the fact that the advisory staffs at both the 2nd ARVN Division and Quang Ngai Province had received a great deal of information about civilian casualties, there was no testimony or documentation to show that it had been passed along to higher headquarters. When we saw copies of the monthly reports we were surprised to find that the province advisory report to CORDS, I Corps, dated March 31, 1968, included this comment: "Task Force Barker and Engineer units of the Americal Division have been extremely active and continue to merit high praise."

Lieutenant Tan said he had informed his senior U.S. advisor, Major Gavin, of the contents of the village chief's report and his letter to Lieutenant Colonel Khien. Captain Rodriguez said he had talked with Captain Clarence J. Dawkins, intelligence advisor, about Tan's letter, and Dawkins verified this in his testimony. Further, when Major Gavin returned Rodriguez said he had told him about Tan's letter, the request from the advisory staff at province headquarters, and his (Rodriguez') "statement" in reply. Although it seems virtually impossible that Tan and Rodriguez would not have discussed a subject of this magnitude with him, Gavin steadfastly denied any knowledge of it.

Major Gavin, who headed the U.S. advisory group at Son Tinh District headquarters from July 1967 to January 1969, told the Inquiry he felt he had had a good working relationship with Lieutenant Tan, and that Tan would have told him if he had known anything adverse about the U.S. forces, but Tan had not done so. Gavin said he had never seen Tan's letters to the district chief until we showed him copies during his appearance before the Inquiry.

Using a map, Gavin pointed out the area in the eastern portion of the district which they considered to have been under complete Viet Cong domination. The Regional Forces/Popular Forces of the district never entered the area except as part of a larger ARVN operation, and the local village and hamlet chiefs did not live there, preferring to be nearer the Son Tinh headquarters. The chiefs got their information from people on their way from the VC area to Quang Ngai City or Son Tinh.

Gavin had been aware of the results of the March 16 Task Force Barker operation only from the operational report. He recalled the number of enemy killed in action as something like a hundred, and hadn't been surprised at the small number of weapons captured because, he said, the VC always made an effort to recover weapons from their dead. In the VC-controlled area it was normal to destroy bunkers and burn hootches, he said, but not to kill livestock, and usually Vietnamese civilians would flee the immediate area when an operation started. When asked whether he thought My Lai-4 would have been free of civilians by 7:00 A.M., he said it was highly unlikely. Some of the women and children might have gone to market, but most of them, along with the old men, would still have been in the hamlet. And, of course, the able-bodied men would have been working in the rice fields and gardens.

Gavin said he had heard nothing about mass exodus of civilians during the Task Force Barker operation and he had not been aware of any civilian casualties. It was his opinion, however, that because My Lai-4 was in a VC-controlled area it was possible that a massacre might have occurred without his knowing about it. During his tour as senior district advisor he had collected several pieces of printed VC propaganda, which he later made available to the Inquiry. None of them mentioned atrocities by U.S. troops, and Gavin was not aware of any such propaganda. Specifically, he had not seen or heard of the VC propaganda accusing U.S. troops of killing a large number of civilians at Tu Cung (My Lai-4) and Co Luy because, as has already been mentioned, he said he had not been shown the district chief's letters.

It seemed incredible to us that, with all the bits and pieces of information coming out of the Son My area, Major Gavin had known nothing about civilians being killed or atrocities being committed there. Several of us felt he knew much more than he had told us.

The command section of the Americal Division should have been alerted to the fact that something most unusual had taken place at My Lai on March 16 from Vietnamese channels, if nothing else. There should have been warning flags flying all over the place, but they seemed to have been lulled into inaction by the impression that Colonel Henderson had investigated it and had not been able to substantiate the VC allegations.

Aside from General Young's verbal report to General Koster on Lieutenant Tan's April 11 letter, Colonel Henderson had testified that he had sent copies of the VC propaganda, with English translations, to the Americal Division. (Initially, Henderson said he had also sent them copies of the district or village chief's letters, but later, when he was shown these documents, he denied ever having seen either of them.) Also, there were many indications that General Koster was personally aware of Tan's April 11 letter. In later testimony, Koster said that he had visited both Colonel Toan and Lieutenant Colonel Khien in mid-April, at which time the atrocities mentioned in the VC propaganda were discussed. This, he said, was what prompted him to have Colonel Henderson put his oral report into writing. Both Colonel Toan and his intelligence officer, Major Pho, recalled a meeting at the 2nd ARVN Division with General Koster, accompanied by the senior U.S. advisor, Colonel Dean F. Hutter, at which Tan's April 11 letter and Pho's enclosure addressed to Toan were brought out and discussed. In his testimony, Koster confirmed the meeting and, generally, the discussion but—because of either the results of Henderson's investigation or Toan's reference to the letter as being propaganda—he did not appear to have recognized its full implication. For his part, Hutter recalled neither attending that meeting nor seeing Tan's letter or the VC allegations. Lieutenant Colonel Guinn also accompanied General Koster to a meeting with Khien at which the same subject was discussed.

Colonel Parson testified that he had seen a copy of a document he thought had been written by either the 2nd ARVN Division commander or the province chief relating to the unnecessary killing of civilians, possibly by artillery. In his testimony to the CID Parson said he had given it to the commanding general. When we showed him copies of Lieutenant Tan's letters of March 28 and April 11, 1968, he wasn't sure which one he had seen. Most likely it was the April 11 letter since because it had been sent to U.S. advisory elements while, to the best of our knowledge, the March 28 letter had never left Vietnamese channels.

Another indication that word of the incident had come from province to division was given by of Captain Donald J. Keshel, civil affairs officer, 11th Brigade. Late in March when he was visiting Lieutenant Colonel Anistranski at division headquarters, Anistranski told him, "Task Force Barker is in big trouble and in fact the entire 11th Infantry Brigade might be in big trouble." Anistranski had also said, "They [Quang Ngai] are up in the air about this and are having an inquiry, they want to get to the bottom of whatever happened in the Barker area." When Keshel asked what had happened, he was told it was all in a white folder, which Anistranski had tapped, saying, "Don't worry about it; it's being taken care of." Keshel had not pressed the point because he had not known whether Anistranski was serious or joking.

Whether there really was anything in the folder and, if so, what it was can only be guessed at. At the end of March it could have been a copy of the village chief's report, Lieutenant Tan's first report, the Census Grievance report or all of them. Later it could have included Tan's second report, some VC propaganda, and possibly several other papers. We were never able to determine the contents of the folder nor to find out how Anistranski had obtained them or what he had done with them. He had left the service, and when we asked him to give us additional testimony he refused, saying that he had already told everything he knew and had nothing to add. Unfortunately, we had no means of requiring him to testify so we had to rely upon Captain Keshel's testimony.

In the process of interviewing people from the province advisory group, we talked with James A. May, province senior advisor. He had been in Danang, Saigon, and other places a great deal during the period we were investigating, leaving Lieutenant Colonel Guinn in charge. According to May, he had not been aware of the incident and had not seen any of the pertinent documents at province headquarters or within the advisory group. Lieutenant Colonel Khien had told us that he had talked with May about Lieutenant Tan's April 11 letter—but May said he did not remember this.

We wanted to talk with some of the CIA personnel attached to the province advisory staff. Agency officials were reluctant at first, primarily because they did not want to reveal the identity of their personnel or their operating methods, but we assured them it would remain confidential and they finally relented. Three agents, all of whom had since been separated from the Agency, testified before the Inquiry. On a roster or organization chart they are shown as members of the Agency for International Development but, in fact, they belonged to CIA.

Donald R. Keating was the senior CIA representative in Quang Ngai Province. The agency served as the sponsor for several programs and participated in a few others in each province of South Vietnam. Essentially, they were Vietnamese programs for which the agency provided advisors as well as some funds and equipment. In some areas, however, the advisors were more aggressive than their Vietnamese counterparts, who were inexperienced and reluctant to accept responsibility, which meant that these advisors were, in effect, program directors. Some of the programs initiated by the agency subsequently were phased into other elements of the CORDS organization. Because of the time required to transfer the programs, which varied from province to province, it would be difficult to state which of them were under agency control at any given time.

Mr. Keating explained that the principal efforts of the agency were focused upon assisting the Vietnamese (1) in the development of effective administration and control within the hamlets and villages in what was known as the Revolutionary Development Program and (2) in the identification and apprehension of members of the VC underground, commonly referred to as the VC Infrastructure. It was Keating's job to coordinate the various agency programs and provide the necessary supporting personnel and material resources.

The agency activities of principal interest to the Inquiry were the Census Grievance and the Phuog Huang (Phoenix) programs.

We were quite surprised when we talked with Maurice M. Prew, advisor to the Census Grievance committees, to find that he was unaware of any reports of the My Lai operation having been submitted by one of the cadreman to Mr. Te, the Census Grievance chief. Te had been quite willing to give us a copy of his report during our trip to South Vietnam, but evidently in 1968 it had remained tightly held in Vietnamese circles, except for the distorted report received by Lieutenant Colonel Guinn.

Both Keating and Prew had high praise for the Census Grievance program, which provided considerable statistical data for use in population control. Along with this data, the Census Grievance committees also garnered a lot of information concerning the identity of Viet Cong and VC sympathizers, which was passed on to other agencies. Some grievances were brought to light but many were not. The Vietnamese were basically stoic about their situation, but they may also have feared retribution if they complained about anything.

Robert B. Ramsdell testified about the CIA's participation in the Phoenix program, which had been developed to counteract the Viet Cong underground government. It was a comparatively new program, having been started in late 1967, and was slow to develop because of the time needed to recruit and train personnel. Ramsdell described the program to the panel —how its agents gathered information on VC Infrastructure suspects from all possible sources; maintained lists of suspects, sometimes referred to as "blacklists," which they furnished to the National Police, Special Police, and interrogation agencies at province and district levels; and worked with other agencies in planning and conducting operations to seize suspects, question them at the interrogation center, and perhaps try them before a court or tribunal.

Ramsdell had arrived in Quang Ngai about a week after the Communist Tet offensive, on January 30, 1968. According to the testimony of some of the advisory staff, he was overbearingly aggressive and flamboyant in both manner and dress. These traits did not exactly endear him to them, and they sometimes suspected that some names on the lists were not Viet Cong. However, they conceded that Ramsdell seemed to have good relations with the Vietnamese.

Ramsdell had never met Lieutenant Colonel Barker, but he had known and talked with Captain Kotouc and Major Gavin before the My Lai operation. He said their discussions had centered on the 48th Local Force Battalion, its movements and location—fairly normal military information one would have expected to be passed to military units. In addition, Staff Sergeant Jones K. Warren, the Task Force Barker military police sergeant, made periodic calls on the Phoenix program office and other province and district intelligence-gathering agencies to pick up any information they might have, serving, in effect, as an intelligence liaison officer. Undoubtedly some of the information from the Phoenix and other programs was used in planning the My Lai operation, but we found no indication that it had any great influence upon it.

A couple of publications have intimated that the My Lai operation was planned by CIA and that I went easy in questioning the CIA representatives. Neither charge can be justified. Lieutenant Colonel Barker was his own planner, and he was not even acquainted with the agency operatives.

As for my questioning, even though I had served in both OSS and CIA, why should I have been more lenient with them than with my military colleagues? I had no such inclination, as is borne out in the full testimony. Moreover, Bob MacCrate and others participated in the questioning, and I am sure they would have spoken out if any attempt had been made to downplay any of the activities of the agency.

The nature of the Inquiry was such that there was not much room for levity. Living with the incident and its aftermath twenty-four hours a day, day in and day out, put a tremendous strain on all of us. Fortunately, everyone seemed to have a good sense of humor, so we could get a laugh from time to time.

One of the most humorous involved the testimony of a former major who had been on the staff of Task Force Barker but had been transferred to another assignment. His testimony was hazy, his speech incoherent, and he couldn't remember very much. We certainly did not get any information out of him. After his testimony we left for a short break, shaking our heads. A little later one of the enlisted men of the witness section brought us an empty pint whiskey bottle he had found behind the witness' chair, which explained why the ex-major hadn't been able to put the pieces together.

An expression we heard from several witnesses as to why they had not taken action that might have led to exposing the incident was CYA: "Don't do anything to rock the boat, CYA." What it meant was fairly apparent; however, one witness was a bit more subtle. To him it meant Cover Your Assets. This comment was another tension breaker.

Occasionally we encountered a witness who, like Warrant Officer Thompson, had maintained his basic integrity in spite of everything that surrounded him, who knew right from wrong and had acted accordingly. These men were bright spots in the generally bleak and depressing picture unfolding before us. They kept alive our faith in the American soldier.

One of these persons was an enlisted man who had been assigned to the 2nd Platoon, Charlie Company, during the Task Force Barker operation. After being discharged from the Army he bought a chicken ranch a hundred or so miles south of San Francisco, where he handled from 10,000 to 20,000 chickens; he enjoyed talking about them in his own quiet, unassuming way, and since I am from rural stock myself, I enjoyed listening to him. He was a large man, about six feet and 210 pounds, and put together like a rock. His hands seemed at least twice the size of mine.

Our chicken farmer's story of his experiences with Charlie Company was both depressing and inspiring. Both while in training in Hawaii and after his unit arrived in Vietnam, they had gotten lost during operations because the platoon leader could not read a compass. He had been embarrassed for the platoon, and because he had a good sense of direction as a result of climbing around the California foothills as a boy, he had volunteered to guide the platoon as "point man" in all operations. This young man had stayed in this most exposed and dangerous position continuously for six months, even though the unenviable job of "walking point" was usually rotated among all the men in a unit.

He told us that shortly after arriving in Vietnam, while the unit was taking a rest break in a Vietnamese village, he had seen one of the "thugs" in the company attempting to rape a Vietnamese girl. He went over to the man, pulled him away from the girl, and told him to stop it. The soldier had obeyed him because no one in the platoon wanted to tangle with him, but a day or so later, after the company had returned to its fire base from an operation, several of the thugs told him that if he did not stop interfering with their "fun" he was going to be "accidentally" shot in the back while walking point. When asked by a panel member why he hadn't reported this threat to his platoon leader, the young man answered that it would have been useless because the platoon leader was one of those who abused Vietnamese women.

Following this incident, and after much soul-searching, he decided that his job in Vietnam was to do what he was told and to try to get home in one piece, so he made no further efforts to stop his fellow soldiers when he saw them mistreating the Vietnamese. He gave us a vivid description of some of the killings and rapes that took place both in My Lai-4 and in Binh Tay. He knew they were wrong but refused to become involved, because of his earlier experiences and his lack of faith in his leaders. Thus the basic humanitarian instincts of this soldier, which should have served to help limit the atrocities committed at My Lai, or at least to see that they were reported and investigated, were suppressed, leaving him confused and frustrated.

All of us came to admire this young man. Thereafter, to ease the tension and disgust we would sometimes feel after listening to other witnesses, someone would say, "What we need around here are a few more chicken farmers."

Perhaps the most surprising testimony we heard throughout the entire Inquiry was that of Major William Ford, who was an advisor and operations officer with the Regional Forces/Popular Forces. In Vietnam, Lieutenant Colonel Khien had told us that although he had not immediately carried out Colonel Toan's order to investigate, he had planned to do so as soon as the troops were properly trained and the tactical situation was favorable. A three-day operation was scheduled to go into My Lai-4 on June 11–13 for an on-site investigation, but according to Khien they had been prevented from doing so by heavy fire received from My Lai-4. In addition, his forces had been diverted to secure a helicopter that had collided with a forward-air-controller aircraft and crashed in a nearby rice field.

Major Ford, a highly competent officer, almost completely refuted Khien's story of the operation. On June 11 he was serving as an advisor to a Regional Forces group. When the helicopter crashed these troops were moved to secure the right and eastern flank of the crash site. They passed through a hamlet and established their defenses along the northeast edge of it, where they remained for about two and a half hours while the crash victims were being removed.

From the location of the crash and Ford's description of the hamlet, it appeared to us that he might have been in My Lai-4. We got out our large air photo, and sure enough it was. He showed us his routes through the hamlet and where they had set up defenses. To our knowledge he was the first American to re-enter My Lai-4, but until we questioned him he had not been aware of where he had been. He said it had been overgrown with tropical vegetation and almost deserted except for some pigs running around and three or four elderly people with whom he exchanged greetings.

During the almost four hours he was in or near My Lai-4 he could have done some checking on the incident of March 16,but he had not been told to do so, nor, he believed, had his Vietnamese counterpart received any instructions to that effect.

The ease with which Major Ford and the Regional Forces group entered My Lai-4 would indicate that whatever the true purpose of Khien's operation, it was not to conduct an on-site investigation of the Task Force Barker incident. This was further substantiated by the interrogation reports of three prisoners who were captured that day. They had been asked nothing about the incident.

During the late February and early March 1970 we recalled between twenty-five and thirty witnesses who had appeared early in our proceedings. Each of these men was again warned of his rights, advised of any suspicions we had against him, and given an opportunity to seek legal counsel. About half of them did accept counsel, which Colonel Miller arranged through the Judge Advocate General's office.

I informed each of them of the status of the Inquiry—that we had interrogated over 350 witnesses, accumulated numerous relevant documents, visited My Lai itself and talked to many people there—and then told them that when we had questioned them earlier we had been seeking information but now we had quite a detailed picture of the incident and were only seeking to fill in some gaps.

For the most part, the recall witnesses basically repeated their original testimony, and those few cases in which critical new information was revealed have already been covered in the discussions of individual testimony.

Aside from Lieutenants Calley and Willingham, who remained silent except on a very limited basis, there were four others who upon recall by the Inquiry refused to testify further.

The first to refuse to do so was Captain Kotouc, Task Force Barker's intelligence officer. From his earlier testimony and that of others, we told him, we had quite a list of offenses we suspected he had committed (failure to obey a lawful regulation, dereliction of duty, maiming of a Vietnamese national, planning and participating in an illegal operation, suppression of information, and murder). Under the advice of his two lawyers, he elected not to respond to any further questioning. Because of the gravity of some of the suspicions against him, this was not surprising.

The second to refuse, Major Calhoun, the task force operations officer, was unexpected. He was informed that he was suspected of having committed four offenses (failure to obey a lawful order, dereliction of duty, participation in planning and executing an illegal operation, and suppression of information). At first he agreed to testify and did so for about four hours; most of his responses were generally consistent with his earlier testimony. But, when we were discussing the twenty to thirty noncombatant casualties and the differences between the Task Force Barker log entries and those of the 11th Brigade, his lawyer suddenly said that Calhoun elected to exercise his rights under Article 31 of the Unified Code of Military Justice to answer no further questions. We took a short recess so that Calhoun could confer with his counsel about answering questions in other areas, but again he chose not to do so.

This greatly bothered me, as it had never occurred to me that a Regular Army officer would not testify when called to do so by a properly appointed investigating officer. It was beyond the realm of what I considered professional military ethics. We had a long session of the Inquiry panel that evening and decided that legal counsel should not be allowed to serve as a spokesman for any witness, although the witness could ask the advice of his counsel at any point in his testimony. The matter of what to expect of a Regular Army officer, however, continued to bother me.

Major McKnight, the 11th Brigade operations officer, was the third to refuse to testify further. After being advised of the suspicions against him (failure to obey a lawful regulation, dereliction of duty, withholding of information, false testimony, and suppression of information) he requested and was provided with legal counsel. They conferred for two days, and on the third day McKnight declined either to make a statement or to answer any questions.

This prompted me to provide some guidance to him and his counsel, which I quote at length because it was subject to criticism later.

> I don't look upon you as the ordinary American citizen. You are a senior Army officer. You're a Regular Army officer, so you cannot be put in the same category with other people. I don't think you realize the enormity and the gravity of the situation that is being investigated by this particular inquiry and the effect this is going to have upon many, many people. Let me tell you what we're looking into so that you might think this over to determine that you might not want to help.
>
> We know at the present time that in this particular operation something in excess of 200 women and children, old men, noncombatants were killed, and it

may get up to as many as 500. I would also say that, in addition to the killings, there were repeated rapes by members of the command. I would also say that what is referred to as My Lai-4 was for all practical purposes leveled, the houses destroyed and burned, and the livestock were killed. In addition to that there were six other subhamlets that were burned. So it is not just Task Force Barker, and it's not you and myself. This gets way beyond the two of us. This is going to have drastic effects upon the United States Army, on our military establishment, upon our country, and upon our people.

Now, I haven't the slightest intent to incriminate you, and I would under no circumstances ask you to testify against yourself. We know a great deal about this situation at the present time, but there are some areas that you can, I feel, testify to without jeopardizing your position, or incriminating yourself. So looking at this situation, and looking at you as a senior officer, and the authority and the responsibility invested in you as a senior officer and a regular officer, having been so designated and approved by Congress, I think it takes an entirely different light.

You recall I mentioned before that this report is going to go to the Secretary of the Army, and it will be confidential. What will happen above and beyond that I do not know, but looking at past history it is likely that the report, including the testimony, or at least parts of the testimony, will become a matter of public knowledge. So I would suggest to you that rather than declining and so on that you might give this some thought as to your own participation in this and your willingness to cooperate on the basis of non-incrimination of yourself.

In 1971, when I was called to testify at the court martial trial of Colonel Henderson, the civilian defense counsel asked if I had made such a statement during the Inquiry. I said I had. The obvious implication was that I had been trying to influence the witness. By that time in the Inquiry I was well aware of the rights of witnesses, and although my statement *was* intended to influence the witness, I did not consider it coercion or unlawful influence. Moreover, it was fully understood that he would not be required to answer questions that might incriminate him. I have thought about this many times since, and feel sure that if I were again faced with the same problem I would follow the same course of action. I take a pretty strong view that any Regular Army officer who refuses to testify in a war-crimes situation is not worthy to hold the commission or to wear the uniform. His legal rights should be fully protected, but in my opinion his refusal to cooperate should automatically disqualify him from further active duty.

In all events, Major McKnight refused to answer any other questions or to make a statement. We took a short recess so that he could confer with his counsel and perhaps reconsider his decision, but when they returned McKnight still declined to make any further statement.

That evening I met with the four senior legal representatives of the Inquiry—Bob MacCrate, Bland West, Jerry Walsh, and Colonel Miller— to discuss this issue. Colonel Miller felt strongly that if an individual elected to remain silent we could ask him no further questions. MacCrate and

Walsh were equally adamant that, with respect to the Fifth Amendment, a witness could refuse to answer only those questions he reasonably believed might tend to incriminate him, and that we would not be infringing on his rights by asking him additional questions because until the questions were asked he would have no basis on which to decide whether the answers might be incriminating. Bland West, who had been a colonel on the Army Judge Advocate General's staff, agreed with them. We discussed the legal ramifications at considerable length. For my part, I was faced with a practical consideration as well. The fact that senior Regular Army officers were refusing to testify made it even more imperative that we do everything possible to insure that no one could later say we had not made every effort to get the facts. By asking these witnesses further questions on the important points, the record would show that we had tried even if none of the questions was answered.

In the end, I was faced with having three highly qualified lawyers saying in effect "Yes, we can address further questions" to the witness and another saying "No, we can't." I decided we would proceed with the questioning, but on a limited, specific basis.

We prepared a list of approximately twenty questions to be put to to Major McKnight to see if he would respond. His legal counsel vehemently protested this procedure, calling it, among other things, intimidation, coercion, and harassment. His objections were duly noted and recorded in the testimony. We proceeded with the questions, but in each instance the answer was, in effect, "I do not have anything to add to my previous statement." It was apparent by about the twelfth question that we were getting nowhere, so we ended the questioning and recessed the hearing.

We followed the same procedure with Lieutenant Colonel Guinn, the fourth man who refused to testify further, but it soon became obvious that we were running into a stone wall. On the advice of counsel he refused to answer any of the questions put to him, so the Inquiry was recessed. By this time it was clear that we would be wasting time in pursuing this course, so we abandoned it.

Major Gavin was also recalled, and was advised of our suspicions against him—failure to obey certain regulations and dereliction of duty. This shocked him, but he nevertheless decided to testify without counsel. It turned out that his new testimony raised further doubts in our minds, and the following day we informed him that he was also suspected of false swearing and suppression of information; at the same time we strongly suggested that he obtain counsel, which he did. There followed several days during which various alternatives were discussed with Gavin and his lawyer, but in the end he agreed to cooperate and answer our questions. Afterward we were still convinced that Major Gavin knew much more than he was telling us, but we admired him for deciding to testify while some other officers refused.

As I look back upon the refusals to testify further, I feel it was most regrettable. Although only the witnesses and their counsel can know which, if any, of their answers might have been incriminating, I believe they could have answered many of our questions without any risk, and could have filled in many of the gaps in our knowledge. In fact, I believe they could have allayed some of the suspicions we had against them. All of these men appeared to be fine, highly qualified, competent officers who had had the misfortune to become inescapably entwined in the tragedy and confusion of My Lai and its aftermath.

chapter 15

What Happened at My Lai-4: Summary

onsiderable information concerning the My Lai operation has already been covered, but there were many gaps and contradictions in the testimony. Therefore, the following résumé is provided to assist the reader in bringing the salient features into proper perspective. It is based upon the testimony of all the witnesses interviewed by the Inquiry, including seventy-two men from Charlie Company.

Task Force Barker's Orders

Although Major General Koster was familiar with the broad aspects of the plan for the operation, he had not reviewed the detailed plan or given it his personal approval as was his normal practice for battalion-size operations.

Both Brigadier General Lipscomb, who commanded the 11th Infantry Brigade until March 15, 1968, and Colonel Henderson, who replaced him on that date, knew the objectives of the plan but may not have been fully acquainted with the details of its execution. When Lieutenant Colonel Barker assembled his commanders and staff on the afternoon of March 15 to issue his orders for the operation, Henderson addressed the men, encouraging them to be aggressive and close rapidly with the enemy. He also intimated that they had an opportunity to eliminate the VC 48th Local Force Battalion "once and for all." He did not remain to hear Barker issue his instructions to his subordinate commanders.

Captain Kotouc, the task force intelligence officer, briefed the group on the enemy situation and the status of the civilian population. Barker later amplified and reinforced Kotouc's briefing, most of which focused upon My

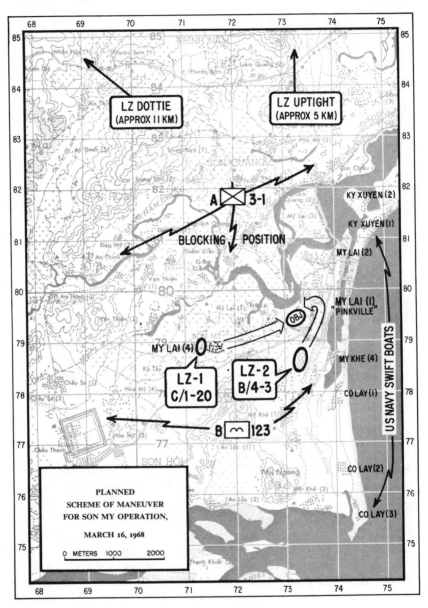

Map 15–1

Lai-4. The civilian population was described as being actively sympathetic to the VC. It was stated that by 7:00 A.M., at least thirty minutes before the airborne assault on the village, all the inhabitants would have departed for the markets in the area of Quang Ngai City. The group was told that the 48th Local Force Battalion was in the Son My area, and that its headquarters and two companies—a combined strength of 200 to 250—was in My Lai-4. There seemed little doubt that Charlie Company would encounter strong enemy resistance.

Major Calhoun, the task force operations officer, presented the scheme of maneuver for the combat elements. Although the operation was to last two to three days, only the first day was discussed; plans for the following days were to be issued later. Barker provided the details of the operation, essentially as follows (Map 15–1).

- Alpha Company was to move south from LZ Uptight during the night of March 15–16 to establish blocking positions along the Song Diem Diem River to intercept any enemy forces leaving the Son My Village area.
- Charlie Company, following an artillery preparation on the landing zone immediately west of My Lai-4 and the western portion of the hamlet, was to be combat-assaulted into the LZ starting at 7:30 A.M. on the 16th (Map 15–2). They were to attack the hamlet, destroy the enemy forces, and drive the remnants to the east. Thereafter they were to move eastward approximately two kilometers to join forces with Bravo Company in a night bivouac area.
- Following Charlie Company's air assault, Bravo Company was to be landed at an LZ south of My Lai-1, preceded by a brief artillery preparation. After landing, they were to move through My Lai-1 and subsequently join Charlie Company.
- An aero scout team from B Company, 123rd Aviation Battalion, was to screen the area generally south of Charlie and Bravo companies.
- A group of U.S. Navy Swift boats was to screen the waters along the Son My Village coastline.

Some testimony indicated that the residents of the My Lai area had been warned of an impending attack a day or two before the operation by propaganda leaflets and radio broadcasts from aircraft. However, nothing was found in any of the records to substantiate this.

There is some question as to the exact instructions issued by Lieutenant Colonel Barker in regard to burning dwellings, killing livestock, and destroying crops and foodstuffs. Calhoun recalled no such instructions, whereas Kotouc remembered them quite vividly. Captain Medina testified that he had received specific orders from Barker to destroy My Lai-4. Apparently no instructions were given as to the handling of civilians. Some

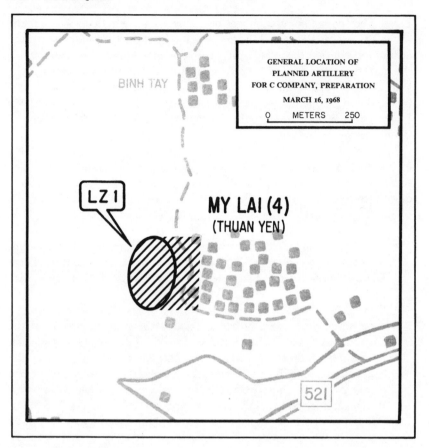

Map 15–2

witnesses felt this was a matter of Standing Operating Procedure, but Task Force Barker had no written SOP so at best it was an informal understanding. There is little doubt, however, that Barker's orders—combined with (1) placing artillery and helicopter gunship fire on the western portion of the hamlet, (2) the absence of any formal warning to the inhabitants, (3) the intelligence briefing portraying a population sympathetic to the VC and their supposed absence from the hamlet at the time of attack, and (4) the expectation of strong enemy resistance—created a potentially dangerous situation.

After the briefing, Barker took his unit commanders and some of his staff on a reconnaissance flight over the My Lai area to point out the landing zones and the planned artillery-preparation areas, and issue additional instructions. Medina said that it was during this flight that Barker told him to destroy My Lai-4. They had been near an open door of the helicopter when Barker said this, and because of the noise no one else in the helicopter could have heard it. Thus, because Barker had been killed, we had only Medina's word to go on. At Colonel Henderson's trial, Medina admitted he had been less than truthful and candid during his appearances before the Inquiry, so there may be serious question as to the validity of his testimony in this instance. Also, we do not know if any additional instructions were given to Captain Michles of Bravo Company because he too was killed in the same aircraft accident that killed Barker.

Orders by Company Commanders

When he returned from the Task Force Barker briefing, Captain Michles assembled the platoon leaders of Bravo Company and some of the key men of his command group to issue his instructions. The general consensus of those who were present was that it was to be a search-and-destroy operation, the population was either VC or VC sympathizers, and they were to burn the settlements. Some felt the instructions were more inclusive than this and that everything was to be destroyed. The platoon leaders then assembled their squad leaders and issued instructions to them, and the squad leaders in turn issued directions to their men. One exception may have been the 2nd Platoon commanded by Lieutenant Roy B. Cochran (killed by an enemy mine the following morning), who was reported to have assembled his entire platoon to brief them on the operation. Testimony taken from the men of the company generally indicated that these briefings had been quite routine. Considerable detail was given about the movements of the units and the techniques and procedures to be followed. Most of the men did not recall any instructions to destroy the villages or kill livestock, or any special instructions about how to handle VC suspects or civilian noncombatants. Some of the men, however, felt they had been instructed to shoot anyone they found in the operational area. The men were worked up for the operation but they did not seem to have developed any "spirit of revenge for past losses," as one of them put it.

Unlike Captain Michles, Captain Medina assembled all the men of Charlie Company to issue his instructions. We questioned a large percentage of these men, and the following represents a consensus of the contents of Medina's briefing. Closely paralleling the Task Force Barker intelligence briefing, he told the men they could expect strong resistance in My Lai-4 from the 48th Local Force Battalion—that, in fact, they would be outnumbered two to one—and there would be no civilians in the hamlet. He told them the location of the planned landing zone and the impact area of the artillery preparation and, by use of a stick or a shovel, outlined the scheme of maneuver on the ground (Map 15–3). After landing at the LZ, the 1st Platoon was to move through the southern sector of the hamlet, sweeping the enemy to the east; the 2nd Platoon had a comparable mission in the northern part; and the 3rd Platoon was to follow behind the other two to mop up. The weapons platoon was to move with the 3rd Platoon to provide mortar support to the company if it were needed. After clearing out My Lai-4, the company was to reorganize and then move to the east to join with Bravo Company in a night bivouac area.

The preponderance of evidence indicated that Medina told his men they were to burn the houses, kill the livestock, and destroy the crops and foodstuffs. There is less unanimity about what he told them concerning noncombatants. However, by telling them that no civilians would be in the hamlet and that the 48th Local Force Battalion would be present in strength, and by not issuing any instructions as to how to deal with civilians, he created the impression in the minds of many men in the company that they were to kill or destroy everything in the area. He also reminded them that they had lost several men to enemy mines and booby traps and this operation was their chance to get even: it was to be a revenge or grudge battle. Colonel Henderson's admonition to be aggressive and close rapidly with the enemy was repeated, and Medina cautioned them to clean their weapons, check their ammunition, and be sure their equipment was in shape.

All the men in Charlie Company were keyed up for the operation (some said they were psyched up), as it had the earmarks of being their first real encounter with the enemy. Their emotions were further heightened by a memorial service for Staff Sergeant George J. Cox, who had been killed by a land mine a day or so earlier. Some recalled the service as taking place immediately before Captain Medina's briefing while others thought it had been held the day before. In either case, Sergeant Cox had been well liked and the service had had a definite psychological impact on the men. Later that evening Medina met again with his platoon leaders (Second Lieutenants Calley, Brooks, and La Cross) and they in turn talked with the men of their platoons. There was nothing in the testimony to indicate that any

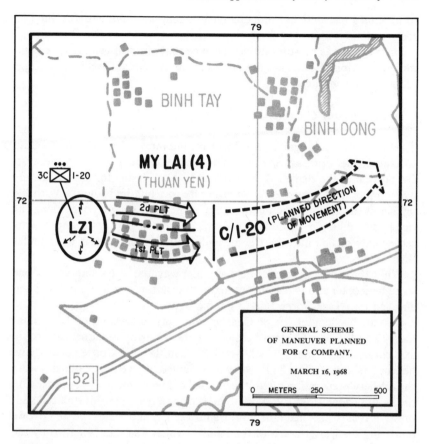

BINH TAY

BINH DONG

3C ☒ 1-20

MY LAI (4)
(THUAN YEN)

LZ1

2d PLT

1st PLT

C/1-20 (PLANNED DIRECTION OF MOVEMENT)

521

GENERAL SCHEME
OF MANEUVER PLANNED
FOR C COMPANY,

MARCH 16, 1968

0   METERS   250   500

Map 15–3

of Medina's instructions were changed or reported differently by the platoon leaders.

Since there was no substantive evidence that any war crimes were committed by Alpha Company, the orders given by Captain William C. Riggs are not discussed here.

Charlie Company Operations, March 16

The combat assault against My Lai-4 on the morning of March 16 began with an artillery preparation on the designated landing zone and the western portion of the hamlet. It began at 7:24 A.M., lasted for approximately five minutes, and consisted of between fifty to a hundred rounds. With the impact of the artillery rounds, workers in the fields sought cover along the rice-paddy dikes or in buffalo wallows. Those in My Lai-4 and nearby settlements rushed into their homemade shelters located near to or under their homes.

While the artillery preparation was under way, the aero scout team of one scout helicopter and two gunships arrived on station south of My Lai-4 and checked into Task Force Barker's radio network.

The first helicopter lift of Charlie Company, consisting of Lieutenant Calley's 1st Platoon, Captain Medina and the company headquarters group, and parts of Lieutenant Brooks' 2nd Platoon, left LZ Dottie aboard nine helicopters at 7:22. The flight was accompanied by two Shark gunships. As the artillery preparation lifted, the first helicopter element was approaching the landing zone from the south. The accompanying gunships placed suppressive rocket and machine gun fire on the LZ and along the hedgerows bordering the western part of the hamlet, which was supplemented by the fire of the door gunners of the lift aircraft. The first element touched down at 7:30. Medina testified that he reported the LZ as being "cold" (receiving no enemy fire); however, one of the helicopter pilots advised him that the LZ was "hot," and they *were* receiving fire. With this, Medina immediately informed his platoon leaders that the LZ was hot.

Upon landing, Calley moved his platoon about 150 yards to the east to set up a defensive position along the west edge of the My Lai-4 to secure the LZ for the next lift. Brooks' platoon moved rapidly to the northwest edge of the hamlet to secure that portion of the perimeter. Medina and the command group remained in the immediate vicinity of the LZ. As the platoons moved from the LZ to their defensive positions several Vietnamese who had left their hiding places were killed. Heavy rifle fire was also directed at suspected bunkers and other hiding places within the hamlet.

The lift helicopters returned to LZ Dottie to pick up Lieutenant La Cross' 3rd Platoon, the remainder of the 2nd Platoon, the mortar platoon, two men of the 52nd Military Intelligence Detachment, and two others from the 11th Brigade public information office. This lift landed at the LZ at My Lai-4 at 7:47 A.M. One of the helicopter pilots advised Lieutenant Colonel Barker that they had received fire from one of the adjacent hamlets as they left the landing zone; thus it was declared hot, and was so recorded at that time.

While the second helicopter lift was under way the two Shark gunships were circling over My Lai-4. They were advised by an Air Force forward air controller that there was an armed VC on a trail just outside the southeast corner of the hamlet, and he was reportedly killed. The air controller also saw two VC in the rice paddy to the north; the gunships killed them. The Sharks also spotted another armed VC south of the hamlet and, after several gun runs, killed him and marked his position with a smoke grenade.

At about 7:50 A.M. the two lead platoons started moving eastward through My Lai-4. (See Map 15–4 for actual movements of Charlie Company units.) Calley's 1st Platoon had only two squads, instead of the normal three, with a total strength of about twenty-five men. The right squad was commanded by Sergeant Mitchell, and Calley and his radio operator followed behind it. Sergeant First Class Cowan followed behind Staff Sergeant Bacon's second, or left, squad. As they moved into My Lai-4 they shot numerous fleeing Vietnamese and bayoneted others; they also threw hand grenades into houses and bunkers, destroyed livestock and crops, and committed other atrocities. As they proceeded further they began rounding up.. groups of civilians (women, children, and old men) and moving them along trails to the south and southeastern part of the settlement. One group of twenty to fifty was moved about twenty yards south of the hamlet along the dirt road leading toward Highway 521 and placed under guard. Another group of approximately seventy was moved into a ditch about a hundred yards to the east. All this took place within about forty-five minutes.

A short time later the group that had been moved south of the hamlet was shot down by members of the fire team[1] guarding them. The fire team then moved through the southeastern part of the hamlet and rounded up about ten other Vietnamese and moved them into the area near the ditch. Subsequent testimony from Vietnamese witnesses indicated that other Vietnamese from nearby settlements either sought refuge in the ditch or were driven into it; some estimates of additional people were as high as fifty. Meanwhile Mitchell's squad, less the fire team guarding the people in the ditch, and Bacon's squad moved another fifty to a hundred yards east of the ditch and set up a defensive perimeter.

Calley reached this area at approximately 9:00 A.M. Shortly after Calley's arrival, at about 9:15, the Vietnamese who had been herded into the ditch were shot down by members of the 1st Platoon. Estimates of various wit-

---

1. An infantry squad normally is composed of an automatic weapons team, which provides a base of fire and two maneuver elements, known as fire teams, to envelop the enemy position. Depending upon the strength of the squad, a fire team consists of three or four riflemen.

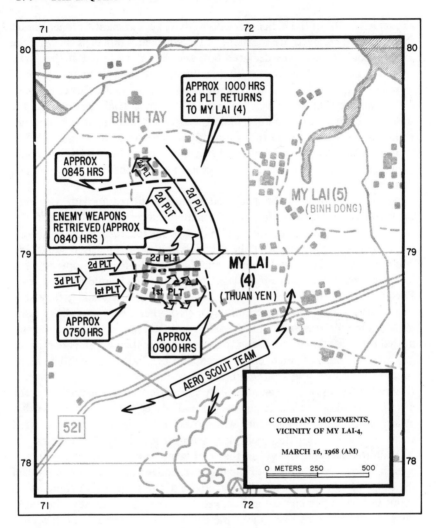

APPROX 1000 HRS
2d PLT RETURNS
TO MY LAI (4)

BINH TAY

APPROX
0845 HRS

2d PLT

2d PLT

2d PLT

MY LAI (5)
(BINH DONG)

ENEMY WEAPONS
RETRIEVED (APPROX
0840 HRS)

2d PLT

2d PLT

3d PLT

1st PLT

1st PLT

MY LAI
(4)
(THUAN YEN)

APPROX
0750 HRS

APPROX
0900 HRS

AERO SCOUT TEAM

521

85

C COMPANY MOVEMENTS,
VICINITY OF MY LAI-4,

MARCH 16, 1968 (AM)

O METERS 250   500

Map 15-4

nesses as to the number killed varied from 75 to 150. Some witnesses told of huge holes being blown into bodies, limbs being shot off, and heads exploding. There is no question that there was ample bloodletting. None of the Vietnamese was armed. In terms of numbers of Vietnamese killed, the ditch episode represented the gravest single atrocity of the My Lai incident.

Brooks' 2nd Platoon moved into the northern part of My Lai-4 with its three squads abreast—Sergeant Hodges 1st squad left, Corporal Schiel 2nd squad center, and Sergeant La Croix 3rd squad right. It was difficult to move in a straight line because of the dense growth and the numerous hedgerows around family plots. As a result, the squads became intermingled with each other and with the left squad of the 1st Platoon. As they moved through the area they shot down fleeing civilians in the hamlet and in nearby rice paddies. In some instances grenades were thrown into family shelters. In others, the occupants were called out and then shot down as they emerged. It was also reported that in at least three instances groups of five to ten persons were rounded up and shot on the spot. No detainees were kept. Because of the intermingling of units it is difficult to assess the number of civilians killed in My Lai-4 by the 2nd Platoon, but it was probably between fifty and a hundred. In addition, livestock, crops, and buildings were destroyed. With this kind of action going on it seems incredible, but at least two rapes were committed by the 2nd Platoon, and in one case the rapist is reported to have then shoved the muzzle of his M-16 rifle into the vagina of the victim and pulled the trigger. Although there may have been some shortcomings in training and leadership, this kind of barbarity was very difficult to comprehend.

At about 8:30 A.M. Captain Medina directed Lieutenant Brooks to move his platoon north into the rice fields to recover the weapons from the two VC killed by the Shark gunships. The platoon left the hamlet, located the bodies, and recovered their weapons. The two VC had been seen running from the small settlement of Binh Tay, just north of My Lai-4, and the platoon was ordered to check it out.

The platoon entered Binh Tay about 8:45 and continued the pattern of atrocities it had begun in My Lai-4. In one instance, ten to twenty women and children were rounded up and forced to squat in a circular formation. Then one of the men in the platoon fired several rounds from his M-79 grenade launcher into their midst. Those who were not killed by the grenade blasts were finished off by rifle fire from other members of the platoon. Other cases of rape and sodomy were reported—one girl was raped by three men in succession, and another was the victim of a three-on-one gang rape. Again, it was a gruesome picture.

At about 9:15 Captain Medina got in touch with the 2nd Platoon and told Lieutenant Brooks to "stop the killing," or words to that effect, and to round up the inhabitants, move them out of the area, and burn the dwellings. With that, a strange transformation took place in the platoon's activities in Binh Tay. The killings and other atrocities ceased, as if a curtain had been drawn, and the men suddenly adopted a somewhat benevolent attitude toward the Vietnamese. The remaining fifty or so inhabitants of Binh Tay were rounded up and directed to move out of the area toward the southwest, which they did without being harmed.

Why Medina issued the cease-fire order to the 2nd Platoon was never made clear to the Inquiry. Such an order does not seem to have been given to the 1st and 3rd platoons, whose members continued the killings for at least another hour.

After leaving Binh Tay, the 2nd Platoon moved to the southeast; some of the men entered the northeast section of My Lai-4 and the remainder moved 150 to 200 yards to the east and set up a defensive perimeter. It was in this sector that the confrontation took place between Warrant Officer Thompson and an American lieutenant, probably Lieutenant Brooks. Thompson had spotted a group of women and children running toward a bunker, closely followed by a group of U.S. soldiers. He landed his helicopter between the bunker and the Americans and told the gunners in his helicopter to cover him. Then he talked with the lieutenant about getting the women and children out of the bunker and was told, in effect, that "the only way to get them out was with a hand grenade." Thompson told the lieutenant to hold his men, and then he went to the bunker and motioned for the Vietnamese—twelve to fifteen women and children—to come out. Subsequently, he had one of his gunships land in the vicinity and these people were flown to safety.

Shortly after the 3rd Platoon landed at the LZ, Lieutenant La Cross was directed to send an element to the south to recover the weapon and web gear of the VC reported killed by the Shark gunships and marked by a smoke grenade. Specialist-4 Grimes' 3rd squad was selected for the mission, accompanied by La Cross and his radio operator. Upon reaching the area, they searched it thoroughly but could not find the body. Medina told them to keep looking. Meanwhile the Sharks had engaged and killed another armed VC running toward a hedgerow south of Highway 521. They marked his location with a smoke grenade, and La Cross' squad was told to recover the equipment.

A large number of Vietnamese civilians—estimates ranged from three to five hundred—were fleeing southwest along Highway 521 to Quang Ngai City. As the 3rd squad moved south toward the highway they fired upon those Vietnamese on the road immediately ahead of them, reportedly killing from three to fifteen people. Upon crossing the road, a woman hiding in a ditch was shot and killed.

The squad continued south and found the dead VC, recovering his weapon and a couple of ammunition boxes. As they were moving back toward the landing zone the 3rd squad killed at least two other Vietnamese trying to flee.

The remainder of the 3rd Platoon had set up a defense perimeter near the landing zone, and the 3rd squad rejoined them at about 8:45 A.M. Then the entire platoon moved into My Lai-4 to conduct its mopping-up operation. They burned or destroyed several homes, killed almost all of the remaining livestock, and destroyed crops and foodstuffs. They also reportedly killed five or six wounded Vietnamese to "put them out of their misery." In one instance, they herded together seven to twelve women and children and then shot them down.

When Warrant Officer Thompson returned to LZ Dottie to refuel at about 8:45 he was given authority to operate in the area north of Highway 521 and, upon returning to the area around 9:00, he noted several wounded Vietnamese in the rice paddies south of My Lai-4. He marked their positions with smoke grenades and, through his gunships, asked the ground elements provide them with medical assistance. Evidently his request was misinterpreted in being relayed from the low gunship to the high gunship and then to Lieutenant Colonel Barker, because the information he received was that "eight or nine dinks with web gear" had been wounded or killed to the south of My Lai-4. He directed Captain Medina to recover the equipment.

After Charlie Company had landed at My Lai-4, Medina moved his command group to the northwest edge of the hamlet. Later they moved south into the hamlet itself. Here an old man was interrogated who told them that thirty to forty VC had stayed in My Lai-4 overnight but had left the area before the combat assault. Medina's information was relayed to Task Force Barker.[2] He then moved the command group farther south and reached the southern edge of the hamlet at about 9:30.

It was at about this time that Medina received word to check into the VC killed and wounded as reported by Warrant Officer Thompson. By this time, all his platoons were occupied so he decided to check it himself with his command group. After moving south a hundred yards or so they saw three dead Vietnamese in the rice paddies, and a bit farther on Medina had his encounter with the young Vietnamese woman whom he killed in what he thought was self-defense. Further search of the area revealed no other dead VC or equipment so they returned to My Lai-4. Near the point where the dirt road met the edge of the hamlet, Medina talked with La Cross, who had come from the northern edge of the hamlet by way of the main north-south trail. La Cross informed Medina that he had seen fifteen to twenty Vietnamese males in the vicinity of Binh Tay and wanted to get the information to Lieutenant Brooks. After some discussion, Medina told La Cross to continue his sweep through the hamlet. While this was going on some of the members of the command group strayed off and were reported to have finished off several wounded Vietnamese, including a small toddler.

2. This information was not entered on the Task Force Barker operational journal but it does appear in the 11th Brigade journal.

As the command group moved along the southern edge of the My Lai-4, the group of bodies of persons executed by the 1st Platoon on the road just south of the hamlet was in clear view, and Medina estimated there were between twenty and twenty-four of them. As the group started to move east, Medina received word that a member of the 1st Platoon (Private First Class Carter) had shot himself in the foot. Some of the men testified that they thought this was accidental while others felt Carter could no longer stomach what he saw going on and had deliberately shot himself. In any case, Medina requested a medical evacuation helicopter, and Carter was flown out at about 10:30 A.M. Barker's command helicopter was used to take Carter out; the pilot and other crew members reported that they could clearly see the stack of bodies on the road south of My Lai-4. The Charlie Company command group, along with the mortar squad, then took a short break, resting along the southern edge of the hamlet.

After the med-evac of Carter, Major Calhoun used the command helicopter to fly over the operational area. According to his testimony, before he reached the area he received an order from Barker to "stop the killing" or "stop the shooting," which he relayed to Medina.

At about 11:00 A.M. Medina and his command group entered My Lai-4 near the point where the road left the hamlet; they proceeded on a trail leading to the northeast to arrive at the east-central edge. Medina testified that he had seen no additional bodies along the trail, but others reported seeing as many as eighteen. Upon reaching the edge of the hamlet, Medina ordered a lunch break for the entire company. At this time he received a report of casualties from his platoon leaders, which totaled ninety enemy killed. He reported this figure to Task Force Barker, but such an entry did not appear in the task force operational journal; he did not report any civilian casualties. At this time Medina and his command group were less than a hundred yards from the ditch containing a large number of dead civilians, but Medina professed not to have seen or known about them.

Shortly after 1:30 P.M. Charlie Company left My Lai-4 and moved east toward the area where they were to join up with Bravo Company. En route the 2nd Platoon passed through My Lai-5 and rounded up fifty to seventy-five civilians. Eight or ten young men of military age were segregated from the group and taken with the company for interrogation, and the rest were told to head for Quang Ngai City. There was no conclusive evidence that any additional burnings or killings took place during Charlie Company's afternoon move. They arrived at the night bivouac area at about 3:30.

When Captain Kotouc flew in to the bivouac area he brought with him three National Police and five ARVN soldiers to help him interrogate the suspects brought in by both Bravo and Charlie companies. Several witnesses testified to having seen Kotouc beat the back of a suspect's hand with a Bowie type of knife he habitually carried, and some said the tip of the suspect's finger was cut off. There was also testimony that when one of the police asked him what to do with one of the prisoners, Kotouc gave an upward spiraling motion with his right hand and index finger, a gesture that to Asians indicates "going to heaven."(Kotouc mentioned none of this during his initial testimony.) A little later they heard shots from a bush-covered ditch and suspected the prisoner had been killed. Other beatings and subsequent killings by the National Police were also reported; some witnesses saw only one, others saw four or five, and some as many as eight.

The actions of Lieutenant Johnson and his interpreter, Sergeant Minh, of the military intelligence detachment, and of Sergeant Haeberle and Specialist-5 Roberts of the public information detachment, have already been discussed. Suffice to say that they all knew atrocities were being committed and that this was not a normal operation. Had any of them reported what they had seen it is conceivable that a chain of events would have been put in motion that would have uncovered the entire tragedy.

Following is a summary of some of the problems and discrepancies relating to reports of casualties during Charlie Company's operation on March 16.

Soon after landing, Charlie Company reported one VC killed, and at about 8:00 A.M. they reported fourteen more killed. The Sharks reported they had killed three, two, and one VC on separate occasions, for a total six. In fact, they killed only three. Initially six weapons were reportedly captured, but this was later revised to three, which coincides with the three armed VC killed by the Sharks.

At 8:40 A.M. Captain Medina informed Lieutenant Colonel Barker that sixty-nine VC had been killed by artillery in the vicinity of the landing zone, and this was recorded in the Task Force Barker operational journal. In reporting this to the 11th Brigade almost an hour later, however, the location was moved approximately five hundred yards northeast, which placed it in the general area where the Sharks killed the two VC in the rice fields. The Inquiry was never able to determine why this change was made in the report to brigade, or why it was neither checked nor questioned at the time.

Some members of the command group testified that while they were searching for bodies south of My Lai-4 they overheard Medina report to someone during a radio conversation that 310 VC had been killed. They did not know to whom he was talking. This information does not appear in any of the journals, Medina denied it, and the Inquiry was unable to confirm that such a report was ever made.

The total of ninety VC killed in action Medina said he had obtained from his platoon leaders is identical to the total reported at different times throughout the morning by elements of Charlie Company and the Sharks. Lieutenant La Cross verified that Medina had asked for a body count but said he had not known what to report and had given the first figure that came to mind—"about fifty." Since Lieutenant Brooks was later killed and Lieutenant Calley refused to testify, the Inquiry was not able to find out what kind of figures they had actually given to Medina or how the total of ninety had been arrived at.

Of the ninety VC reportedly killed, only the three killed by the Sharks could legitimately be termed enemy killed in action. It is possible that some active VC may have been included in the remaining eighty-seven, but there was nothing in any of the testimony to verify it.

From the testimony of many witnesses from Charlie Company and others who participated in the operation, the Inquiry arrived at what must be characterized as a very conservative figure of 175 to 200 women, children, and old men, all noncombatants, killed by Charlie Company during the morning of March 16.

Although it cannot be accepted as solid evidence, during the course of their investigation the Criminal Investigation Division conducted a census type of evaluation. They constructed a model of My Lai-4 and, using it, identified the number of people living in each house prior to the operation. Then through questioning they determined which of these people had been killed and which had not, arriving at a figure of 347 civilians killed. This figure was only for My Lai-4, and did not include those who had been killed by the 2nd Platoon in Binh Tay or anyone who might have been in My Lai-4 from other hamlets.

At no time was enemy fire received by Charlie Company after it landed at My Lai-4. In fact, the only reference to enemy fire during the day was that reported by the lift helicopters when they called the landing zone "hot," but even this is questionable because not one helicopter was hit.

The three recovered weapons were of U.S. manufacture and had probably been captured during earlier ARVN or even U.S. operations. Because weapons supplied from Russian and Chinese sources make a different sound than do U.S. weapons, there was some speculation that if enemy forces were using U.S. weapons it would have been impossible to distinguish between enemy and friendly fire. This hypothesis does not hold water, however, because when one is being *shot at* one hears a sharp cracking sound that is clearly different from the sound of one's fellow soldiers shooting at the enemy, regardless of the origin of the weapons being used.

During the afternoon when Medina was questioned about casualties by Task Force Barker he said no women or children had been included in his previously reported body count but that ten or eleven women and children were reported to have been killed by artillery fire or gunships.

Even though the enemy was supposed to be the combat-wise 48th Local Force Battalion in strongly fortified position, the U.S. forces received no enemy fire and requested no fire support. These contradictory facts, together with Charlie Company's reported ninety VC and ten or eleven civilians killed, three weapons captured, no U.S. troops killed and only one wounded (self-inflicted), should have alerted responsible individuals at every higher level of command (Task Force Barker, 11th Brigade, Americal

Division, and even higher) that something was seriously wrong. They should have questioned the reports, but nobody did. Perhaps nobody cared; perhaps they were afraid of what they would find out; perhaps no one had enough combat sense to recognize these irreconcilable factors in the situation; or perhaps it was all part of a coverup.

During the morning several men in positions of authority were flying over and around the area in their helicopters. Why none of them landed to check personally on what was happening in My Lai-4 is difficult to understand.[3] The hamlet was surrounded by rice paddies, so there were plenty of places to land, and no enemy fire was being received. Furthermore, there were seven helicopter landings that morning in the immediate vicinity—three by Warrant Officer Thompson, two by Warrant Officer Millians, one by Lieutenant Colonel Barker's command helicopter (but without Barker himself) to evacuate Private First Class Carter, and another to pick up the military intelligence and public information teams.

Barker, who had the reputation of being a courageous and fearless leader, was over and around the area at comparatively low altitudes to direct the operation; he should have known something unusual was taking place but did not land to check it out. Colonel Henderson was over the area several times during the morning and early afternoon; he even landed nearby to pick up the two VC suspects south of My Lai-4. At times Henderson was flying low enough to have seen two armed VC bodies in the rice paddy north of the hamlet, and, he told General Koster, he had seen six or eight bodies he thought were civilians. (Others in his helicopter testified they had seen fifteen to twenty dead noncombatants—one man said it was more like thirty to forty.) A normally curious commander would either have landed to find out why they had been killed or at least have directed others to do so. Henderson did neither.

When General Koster flew over the area his helicopter was at about two thousand feet so he might not have been able to see bodies on the ground. He could not, however, have missed seeing numerous buildings on fire, which was against his division policy. He had also had word of six or eight civilian casualties from Henderson and a report of enemy casualties from Barker but apparently took no action at the time to have the situation on the ground checked into. Further, that afternoon—although he knew that at least twenty civilians had been killed—he countermanded Henderson's order for Charlie Company to return to My Lai-4 and conduct a body count.

3. With the ready availability of helicopters in South Vietnam it was quite easy—and it was normal practice—for commanders to land to review the progress of an engagement with the ground commander. In some cases this might have been overdone, but leadership is most effective with person-to-person contact and a close-up view of the actual situation on the battlefield. Flying around an area communicating with the ground by radio does not fulfill the requirement.

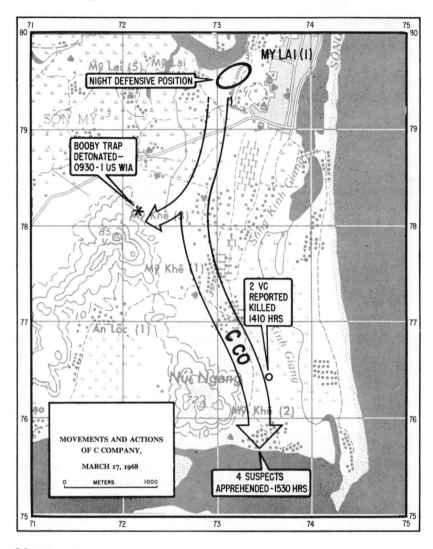

Map 15–5

Major Watke testified that after Thompson and others had told him what they had seen at My Lai-4 and he (Watke) had reported it to Barker, he was still concerned about the civilian casualties. I understand his concern but not his lack of action. He could have pressed Barker to investigate or he could even have suggested that he be permitted to use his reaction team to check into the matter. But he felt that since he was acting in a support capacity he would be exercising too much authority if he did so, so he ended up doing nothing.

All in all, the failure of any person in a position of authority to get on the scene and look into the operation remains a complete enigma. All the signs of a fouled-up operation were certainly present at the time.

Charlie Company Operations, March 17–18

The Task Force Barker journal indicated that on the evening of the 16th the 1st Platoon of Charlie Company moved about eight hundred yards southwest of the night bivouac area to establish a night defensive position. The following morning the entire company began a southern movement toward the Song Tra Khuc River (Map 15–5). While the 1st Platoon was moving to set up an observation post on Hill 85, one of its men stepped on an enemy mine and part of his foot was blown off. Attempts to set up the post were abandoned and the platoon rejoined the company. As the company moved south, it was reported to have burned the subhamlets of My Khe-3 and My Khe-1, both possibly deserted, and to have engaged and killed two VC and apprehended three suspects, two men and one woman. Another male suspect was found hiding in a cave outside My Khe-2. It was he whom Captain Medina subsequently forced to talk by strategically placing several M-16 rounds above his head.

Later in the afternoon the company moved north from My Khe-2 to a location east of My Khe-3 and established a night defensive position.

The following morning, March 18, the company again moved northward. Two if its men were injured by mines or booby traps and evacuated by helicopter. Outside of My Lai-1 they stopped and set up a defensive perimeter while Colonel Henderson conferred with Captain Medina.

In the area of My Lai-3 they established a pick-up zone, where the company began its evacuation to LZ Dottie with a flight of two or three UH-1 helicopters. The evacuation began at about 2:20 P.M. and was completed by 4:30. Charlie Company's tragic operation had drawn to a close.

chapter 16

The Bravo Company Operation

One of the most difficult tactical situations we had to piece together was that relating to Bravo Company, and it was done by a group headed by Jerry Walsh and Colonel Wilson, with others of the panel participating in the questioning from time to time. The report writers also contributed substantially in plotting the locations of the units and individuals involved.

About the only indication we had before we went to South Vietnam that something irregular might have occurred during the Bravo Company operation was a reference in the statement appended to Colonel Henderson's report of April 24, 1968. It was tenuous at best, alluding to the fact that civilians had been gathered together and killed in Tu Cong (My Lai-4 or Thuan Yen) and in another hamlet named Co Luy. We had studied several maps and charts of U.S. origin trying to locate a Co Luy but there was none to be found in the Bravo Company area. There were three hamlets of Co Lay—1, 2, and 3—but none of these seemed to fit. Several miles to the south, in Tu Binh District across the Song Tra Khuc River, we located Co Luy-1, but it was so far from the area that it seemed unlikely to have been the scene of any action.

But once we had clarified the geographic terminology while we were in South Vietnam, we realized that Co Luy was one of the four hamlets that made up Son My Village. It was located along a narrow coastal strip in the southeast corner of the village and comprised the subhamlets of Co Lay-1, 2, and 3. Just across its northern border lay the subhamlet of My Khe-4, which was in the hamlet of My Lai. To get to Co Luy by land one had to pass through My Khe-4, so many people thought that My Khe-4 was part of Co Luy. With this data, we at least had a start in understanding Bravo

Company's operation.

It should be recalled that while we were in South Vietnam we talked with:

- Lieutenant Tan, Son Tinh District chief, about his letter of April 11, 1968, alleging that U.S. forces had killed ninety civilians in Co Luy Hamlet on March 16.
- Luyen Dinh Do, chief of Son My Village, who had provided the information to Lieutenant Tan.
- Ngo Tan Hai, chief of Co Luy Hamlet, who, although he had not actually been in Co Luy, had reported from his conversations with residents from the area that ninety people had been killed there.
- Nguyen Duc Te, Census Grievance chief, who had received a report from a cadreman on March 18, 1968, alleging that U.S. forces had killed eighty people, young and old, in Co Luy Hamlet.

We also obtained from the Americal Division a recently found National Liberation Front Committee notice, dated March 28, 1968, stating that ninety civilians had been killed in Co Luy Hamlet. In addition, Jerry Walsh had talked with several civilians from the area who, in broad terms, confirmed what had been reported in the various documents.

Within the limited time they had, after returning to Washington, Jerry Walsh and Colonel Wilson did a truly remarkable job of assembling information of Bravo Company's operation. All told, they interrogated fifty-eight officers and men of the company, but they were faced with many constraints, one of the main ones being that Captain Earl C. Michles, the company commander, had been killed and so we were not able to know his version of the events. The principal action centered around the 1st Platoon commanded by 1st Lieutenant Thomas K. Willingham. Because it consisted of only twenty-two men, it was organized into two squads, instead of the normal three, a point team[1] of four men who had volunteered to serve in that capacity on a permanent basis, and a small command group. Of these men, two subsequently were killed in South Vietnam, eight others had been discharged from the Army and refused to testify, and some of those who did testify had poor memories or were deliberately misleading. Also, only one of the four men on the point team testified and, for reasons known only to himself, provided little information. Moreover, when we flew over Co Luy Hamlet while we were in South Vietnam, there had been little sem-

---

1. As the name would imply, the point is the leading element while the unit is advancing in a column formation. Its mission is to locate the enemy and his defensive works, ambushes, mines, booby traps, and the like and to give warning to the unit to its rear. The number of men in the point is flexible, from one man to a team of four or five, and its formation will vary depending upon the terrain. In close jungle terrain they will follow one another, while in open terrain they tend to spread out somewhat. Since the point leads the formation, it is in the most vulnerable position to receive enemy fire or to encounter mines and booby traps. It is not an enviable job and requires persons with special qualifications and fortitude.

blance of any life or previous habitation. A combination of the shifting sands from the ocean winds and the growth of grasses and jungle had all but obliterated it. Thus, despite the staunch efforts of Mr. Walsh and Colonel Wilson, there were many details of Bravo Company's operation we still did not know when we submitted our final report.

Bravo Company's task on March 16 had been to intercept any of the 48th Local Force Battalion that might withdraw from the area of My Lai-4 as a result of Charlie Company's assault and to search the enemy stronghold of My Lai-1, also known as Pinkville (Map 16–1). The company was supposed to have been air-assaulted into its landing zone five hundred meters southwest of My Lai-1 starting at 9:00 A.M. but, probably because Charlie Company's assault at My Lai-4 had gone so well, Lieutenant Colonel Barker had advanced it one hour. The first lift was picked up at LZ Uptight shortly after 8:00, left at 8:08, and was supposed to have landed at 8:12. The helicopter formation flew southeast over the South China Sea to avoid the tragectory line of the artillery preparation being fired into the landing zone. As the helicopters approached the LZ the artillery failed to lift and the helicopter formation was forced to make a full-circle turn until Barker could issue instructions to cut off the artillery. He then marked the LZ with a purple smoke grenade and the first lift landed at 8:15. A second lift with the remainder of the company was completed at 8:27. There had been no hostile ground fire, and the LZ was noted as being "cold."

As the platoons had moved from the landing zone on their assigned missions some of the men heard rifle shots and thought they were receiving enemy small-arms fire. In all likelihood what they were hearing was the firing of Charlie Company in My Lai-4, less than a mile to the west.

First Lieutenant Roy B. Cochran's 2nd Platoon had the mission of going into My Lai-1. Soon after crossing Highway 521, with Cochran in the lead, the platoon had started moving over a hedgerow when it encountered a land mine. Cochran was killed instantly and four men were wounded. A medical evacuation helicopter was called in to take out the dead and wounded. The platoon was reorganized under the command of the platoon sergeant. It had moved only 100 to 150 meters toward My Lai-1 when a second land mine was detonated, at about about 9:30 A.M., wounding three additional men. Barker was flying over the area at the time and landed nearby to pick up the wounded to take them to LZ Dottie for subsequent evacuation to Chu Lai. The platoon, having received heavy casualties, although there had been no hostile fire, was directed by Michles, and probably Barker, to retrace their steps and withdraw from the area of My Lai-1.

The 3rd Platoon, commanded by the Staff Sergeant Franklin McCloud (the platoon leader did not accompany the operation), had proceeded northwest and crossed Highway 521, closely followed by the weapons platoon and Captain Michles' command group. They were halted at a trail junction just north of the highway when they heard the mine explosions and, since they

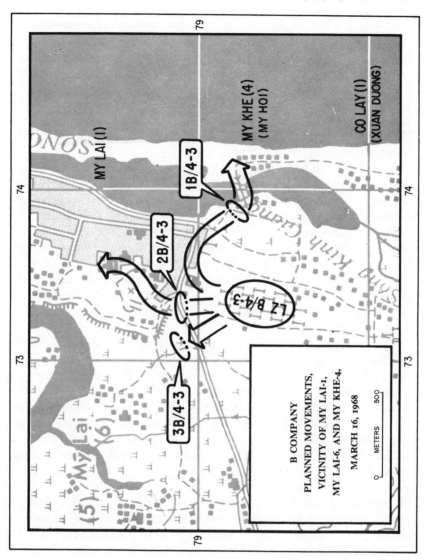

B COMPANY
PLANNED MOVEMENTS,
VICINITY OF MY LAI-1,
MY LAI-6, AND MY KHE-4,
MARCH 16, 1968

0   METERS   500

Map 16-1

were within sight of the 2nd Platoon, they could clearly see what was happening. It seriously affected their morale as well as that of the 1st Platoon, which was still farther to the east on a screening mission.

For all practical purposes, the withdrawal of the 2nd Platoon left Bravo Company with nothing to do but cover the VC escape routes from My Lai-4. The company, except for the 1st Platoon, moved north. The 3rd Platoon entered My Lai-6 and screened its inhabitants, detaining several of them, and then moved to the company's nearby night bivouac area. (Map 16–2.)

The 1st Platoon had moved north from the landing zone in advance of the 2nd Platoon. When it reached Highway 521 it turned eastward toward the area of My Khe-4, which it was supposed to search and then establish blocking positions against any VC that might be escaping south out of My Lai-1. The platoon's movement from the LZ to the concrete bridge across the Song Kinh Giang (an inland body of water separated from the ocean by a narrow spit of land) was without major incident. Although no enemy fire was received, some men reported that a couple of grenades had been thrown at them and they had responded with fire. The grenades did not explode, and the men were unable to find either the grenades or the persons who had thrown them.

The four men of the point team, who were well respected within the platoon and noted for both their bravery and their ability to locate and detonate enemy mines and booby traps, reached the concrete bridge at about 9:00 A.M. The point team was also equipped with a radio with which it maintained contact with Lieutenant Willingham, who requested gunship support to assist his platoon in crossing the bridge. The gunships, however, had returned to LZ Dottie to rearm, so upon the advice of Lieutenant Colonel Barker, Captain Michles directed the 1st Platoon to use mortar fire to cover the crossing in lieu of the gunships. The 81-mm. mortars of the company weapons platoon fired several rounds, adjusted by a forward observer of the weapons platoon who had joined the 1st Platoon. The mortar rounds appeared to be duds and the fire mission was called off. Later some of the men on the Navy Swift boats reported they had seen some of the rounds impact upon the beach beyond a ridge of sand dunes.

Under Michles' direction, Willingham placed his two machine guns to cover the eastern end of the bridge and deployed his men so that they could use their M-16 rifles to cover the crossing. The men of the platoon were exceptionally cautious, as they would be fully exposed during the bridge crossing; their apprehension was probably heightened because of the casualties within the 2nd Platoon.

There was considerable disagreement among the witnesses as to whether they had received enemy rifle or sniper fire either before or during the crossing. Some witnesses thought they had received intensive fire and had been driven back and had had to try a second time. The platoon sergeant

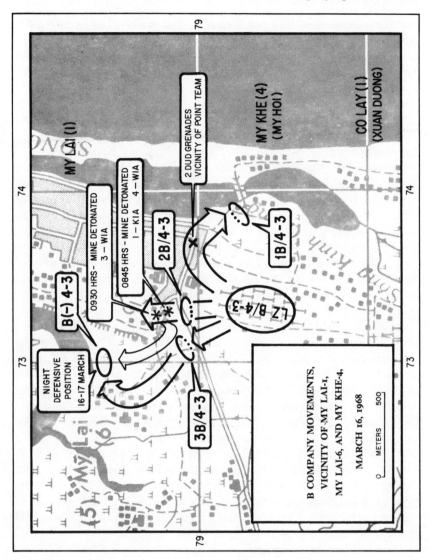

MY LAI (1)

MY KHE (4)
(MY HOI)

CO LAY (1)
(XUAN DUONG)

2 DUD GRENADES
VICINITY OF POINT TEAM

0930 HRS – MINE DETONATED
3 – WIA

0845 HRS – MINE DETONATED
1 – KIA   4 – WIA

B(–) 4-3

2B/4-3

1B/4-3

3B/4-3

LZ B/4-3

NIGHT
DEFENSIVE
POSITION
16-17 MARCH

(5) My Lai (6)

B COMPANY MOVEMENTS,
VICINITY OF MY LAI-1,
MY LAI-6, AND MY KHE-4,

MARCH 16, 1968

0   METERS   500

Map 16–2

and some others said they had received a few rounds. However, the rifle squad leaders and still others did not recall any enemy fire at all, and there was no record in any of the logs or journals that hostile fire had been received. In all events, with the point team in the lead, the entire platoon completed its crossing by about 9:35.

Leaving a couple of men to guard the eastern approach to the bridge, the 1st Platoon moved east and then south along the main trail toward My Khe-4. According to testimony of members of the platoon, when they were between seventy-five and a hundred meters from My Khe-4, which consisted of about twenty thatched huts, the lead point and the 1st Squad opened fire on the hamlet with a machine gun and M-16 rifles. We were never able to determine why they had begun firing at that time. It could have been a reaction to sniper fire, although nobody testified to having received any, or it could have been part of a prearranged plan, or it might simply have been the impulsive act of one of the men. The firing into and around the hamlet continued for four or five minutes. As the inhabitants, mostly women and children, fled they were cut down, many of them on the sand dunes near the ocean. A radio report was received from the Swift boats that a lot of firing was coming off the beach from that direction.

At about 9:40 A.M. Willingham issued an order to stop firing. This is about the same time that a similar order was issued in Charlie Company and may have been the result of Barker's order to stop the killing. It was also reported that at about this time Michles cautioned Willingham "not to kill any women and children." Michles was said to have had considerable sympathy for the Vietnamese and was reported to have stressed their protection to his men, so his instructions to Willingham may have been on his own accord. There was even some testimony from a radio operator that Michles had issued the instructions before the platoon crossed the bridge.

A few minutes later, Willingham notified Michles that twelve VC with web equipment had been killed. Although this report and subsequent reports by Willingham of additional VC killed were entered into unit logs and reported to higher headquarters, we found no credible evidence of any kind that the persons killed were in fact VC.

The point team, followed by the 1st Squad, then moved into My Khe-4 (Map 16–3), where they threw demolition charges of one or two pounds of TNT into the bunkers and shelters the local Vietnamese had constructed. Reportedly, this was done without any attempt to find out if these structures were occupied, and some women and children were shot as they ran out. Then all the shelters were burned.

It was difficult to obtain precise information as to what actually happened in My Khe-4. The best information came from ex-Specialist-4 Mario D. Fernandez, who had been a radio operator, and Specialist-4 Rodney I. Linkous, the leader of the 2nd Squad. It seems that only ten men had participated in the action. Two of them were later killed and the others

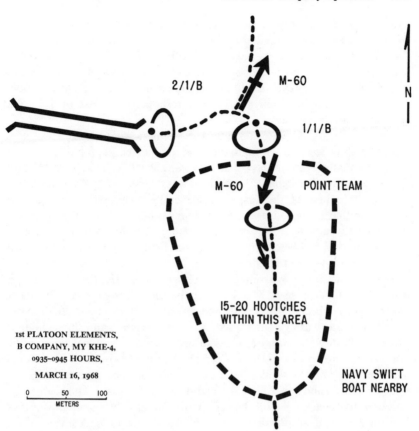

2/1/B

M-60

N

1/1/B

M-60   POINT TEAM

15-20 HOOTCHES
WITHIN THIS AREA

1st PLATOON ELEMENTS,
B COMPANY, MY KHE-4,
0935–0945 HOURS,

MARCH 16, 1968

0   50   100

METERS

NAVY SWIFT
BOAT NEARBY

Map 16–3

either refused to testify or said they didn't remember anything about it. However, at 10:25 A.M. Lieutenant Willingham reported that eighteen more VC had been killed, and at 2:25 P.M. another eight—for a total of thirty-eight credited to the 1st Platoon on that date. An idea of the amount of explosives and firepower used can be gained from the fact that at noon Willingham had requested a helicopter resupply of a case of TNT and additional ammunition.

During the My Khe-4 episode no U.S. soldiers were killed or wounded and no enemy weapons or equipment were reported captured.

The 1st Platoon did not report any civilian casualties to Captain Michles. Moreover, when Lieutenant Willingham was questioned by Colonel Wilson during the course of the Inspector General's investigation, he gave no indication that there had been any civilian casualties during the operation. However, his radio operator, who had accompanied him on a walk through the hamlet, testified before the Inquiry that he had observed about twenty bodies, all women and children.

In her testimony to Warrant Officer Feher of the CID, Mrs. Nguyen Thi Bay said she had been in My Khe-4 at the time of the attack. She stated that no VC had been in the hamlet and that ninety women and children had been killed. She was in a shelter with two other women and three children, none of whom were shot, but she had been raped by two soldiers and hit with a rifle butt by one of them. Then she had been taken to a hootch, she said, and shown a facsimile of a booby trap (two cartridges tied together with a rubber band), of which she had denied having any knowledge. She had been forced to stay with the platoon during its subsequent movements. With a rope tied around her waist, she was made to walk ahead of the platoon, serving as a guide to avoid booby traps. Evidently they thought she knew where booby traps were located and would lead the platoon around them.

Mrs. Bay's account was corroborated in certain respects by several members of the platoon. They recalled the booby trap device as well as a Vietnamese woman leading the platoon until it rejoined the remainder of Bravo Company, when she was turned over to some ARVN soldiers who had joined Bravo Company in the field with the Vietnamese National Police.

The 1st Platoon remained in the My Khe-4 area until about 3:00 P.M. Then, still led by Mrs. Bay, it began moving north along the same spit, passing My Lai-1 and finally stopping just east of My Lai-2 (Map 16–4) where six sampans had been forced ashore by the Navy Swift boats. The occupants of the sampans, about twenty men and boys, were held until an interrogation team could be helicoptered in from Bravo Company. Five of them were detained, flown first to Bravo Company's night location and then to Duc Pho for further interrogation. The 1st Platoon bivouacked at that point, the night of 16–17, and engaged in no other significant activity.

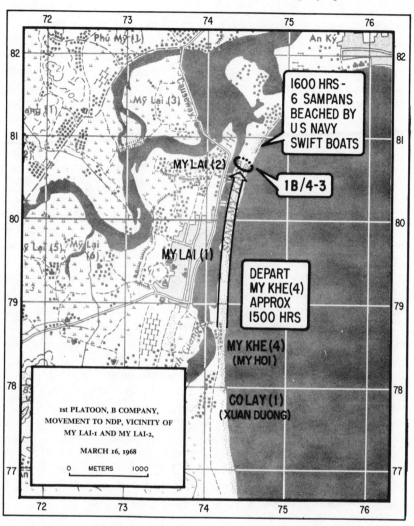

1st PLATOON, B COMPANY,
MOVEMENT TO NDP, VICINITY OF
MY LAI-1 AND MY LAI-2,

MARCH 16, 1968

Map 16-4

It will be recalled that at about noon on the 16th Specialist-5 Roberts and Sergeant Haeberle of the 11th Brigade public information office, along with Lieutenant Johnson of the brigade military intelligence detachment and his Vietnamese interpreter, Sergeant Minh, arrived at the Bravo Company night bivouac area. The rather idyllic pictures Haeberle took while he was with Bravo Company were in sharp contrast to the gruesome ones he had taken with Charlie Company. Johnson helped interrogate some of the detainees brought in by Bravo Company after its search of My Lai-6. Charlie Company joined Bravo Company at about 3:30 to establish their night location. Captain Kotouc, the Task Force Barker intelligence officer, arrived at about 5:00 P.M. accompanied by some National Police and ARVN soldiers.

The next morning the 1st Platoon, again led by a Vietnamese woman (presumably Mrs. Bay), moved southward to join the other elements of Bravo Company on the east end of the concrete bridge. Shortly before this time one man of the platoon was wounded by a booby trap and soon thereafter sniper fire was reportedly received from My Khe-4. The 3rd Platoon remained in the general vicinity of the bridge while the remainder of the company, with the 1st and 2nd platoons abreast, moved south through Co Lay-1, 2, and 3 (Map 16-5). There were only a few inhabitants in these settlements, where all dwellings were burned. In the area of Co Lay-2 the 1st Platoon sighted two VC and reportedly killed one of them, although no body was found. During the afternoon Bravo Company retraced its steps to the north and bivouacked for the night in the vicinity of the east end of the concrete bridge.

The following day—March 18—the company moved north along the Song My Khe (Map 16-6). For some reason never explained, their operations were radically different from those of the previous days. There was no destruction or burning, and in the area of Ky Xuyen-1 and 2 they gathered up all the inhabitants, about a thousand of them, and had a medical assistance team flown in to attend to their medical needs.

They spent the night of March 18–19 north of Ky Xuyen. During the night they received a six- to ten-round mortar attack, which killed one man and wounded five, and fired counter mortar fire with their 81-mm. mortars. The dead and wounded were evacuated by a medical helicopter and a helicopter fire team was called in to overfly the area. The company, suspecting a major attack was imminent, was told to "really dig in." The helicopter fire team was later replaced by an Air Force C-47 (Spooky) aircraft equipped with Gatling guns, each capable of firing six thousand rounds per minute. The Spooky aircraft periodically "hosed down" the area from which the mortar attack had come. Two additional mortar rounds were received just before dawn, but there were no casualties.

The following morning the company searched the area. The VC mortar position was located, but nothing else. It was reported that during this

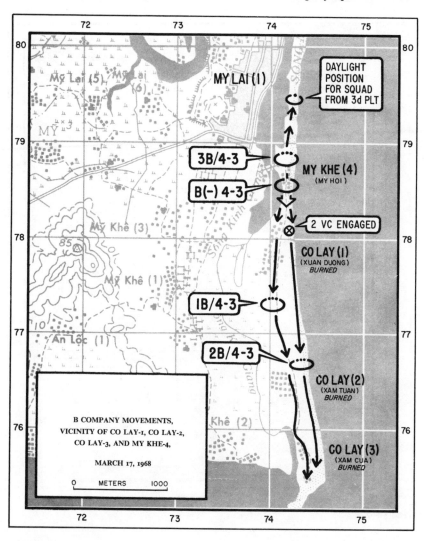

Map 16–5

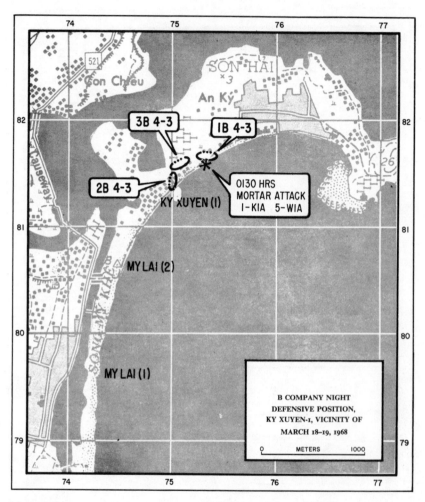

Map 16–6

period an American with an ARVN interpreter used a battery-operated field telephone to produce electric shocks on one of the detainees in an attempt to get him to talk. Also, an American (perhaps the same one who administered the shock treatment) rubbed salt in the open knife wounds he had inflicted on the hand of a detainee.

Later in the day the 1st Platoon was taken by helicopter to LZ Uptight and the remainder of the company was flown to LZ Dottie, thus ending Bravo Company's participation in the Task Force Barker operation.

During the Bravo Company operation two men were killed and thirteen wounded by booby traps and mortar fire; there were no casualties from enemy small-arms fire. The company claimed thirty-eight VC killed, all by the 1st Platoon, and no weapons captured. Captain Michles had reported to Task Force Barker on the 16th that none of the VC reported killed were women or children.

The Inquiry was aware that Lieutenant Willingham's three-year tour tour of active duty was to terminate in early February. We had reasonably good information that a large number of women and children (as few as thirty-eight but possibly over ninety) had been killed by members of his platoon in My Khe-4, and even though he might not personally have killed any of them, anything done by members of his command was his responsibility.

The details of Bravo Company's operation and Willingham's imminent separation from military service were called to the attention of the Army General Counsel, the Judge Advocate General, and the Provost Marshal. After their review of all pertinent testimony, charges for trial by court martial were prepared against Willingham under the 118th Article of the UCMJ (murder) and were served by the CID on February 10, 1970, the day he was to be released from active duty, but not announced until the 12th because he sought a delay in order to obtain civilian legal counsel. This effectively retained him on active military service and subject to military jurisdiction and also gave the Inquiry time to find out more about the Bravo Company operation.

The crime for which Willingham was charged was a war crime under the Law of War for which, theoretically, there is no statute of limitations. However, the attitude of the American people and the climate within the government at the time were such that had he been released to civilian status, it was highly unlikely that he would have been prosecuted at all.[2]

Willingham came to testify before the Inquiry on February 20. He appeared with military legal counsel, upon whose advice he elected to remain silent except for this statement: "Subsequent to the completion of the operation 16 to 18 March 1968, I was never interrogated by any superior officer in Task Force Barker or any other member of an echelon of command,

2. The disposition of Lieutenant Willingham's case, and those of others, is covered in Part III.

other than Colonel Wilson on 8 May 1969."

It should be noted that the My Khe-4 atrocities were not mentioned in Colonel Henderson's report. The information was so tightly held within the 1st Platoon, and perhaps by certain other members of Bravo Company, that I doubt that Colonel Henderson or General Koster had any knowledge of it. Nobody on the Americal Division headquarters staff professed awareness of it. It was reported that there was some talk within Bravo Company but it soon died out. Taken as a whole, the information of the operation was more deeply suppressed than even that of Charlie Company. It was an almost total coverup.

chapter 17

The Coverup Evidence: Summary

The requirements placed upon the Inquiry were to determine the sufficiency of reviews and reports within the chain of command, the adequacy of investigations, and the possible suppression of information. The reports and investigations have been discussed at length in earlier chapters; here I would like to review the suppression of evidence—the coverup—as revealed during the Inquiry.

Action to conceal the incident was taken at every level, from the individual soldiers of Charlie Company and the 1st Platoon of Bravo Company through the company, task force, brigade, and division commands. Some did it deliberately, others unknowingly. Some actively suppressed information, others withheld it, and still others were responsible by merely not wanting to become involved. Many commanders were aware of at least some of the troubling aspects of the operation (see accompanying chart for a partial listing). In addition, some of the blame must be placed upon the inadequate enforcement of established policies.

It is doubtful that any of those who attempted to conceal the incident realized its full magnitude. Those who participated in the action knew what they had done and perhaps had seen some other acts, but they hadn't been aware of what had happened in other areas. Several persons in higher positions knew some civilians had been killed, but the numbers they were dealing with were minuscule compared to the two hundred—and possibly over four hundred—noncombatants killed that day.

There was little need for individual infantry soldiers participating in the action to report to their platoon leaders since these leaders were already aware that war crimes had been committed, and in some instances had been

KNOWLEDGE OF INCIDENTS RELATED TO THE SON MY OPERATION

Columns (left to right):
- MG KOSTER, CG AMERICAL DIV
- BG YOUNG, ADC AMERICAL DIV
- COL PARSON, CofS AMERICAL DIV
- COL HENDERSON, CO 11TH BDE
- LTC BARKER, CO TF BARKER
- LTC HOLLADAY, CO 123D AVN BN
- CHAPLAIN (CHAP) LEWIS, AMERICAL DIV
- LTC LUPER, CO 6-11TH ARTY
- MAJ CALHOUN, XO, 3, TF BARKER
- MAJ MCKNIGHT, S3 11TH BDE
- MAJ WATKE, CO CO B, 123D AVN BN
- CHAPLAIN (CHAP) CRESSWELL, AMERICAL DIV
- CPT JOHNSON, DIV INTERROGATOR, 52D MI
- CPT KOTOUC, S2 TF BARKER

Rows (incidents):
- ARTILLERY PLANNED AND FIRED ON MY LAI (4)
- GUNSHIPS AND LIFTSHIPS FIRE ON MY LAI (4)
- REPORTS OF DEPARTURE OF VC FROM MY LAI (4)
- EXODUS OF CIVILIANS FROM MY LAI (4)
- REPORTS AND OBSERVATIONS OF NONCOMBATANT CASUALTIES
- REPORTS AND OBSERVATIONS OF BURNING BUILDINGS
- INITIAL REPORT OF HIGH VC BODY COUNT
- REPORT OF 69 VC KIA BY ARTILLERY
- ABSENCE OF REPORTS OF ENEMY CONTACTS & REQUESTS FOR FIRE SUPPORT
- LOW RATIO OF US CASUALTIES TO VC CASUALTIES
- LOW RATIO OF WEAPONS CAPTURED TO VC KIA
- WO1 THOMPSON'S COMPLAINT
- COMMANDER'S ORDER TO RETURN TO MY LAI (4)

LEGEND
◼ CONFIRMED
▨ PROBABLE

M = MARCH
A = APRIL

KNOWLEDGE OF INCIDENTS RELATED TO THE SON MY OPERATION

personally involved themselves. Of course, those soldiers involved in the killings, rapes, and destruction of homes and property had been unwilling to report outside their own units since it could have led to their indictment, but it is difficult to understand why those who had not been involved in any way had not done so. Even after Task Force Barker was inactivated and the companies had returned to their parent battalions, no one took action.

Captain Medina was fully aware that a far greater number of noncombatants had been killed than the twenty to twenty-eight he had reported as resulting from artillery and gunships. Also, after Charlie Company returned to LZ Dottie, Medina told his men that the operation was being investigated and it would be best if they did not discuss it, and he advised Private First Class Michael A. Bernhardt not to write to his congressman about the operation until the investigation was completed. In this way he kept information from going outside the company and reduced internal discussion.

Whether Captain Michles knew or even suspected that the thirty-eight VC reported by his 1st Platoon were noncombatants is a matter of conjecture. There was evidence, however, that the platoon leader, Lieutenant Willingham, was aware that many noncombatants had been killed. It was only during the CID investigation and our Inquiry, almost two years later, that anyone became suspicious of what had transpired at Co Luy (My Khe-4).

Within Task Force Barker headquarters several actions were taken to cover up the incident. During the morning of the 16th there were a number of radio conversations initiated by helicopter pilots alluding to the killing of noncombatants, including such statements as "From up here it looks like a blood bath" and "If you shoot that man, I'm going to shoot you." These transmissions were heard by persons in the task force operations center, and some of them were heard at the 11th Brigade. The resulting actions included a telephone call from the brigade to the task force to find out what was going on. The importance of these conversations is that they were heard by many people, and both Task Force Barker and 11th Brigade should have recognized that something most unusual was going on and initiated immediate corrective action.

Early that morning task force headquarters had been made aware of of noncombatant deaths and had put out the word to "stop the killing." Later in the day they received reports of from ten to twenty-eight civilian casualties, but did nothing to clarify the count or confirm it by a physical check. The ten or eleven civilian casualties reported by Charlie Company were entered in the task force log with a note that the information had been passed on to the 11th Brigade, but there was no corresponding entry in the brigade log. Perhaps the most blatant of all Task Force Barker's deceptions was to change the location of where the sixty-nine VC were reportedly killed by artillery. In addition, Warrant Officer Thompson's allegations were tantamount to the reporting of war crimes, but his report was never transmitted by radio or in any written form to the 11th Brigade or higher head-quarters.

Lieutenant Colonel Barker's Combat Action Report of March 28 was replete with false and misleading statements, creating the impression that there had been contact with a substantial enemy force. In part it stated, "Co C then immediately attacked to the east receiving enemy small arms fire as they pressed forward." In all the testimony there was no indication that Charlie Company had received any enemy fire—their action was unop-posed. Although the report did not mention any civilian casualties, it did allude to two hundred civilians supporting the VC and said that some of them had been caught in crossfires. Then there was an unusual statement: "The infantry unit on the ground and helicopters were able to assist civilians in leaving the area and in caring for and/or evacuating the wounded." To anyone unfamiliar with the operation, the report made it seem to have been a normal combat operation in a populated area—an obvious attempt to obscure the true nature of what had happened.

Aside from the killing and raping in My Lai-4 and My Khe-4 on March 16 there was extensive destruction of property and burning of dwellings; the billowing smoke could be seen for several miles. The following day Bravo and Charlie companies burned out five other hamlets. Although there were strong prohibitions against the destruction of homes and property, no re-ports of this kind of activity were transmitted to the 11th Brigade or the Americal Division.

Within the 11th Brigade there were also efforts to conceal the extent of the noncombatant casualties and other war crimes committed by Task Force Barker. One of the most serious was the failure to report the twenty to twenty-eight noncombatants known to have been killed. General Koster was aware of the civilian casualties, but he did not pass on the information to his staff. However, the fact that General Koster had been advised is no substitute for official transmission by the 11th Brigade to the Americal Division and then to higher headquarters. In all probability it would have started a formal investigation by either MACV or USARV.

Colonel Henderson's efforts to investigate Thompson's allegations were cursory and in some respects futile. Yet in orally presenting his findings to Generals Young and Koster, he led them to believe he had conducted a thorough, in-depth investigation. Whether he did this knowingly or unwit-tingly, it eliminated, at least for the time being, the need for any further action.

If the intention of Colonel Henderson's so-called Report of Investigation dated April 24, 1968, was to put his oral report in writing, it was totally inadequate. It made no reference whatsoever to Warrant Officer Thomp-son's allegations, which had prompted Henderson's investigation and his oral report. It addressed only the charges in the VC propaganda and in the unsigned statement, which appeared to be of Vietnamese origin—although it had been prepared (and originally signed) by Captain Rodriguez of the

Son Tinh District advisory group. Moreover, despite its title, it was not a report of investigation by any stretch of the imagination, which even Colonel Henderson acknowledged. One copy had been delivered to division headquarters and two or three others had been kept in a folder in Sergeant Major Gerberding's desk with instructions to "keep it confidential." This was an unusual procedure for handling and filing such a document. Another indication that the report was given special handling was that no entries were made in the logs or journals indicating its dispatch by brigade or its receipt by division. The only copy of the report ever located was found in the 11th Brigade intelligence files.

General Koster said that this report had been so unsatisfactory that in early May he had directed either General Young or Colonel Parson to have a formal investigation conducted. Henderson recalled receiving verbal instructions from General Young and his tacit approval to have Lieutenant Colonel Barker conduct the investigation, but Young denied having any such conversations. Henderson and Koster described the report as being three or four pages long with fifteen or twenty sworn statements attached. The conclusions, Henderson said, were about the same as those of his own investigation—twenty civilians had been killed by preparatory fire and crossfire but there had been no unnecessary killing of noncombatants. He had approved the report and hand-carried three copies to Colonel Parson. No copy was kept at brigade nor was an approved copy ever returned from division. Henderson assumed the report had been approved but he never discussed it with Koster.

We hoped to find a copy of the formal report or at least some strong, positive evidence that such a document had actually existed, but General Koster and Colonel Henderson were the only witnesses who claimed any knowledge of it. Both General Young and Colonel Parson (who had been implicated through the testimony of Henderson and Koster) vigorously denied any knowledge of it. We questioned many of the men Henderson said had made sworn, signed statements for this report; they all denied ever having done so at any time.

We also talked with numerous brigade and division staff officers, including the Inspector General and the Judge Advocate General, as well as the officers and clerks who received and routed documents. Not a single one testified to having seen the document or having any knowledge of it.

Colonel Henderson contended that he submitted an interim report on April 4–6, and both he and General Koster testified as to a formal report that was submitted in May. However, there was no persuasive testimony or other evidence to support their claims. The so-called formal report, supposedly prepared by Lieutenant Colonel Barker, was discredited almost completely by the fact that all those named by Henderson as having prepared a signed statements denied having been questioned or having signed such statements.

Henderson said he had been suspicious of the civilian casualties as reported by Barker and had ordered Charlie Company to return to My Lai-4 to make another body count, but his order had been countermanded by General Koster. If Henderson had really wanted to learn the facts, he had several other means of obtaining more accurate figures, but in fact he did nothing. About a month later he volunteered some of his troops to assist the Vietnamese in investigating the incident, but when the Vietnamese authorities did not appear to be interested he made no effort to employ his own assets to conduct his own on-site investigation. This lack of action was still another facet of the coverup.

The concealment was also furthered by Henderson's failure to initiate an Artillery Incident Report or to have Lieutenant Colonel Luper do so. In his own testimony as well as in his Report of Investigation, Henderson claimed that some of the noncombatant casualties had been caused by artillery fire, which, by regulation, should have triggered such a report.

The log of the 61st Artillery Battalion, commanded by Lieutenant Colonel Luper, had been stripped of the page or pages covering March 16, 1968. We never found out who had removed the material, why it had been removed, or what the entries had contained. However, it did not appear as an unusual coincidence, but rather an effort to destroy information concerning the incident.

Others of the 11th Brigade also contributed to the concealment of war crimes:

- Lieutenant Johnson, the military intelligence officer who accompanied Charlie Company during part of the morning of the 16th, by failing to report his observations to Captain Medina, Captain Kotouc, or to his superiors.
- Sergeant Haeberle, by submitting his rather innocuous black-and-white photos but keeping the color photos that showed extensive evidence of war crimes.
- Specialist-5 Roberts, by preparing and submitting a false and misleading article that gave a glowing account of the operation but made no mention of civilian casualties.
- These three men were not assigned to Task Force Barker and thus did not have to fear possible reprisals had they reported what they had observed. Yet they did nothing.

Within the aviation battalion of the Americal Division there were acts of commission and omission that helped conceal the incident. Major Watke's delay in informing Lieutenant Colonel Holladay of Thompson's allegations and the added delay in transmitting this report to the division command group may have prevented the initiation of a full and proper investigation by a disinterested senior officer. Moreover, when he did transmit the report, Watke gave a watered-down version rather than the complete story, which may have misled Generals Koster and Young as to the full implications of what Thompson had seen.

Upon his return to Chu Lai on the afternoon of the 16th, Thompson filed an After Action Report giving the details of what he had observed during the day. Captain Lloyd said he had highlighted Thompson's report and put the word "notice" on it in capital letters to make sure that it was called to the attention of his superiors. Other Aero Scout Company personnel submitted comparable reports, one of them claiming there had been 150 civilian casualties. If these reports had been seen by the proper authorities they would have prompted a full investigation.

Watke had been aware that Henderson was conducting an investigation and had no reason to suspect it would not be a complete one. On at least two occasions, however, he quelled unrest within his Aero Scout Company by telling his men that the incident was being investigated and not to discuss it any further. Although perhaps it was unintentional, this served to keep information within the company.

Both Watke and Holladay became convinced that a proper investigation had not been made and that a "coverup" was taking place. Holladay expressed this opinion to the Chief of Staff, Colonel Parson, when he saw Colonel Henderson's Report of Investigation of April 24, but aside from that, Holladay and Watke made no effort to obtain and document information from the crewmen, report the facts to the division Inspector General or Staff Judge Advocate, or discuss it with Generals Young or Koster.

Within the Americal Division headquarters, knowledge that civilians had been killed at My Lai was confined primarily to members of the command group—Generals Koster and Young and Colonel Parson. No reasonable explanation was ever given for General Koster withholding information from his staff that twenty to twenty-eight civilians had been killed. He was aware of the casualties by about 3:30 on the afternoon of the 16th and attended the evening briefing where the results of the Task Force Barker operation were presented, along with other operational reports. The fact that Koster did not tell his staff what he knew at that time was the first indication that he wanted to restrict this information to just a few men in his headquarters.

General Koster's action to countermand Colonel Henderson's order for Charlie Company to return to My Lai-4 and make another body count was most regrettable in that it could have resulted in a full disclosure of the incident. Instead, it seemed to have set the stage for the coverup. To countermand an order is a most serious matter, and Koster should have spoken personally to Colonel Henderson; instead, he asked the task force to inform him. He did not even mention it to his staff, nor did he explain his reasoning to Henderson that evening when Henderson talked with him on the telephone about the civilian casualties. Koster did not forbid the 11th

Brigade from returning to My Lai-4 at some other time, but it was never done.

There were specific requirements from higher headquarters that immediate spot reports be submitted on all civilian casualties, with follow-up reports. The division staff did not comply since they had not been notified by brigade of any civilian casualties, and General Koster withheld the information from them. Under these circumstances the responsibility rested solely with General Koster. He thought the noncombatant deaths had been part of the normal course of battle, caused by artillery, gunships, and crossfires. However, that in no way relieved him of the requirement to report them. If nothing else, his personal knowledge of General Westmoreland's intense interest in reducing civilian casualties and the destruction of property should have prompted him to report.

By noon of the 17th, Generals Young and Koster had been informed of Thompson's allegations, including the "unnecessary killings." MACV directives in force at the time made clear that any suspected war crime should be reported immediately. This was not done.

Knowing that at least twenty to twenty-eight noncombatants had been killed and having been informed of Thompson's allegations, General Koster still did not make sure that a complete and impartial investigation was conducted by the division Inspector General or some disinterested senior officer; instead the task was given to Colonel Henderson, and with no specific instructions. Both Young and Koster thought Henderson would make a complete, formal investigation, but it turned out to be very superficial, with the results submitted orally to and accepted by Koster. I found it most difficult to understand why senior officers of the caliber of Generals Young and Koster had settled for this and had not themselves talked to Thompson and other crewmen to obtain a firsthand account.

In all probability, the division command group did not recognize the magnitude of the numbers of noncombatant casualties, possibly in excess of four hundred. They may have thought they were dealing with the death of fewer than thirty—a sizable number that should of course have been reported, but lacking the impact of the figures in the hundreds. In mid-April, both General Young and General Koster, and perhaps Colonel Parson, were apprised of a far greater number of civilian casualties, four to five hundred, in Lieutenant Tan's letter of April 11 and the VC propaganda statement. This should have alerted them to the possibility of a much more serious incident, but all they did was to have Henderson put his oral report into writing. This too seems so inconsistent with what would be expected as to be almost incomprehensible.

General Koster testified that he found Colonel Henderson's April 24 Report of Investigation unacceptable, yet there is no conclusive evidence that he made any effort to insure that a proper investigation and report were undertaken.

Little need be said about Lieutenant Colonel Lewis' efforts to investigate Thompson's allegations through chaplains' channels. They were futile at best, although Lewis was in a position to have gotten them into proper channels and insured a full investigation. His actions were forestalled to some extent, however, when Colonel Parson told him the incident was being investigated and not to talk about it.

Even General Westmoreland was peripherally involved with these events. In his book *A Soldier Reports,* Westmoreland mentions that he visited the Americal Division and the 11th Infantry Brigade on April 20, 1968, but was told nothing about any killing of noncombatants or any other war crimes committed during the My Lai operation.

None of the witnesses referred to this visit, nor did General Westmoreland tell me about it. After reading the book I wrote to him to ask what had happened. He responded with:

> As to my visit to the 11th Brigade on 20 April 1968, I will add what I can to my recollection of that stop on my active itinerary that day. Accompanying me was the Division Commander, Major General Koster. The Brigade Commander, Colonel Henderson, met us at the helicopter pad and escorted us to the briefing tent. Colonel Henderson's staff, as I recall, briefed me on the status of the Brigade and on recent operations. I do not recall reference to the Task Force operation at My Lai. There was no mention of civilian casualties. The only thing out of routine was the complaint by the Red Cross representative about poor mail delivery.

Later I talked with Major General Hunt, who had conducted the Article 32 investigation of Colonel Henderson. He confirmed General Westmoreland's visit to the 11th Brigade, where he had been briefed by Colonel Henderson and Major McKnight on three successful operations: My Lai-4 (which General Westmoreland had not recalled), Norfolk Victory, and a North Vietnamese ship that had been forced to beach and was blown up by its crew. The briefing on My Lai-4 cited the body count of 128, but did not mention civilian casualties (not even the twenty that had been confirmed by Captain Medina). This is difficult to comprehend since these men, and especially General Koster, were well aware of General Westmoreland's interest in minimizing civilian casualties. Moreover, only a few days before his visit, both Colonel Henderson and General Koster had become aware of the strong allegations contained in Lieutenant Tan's letter. Failure to acquaint General Westmoreland with such information thus became part of the coverup.

Putting all of this together, the Inquiry could only conclude that by design or by failure to recognize and act upon the many indications they had of a most serious situation, the division command group effectively restricted knowledge of the incident from leaving the division.

Within the U.S. advisory groups at Quang Ngai Province and 2nd ARVN Division headquarters, some of the senior officers were acquainted with the allegations made in Lieutenant Tan's letters and the VC propaganda. The province advisory group should have reported immediately to CORDS, I Corps, but they did not. However, CORDS, I Corps, included a complimentary statement about Task Force Barker in their monthly report. The advisory group with the 2nd ARVN Division should have reported the contents of the documents to Lieutenant General Cushman in his capacity as senior advisor to the Vietnamese commander of I Corps. By failing to inform their higher headquarters, both advisory elements contributed to the concealment of the operation. (It should be noted that General Koster told us he thought he had mentioned the incident and the subsequent investigations to both Lieutenant General Cushman and Cushman's Vietnamese counterpart, Lieutenant General Lam, but neither of them remembered any such discussion.)

The Vietnamese acted with their customary restraint. Not wanting to offend the Americans, they did not make any explicit accusations or conduct any investigations of their own. However, at district, province and 2nd ARVN Division headquarters they made available pertinent information about civilian casualties to some of their U.S. advisors as well as to Generals Young and Koster and to the Inquiry.

In summary, there were numerous people within the Americal Division and elsewhere who realized, to some extent, that something most unusual had occurred at My Lai on March 16, 1968. For example, the report to MACV headquarters that Task Force Barker had killed 128 VC and captured only three weapons should have raised some suspicions among the MACV staff. Rarely was one weapon captured for every VC reported killed in action, but a ratio of forty-three enemy dead to one weapon captured was completely out of line. The operations section should have noted the disparity and called it to General Westmoreland's attention, and an inquiry should have been initiated. Instead, a message of congratulations was sent to the unit. People were apparently so interested in favorable reports that they sometimes overlooked the obvious and failed to check into questionable reports from subordinate commands. Also, many of the men who had participated in the operation and were aware of the facts would have willingly testified if they had been asked to. One of the things that bothered me and other members of the Inquiry very much was the lack of concern on the part of so many people. Only a few, such as Warrant Officer Thompson and Lieutenant Tan, on either the American or Vietnamese side, seemed to care that Vietnamese noncombatants (women, children, and old men) had been killed.

If by some means information of the incident had gotten outside of the Americal Division to higher headquarters, almost certainly a proper investigation would have been conducted and the gruesome details of the operation brought to light. This was one of the great tragedies of the aftermath of My Lai. Another, as Bob MacCrate expressed it, was the haunting problem of the destruction of records and the "cleansing" of files. Additionally, there were the several telephone calls between General Koster and Colonel Henderson immediately before and during the early days of the Inquiry in which they discussed investigations and reports. These calls may have only have served to refresh General Koster's recollection of events, but in another light they appeared to be a continuation of the efforts to mislead and deceive.

To this day the matter that most greatly concerns me is that so many people in command positions—perhaps as many as fifty—had information that something most unusual had occurred during the My Lai operation and yet did nothing about it. To my mind this has had the most damaging effect upon the image of the U.S. Army as a professional institution and has cast doubt upon the integrity of all its officers and men. Had any of of these persons made their knowledge known to the proper investigative authorities, the whole blanket of obscurity covering the incident would have been rolled back and the true facts brought to light. It might be said that Warrant Officer Thompson and Lieutenant Tan submitted their allegations through proper command channels, even though their actions came to naught. I accept that, and admire them for trying, but this in no way relieves responsibility from those others who should have done something but in fact did nothing.

chapter 18

Final Days of the Inquiry

It was an unwritten rule that we would not talk with anyone outside the Inquiry about our findings. Thus I never discussed the investigation with any of my counterparts on the Army staff, and when I talked with Secretary Resor or General Westmoreland it was only of organization and procedural matters, nothing about what we had uncovered. But as we became aware of the enormity of the My Lai incident and the failures within the command to investigate and report it, I became concerned that our report would come as a horrendous shock to both Secretary Resor and General Westmoreland.

To soften the blow, so to speak, in mid-February we sent them a short preliminary report. It told, in abrupt and brutal terms, of the actions at My Lai-4 and My Khe-4 on March 16 and of the burning of other hamlets on the 17th, and provided a short résumé of the efforts made (or not made) within the Americal Division to investigate and report the incident. For about three months we had been immersed in testimony about women and children being killed, murder, rape, piles of bodies, and the destruction of crops, livestock, and homes. We had strong, but I think objective, views of the overall My Lai incident, so it was only natural that a preliminary report would be expressed in equally strong terms.

The reaction was not long in coming. A couple of days later Secretary Resor asked Bob MacCrate and me to see him. As expected, the preliminary report had come like a bolt out of the blue. He did not question the magnitude of the tragedy, nor did he want in any way to control the contents of the final report. To do so would have downgraded and in-validated the purpose of the Inquiry and would be certainly be regarded as "command influence." He did, however, have some suggestions for minimizing what might be termed emotionalism or overly strong language in the final report. In several places we had described the casualties as women, children, babies, and old men. He suggested that whenever possible we use such terms as "noncombatant casualties." We had also described some of the rapes in rather vivid terms, and he felt we might tone down these descriptions a bit. This would not detract from the report, he said, but if we avoided "overemotionalism" the report would be more acceptable to readers outside the senior Army staff. He emphasized that he was by no means trying to influence the final report and that he was only making suggestions. I appreciated his guidance, and in preparing the report we kept his suggestions in mind; I believe they improved our end product.

The final two weeks of the Inquiry were pure bedlam. Seldom did we get home before 10:00 P.M. or midnight. We were still taking testimony from some new and recalled witnesses as well as writing, editing, and reviewing the report.

Although I was personally responsible, as the investigating officer, for the contents and findings of the report, I wanted to make sure that the views of the other panel members were included and hoped that all the senior panel members would endorse the report. Thus, when each chapter was completed, its writers, along with Colonel Franklin, would meet with the senior panelists to go over it word for word. The initial chapters covering background and the operation of Task Force Barker did not take much time, since they were fairly cut and dried and it was only a matter of how the material should be expressed.

This was not the case, however, with the final three chapters dealing with reports and investigations, suppression of information, and findings and recommendations. They were the guts of the report and contained a myriad of controversial issues. (The chapters dealing with reports and investigations and suppression of information, for example, each required the better part of three days and nights to review.) We went over each chapter paragraph by paragraph, discussing it and making changes so that it said exactly what was intended. Then the typist retyped the new version and we reviewed it again before the final draft was typed.

Some of our guidelines were to make the report as brief and concise as possible and yet include the essential details; to follow Secretary Resor's suggestions where applicable and yet not hesitate to call a spade a spade; and to tell the story as we saw it in an intelligible manner.

Nearly everybody on the Inquiry panel had a hand in the preparation of the final chapter on conclusions and recommendations. Initially, we met with Colonel Franklin and the writers to discuss what we considered to be the principal findings. Then we discussed each of the findings in detail to make sure the writers fully understood the views of the senior panel members. Then, of course, after the chapter was written, we reviewed, reviewed, and reviewed it again to make certain it expressed precisely what we intended.[1]

That portion of the chapter dealing with individual commissions and omissions was by far the most difficult. Here we were dealing with *people* and expressing our views of how they performed in regard to the My Lai incident. We first discussed whom we thought should be included, a time-consuming process. Some cases were obvious and required little discussion, but the marginal ones took a great deal of time. We reviewed pertinent testimony and went over the man's actions from start to finish, trying to be fair both to him and to the Army.

Finally we came up with a list of thirty persons who, we felt, had known of the killing of noncombatants and other serious offenses committed during the My Lai operation but had not made official reports, had suppressed relevant information, had failed to order investigations, or had not followed up on the investigations that were made. These men were:

American Division
   Major General Samuel W. Koster, Commanding General
   Brigadier General George H. Young, Assistant Division Commander
   Colonel Nels A. Parson, Chief of Staff
   Lieutenant Colonel Francis Lewis, Division Chaplain

American Division Artillery
   Lieutenant Colonel Robert B. Luper, Commander, 6th Batallion, 11th Artillery
   Captain Carl Creswell, Chaplain

11th Infantry Battalion
   Colonel Oran K. Henderson, Commanding Officer
   Major Robert W. McKnight, Operations Officer
   1st Lieutenant Dennis H. Johnson, Intelligence Officer, 52nd Military Intelligence Detachment
   Sergeant Ronald L. Haeberle, Public Information Officer (photographer)
   Specialist-5 Jay A. Roberts, Public Information Officer (reporter)

Task Force Barker
   Lieutenant Colonel Frank Barker, Commanding Officer (deceased)
   Major Charles C. Calhoun, Executive and Operations Officer
   Captain Eugene M. Kotouc, Intelligence Officer
   Captain Dennis R. Vasquez, Artillery Liaison Officer

1. The major portion of this chapter will be found in the Appendix, page 000. Volume I of the report (officially titled *Report of the Department of the Army Review of the Preliminary Investigations into the My Lai Incident,* Volume I: "The Report of the Investigation") is available in the Army Library of the Pentagon or may be obtained from the Office of the Army Adjutant General. In addition to the principal findings, there were some other issues of lesser importance that we felt to be significant enough to include as an appendix to the report.

123rd Aviation Batallion
Lieutenant Colonel John L. Holladay, Commanding Officer
Major Frederic W. Watke, Commanding Officer, Company B

B Company, 4th Batallion, 3rd Infantry
Captain Earl C. Michles, Commanding Officer (deceased)
1st Lieutenant Kenneth W. Boatman, Forward Observer, Command
    Group
1st Lieutenant Thomas K. Willingham, Platoon Leader, 1st Platoon
2nd Lieutenant Michael L. Lewis, Platoon Leader, 2nd Platoon (deceased)
2nd Lieutenant John E. Mundy, Executive Officer

C Company, 1st Battalion, 20th Infantry
Captain Ernest L. Medina, Commanding Officer
2nd Lieutenant Roger L. Alaux Jr., Artillery Forward Observer
2nd Lieutenant William L. Calley Jr., Platoon Leader, 1st Platoon
2nd Lieutenant Stephen K. Brooks, Platoon Leader, 2nd Platoon (deceased)
2nd Lieutenant Jeffrey U. La Cross, Platoon Leader, 3rd Platoon

2nd Division, Army of Vietnam
Colonel Dean E. Hutter, Senior U.S. Advisor

Quang Ngai Province
Lieutenant Colonel William A. Guinn, Deputy U.S. Advisor

Son Tinh District
Major David C. Gavin, Senior U.S. Advisor

Then came the problem of determining specifically what each person had or had not done. The responsibility of preparing an initial draft relating to each man was assigned to the various panel members, but it did not make much difference who prepared these drafts as we all went over them again and again. Some of them were relatively brief, with only one or two items, while others required up to three pages of the report.

It is important to note that through the process of review everything in the report, including the findings and recommendations, was fully agreed upon by all of the members of the panel, military and civilian alike.

We were still working on the final chapter on March 12, 1970, yet we knew we had to get it to the printer so that Volume I, the report proper, could be submitted no later than the 14th. Needless to say, the printers did a yeoman's job in putting it all together and printing and binding it under a very short deadline. In all events, Volume I was submitted as scheduled on March 14, 1970.[2]

2. Document 18–1: Memorandum from Special Counsel Robert MacCrate Attached to Final Report (March 14, 1970). See page 286.

As we were finishing Volume I, we were also assembling and preparing the back-up materials: Volume II—Six books of documentary evidence, including directives, regulations, reports, photos, and miscellaneous documents; Volume III—Testimony of the 403 witnesses who appeared before the Inquiry, consisting of approximately twenty thousand pages. Because of the magnitude of the task (a complete copy is six feet thick), this work was not submitted until some time after the Inquiry had ended; Volume IV —Statements taken from approximately a hundred men during the CID investigation, which we had used in our deliberations.

As the Inquiry was nearing its end, I became concerned about the preparation of courts martial charges against those who might have committed illegal actions. Time was running out: the two-year statute of limitations on military offenses would expire on March 15, 1970, so charges had to be preferred before that date. This was called to the attention of General Westmoreland and Mr. Jordan, the Army General Counsel, and as a result Colonel Hubert Miller from the Office of the Judge Advocate General was appointed to draft the charges.

Colonel Miller had a tremendous task ahead of him. He was not empowered to recommend action against those men who might have committed war crimes, which was being handled by the CID, but was to identify everyone whom he felt had been derelict in the areas of reporting, investigations, and other military types of offenses. He was not, of course, limited to the thirty persons cited by the Inquiry, and so had thousands of pages of testimony and numerous documents to review before he could arrive at any sound judgment. We helped him as best we could by providing him with drafts of those portions of the report that had been completed as well as copies of pertinent documents. Almost immediately it became apparent that he could not do the job alone, so three other Judge Advocate General officers were designated to work with him.

Colonel Miller submitted charges against the following eleven men:

Major General Samuel W. Koster
Colonel Oran K. Henderson
Lieutenant Colonel William D. Guinn
Lieutenant Colonel Robert B. Luper
Major David C. Gavin
Major Robert W. McKnight
Major Fredric W. Watke
Captain Eugene M. Kotouc
1st Lieutenant Kenneth W. Boatman
1st Lieutenant Dennis H. Johnson
1st Lieutenant Thomas K. Willingham

The fact that certain men were not on this list greatly disturbed the members of the Inquiry panel. (It should be noted that Captain Medina and

Lieutenant Calley were not included because court martial charges had already been preferred against them.) While it is true that we had lived with the problem for over three months and had strong convictions, the panel members knew far more about the individual men and their actions than any outsider could possibly have absorbed in a few days. The Uniform Code of Military Justice permits anyone in the military to prefer charges against any other serviceman whom he considers to have committed an offense chargeable under the articles. Moreover, there was nothing in the directive establishing the Inquiry that prohibited any of the military members of the Inquiry from preferring charges. Thus, Colonel Robert Miller prepared charges against:

Brigadier General George H. Young
Colonel Nels A. Parson

and Lieutenant Colonel Charles Bauer against:

Lieutenant Colonel Francis Lewis
Major Charles C. Calhoun

The charges that had been prepared against Lieutenant Colonel (Chaplain) Lewis were subsequently withdrawn by Secretary Resor and never preferred. That was within his prerogative, but I nevertheless voiced my objections to him. The Secretary was concerned about the damage a court martial trial might do do to the chaplains corps, and also felt that the charges against Lewis were somewhat marginal. My view was that when it comes to taking action in cases involving war crimes, chaplains are no different from anyone else. In fact, I feel that because of their position they may have a greater responsibility than the average serviceman (officer or enlisted man) to make sure that any suspected war crime is properly reported and investigated. Lieutenant Colonel Lewis had been told a great deal about the My Lai incident, but he neither acted properly on this information nor followed through on the matter. Secretary Resor heard me out but stuck by his decision, and that ended it.

Although the report of the House Armed Services Investigating Subcommittee has some kind words to say about the Inquiry report ("an outstanding and scholarly piece of work and a credit to all who participated in its preparation"), it took the Inquiry to task regarding the additional charges prepared by members of the panel. The concluding summary of their report explains the position taken by the investigating subcommittee:

Since the Department of the Army had taken the unusual step of having the sufficiency of the evidence reviewed by legal officers in anticipation of the filing of charges, it is unfortunate their findings were not accepted. The recent dismissal of charges in two cases in which they had recommended against the filing confirmed their assessment of the evidence. If the investigators had acted in accordance with the advice of the professional legal officers, several officers would have been spared the agony of public announcement of charges which were subsequently dismissed.

Be that as it may, the subcommittee overlooked the fact that the Inquiry members included some highly competent legal authorities in Bob Mac-Crate, Bland West, Jerry Walsh, and Colonel Robert W. Miller, and it was Colonel Miller who had prepared the charges against two of the men. With respect to the dismissal of charges, the same reasoning could be applied to ten of the eleven charges prepared by Colonel Hubert Miller, since they were later dismissed and only one of these men—Colonel Henderson—was ever brought to trial.[3] I should also mention that there was no undue influence upon either Colonel Robert Miller or Lieutenant Colonel Bauer. The senior panelists had discussed this issue at length, but they had acted voluntarily. However, I was in full agreement with them, and had they not prepared the charges I might have done so myself.

General Westmoreland, in his capacity as Chief of Staff, took action to have twelve of these fourteen men assigned to the First U.S. Army headquarters at Fort Meade, Maryland. Lieutenant General Jonathan O. Seaman was the commanding general and, as such, had general courts martial jurisdiction. At the same time, General Westmoreland designated Third U.S. Army headquarters at Fort McPherson, Georgia, to handle cases involving war crimes. Since Kotouc and Willingham had been cited by Colonel Hubert Miller for war crimes, they were transferred to that jurisdiction.

When the Inquiry ended, we still had one other matter to attend to. On the evening of March 15 we were notified that there was to be a press conference at 11:00 A.M. on the 17th with Secretary Resor, General Westmoreland, Bob MacCrate, Jerry Walsh, and myself. A hassle started the next morning when representatives from the Office of the Chief of Information arrived to find out what I was going to say. I had drafted a short introductory statement of what I thought the American public should be told, and in it I had used the term "massacre" without being specific as to how many people had been killed. I was requested not to include that portion my statement. Personally, I felt very strongly that we had to inform the public or else we would be deceptive. It was not long before Major General Sidle, the Chief of Information, was in on the act. I don't know who had given him his instructions, but it seemed as though they had come from the General Counsel and the Office of the Secretary. He gave us all kinds of reasons why we should not intimate that My Lai had been a massacre —the impact it would have upon the Army's image, its effects upon on-

3. Of the three cases questioned by the investigating subcommittee, Major Calhoun received a letter of admonition from Lieutenant General Seaman, and Colonel Parson and General Young were subsequently given letters of censure through the administrative action of the Secretary of the Army, and their awards for service in Vietnam were withdrawn.

going and future courts martial and judicial litigation, and on and on. We could not agree on an acceptable alternative, so the meeting ended in a stalemate.

We were at it again the following morning, the day of the news conference. I was not about to present a watered-down version and in effect said that if that was what they wanted, please leave me out. Bob MacCrate and Jerry Walsh felt just as strongly about it. Of course, in my case if the Chief of Staff had ordered me to be present, I would have appeared, but under duress. But at about 10:00 o'clock Jerry pointed out that there didn't seem to be any objection to the word "tragedy," which appeared elsewhere in my prepared statement, and suggested that I use the phrase "a tragedy of major proportions." General Sidle had it checked out at the top level, and gave me the go-ahead less than a half hour before the conference was to begin, but I was still in an irritated and apprehensive mood as it started.

All in all, the conference went quite well, with the three of us from the Inquiry answering most of the questions. Perhaps because of the restraint, I did not feel that all of my answers were as clear and responsive as I would have liked, but the newspeople seemed satisfied, and that, after all, was the purpose of the conference.

When the press conference was over I returned to the Inquiry office to pick up my personal belongings, say goodbye, and thank the other panelists and the clerks, typists, and others without whom the investigation could not have been carried out. It had been a fine team and I appreciated their efforts and the opportunity to work with them. Then it was back to my assignment as chief of Office Reserve Components.

part III

The
Aftermath

chapter 19

Disposition of Charges

Twelve of the fourteen persons against whom charges were prepared as a result of the Inquiry—those suspected of military types of offenses—were placed under the general courts martial jurisdiction of the First Army, commanded by Lieutenant General Jonathan O. Seaman. The other two, charged with war crimes, were assigned to the Third Army, commanded by Lieutenant General Albert O. Connor. The action taken in each case was as follows.

Military Offenses

Major General Samuel W. Koster
Charges dismissed January 29, 1971. General Seaman issued a letter of censure. Subsequently the Secretary of the Army vacated his rank of temporary major general, reducing him to his permanent grade of brigadier general, and withdrew his Distinguished Service Medal. (Retired from the Army January 1, 1973.)

Brigadier General George H. Young
Charges dismissed June 23, 1970. Subsequently the Secretary of the Army issued a letter of censure and withdrew his Distinguished Service Medal.

Colonel Oran K. Henderson
Charges preferred for trial by general court martial; acquitted on December 17, 1971.

Colonel Nels A. Parson
Charges dismissed June 23, 1970. Subsequently the Secretary of the Army issued a letter of censure and withdrew his Legion of Merit.

Lieutenant Colonel Robert B. Luper
Charges dismissed July 28, 1970.

Major Charles C. Calhoun
Charges dismissed January 6, 1971. General Seaman issued a letter of reprimand.

Major David C. Gavin
Charges dismissed January 6, 1971.

Major William D. Guinn
Charges dismissed January 6, 1971.

Major Robert W. McKnight
Charges dismissed June 23, 1970.

Major Frederic W. Watke
Charges dismissed January 6, 1971. General Seaman issued a letter of administrative admonition.

1st Lieutenant Kenneth W. Boatman
Charges dismissed July 28, 1970.

1st Lieutenant Dennis H. Johnson
Charges dismissed February 26, 1971. Subsequently the Secretary of the Army issued a letter of reprimand.

War Crimes

Captain Eugene M. Kotouc

1st Lieutenant Thomas K. Willingham

The charges against Young, Parson, Luper, McKnight, Boatman, and Willingham were dismissed for lack of sufficient evidence by the commanding generals after their own evaluation and upon the advice of their Staff Judge Advocates; no independent Article 32 investigating officers were involved. The remainder of the cases were subjected to Article 32 investigations.

I found the dismissal of charges, particularly those without benefit of an Article 32 investigation, most difficult to understand. We of the Inquiry were intimately familiar with each of the cases, and not only I but all members of the panel felt the commissions and omissions, as listed in the report, were valid and should have been subject to the most rigorous examination. Had these men undergone trial by courts martial and been acquitted there would have been no remaining doubts. However, for a single individual to make such decisions seems inappropriate. While I know that Lieutenant Generals Seaman and Connor were highly effective, competent officers who deliberated long and carefully before deciding to dismiss charges, to this day I cannot agree with them, whatever their reasoning may have been.

I was especially disturbed by General Seaman's dismissal of charges against the senior officers, particularly in General Koster's case. When General Westmoreland informed me of the proposed action against General Koster (the letter of censure), I told him, in effect, that it was a travesty of justice and would establish a precedent that would be difficult for the Army to live down. Of course, there was nothing either Secretary Resor or General Westmoreland could have done about it. Had they interfered in the slightest way, or even given any guidance, they could have been accused of command influence—strictly taboo within the system of military justice.

General Koster's Article 32 investigation was conducted by Brigadier General B. L. Evans, an engineer officer who had served in Vietnam but had not been involved in combat operations. His report, which was submitted to General Seaman on October 27, 1970, justified General Koster's actions in each of the charges filed against him. While this report acknowledged that he may have been remiss in not reporting the twenty known civilian casualties and in not ordering a proper investigation, it stressed General Koster's fine character and his long career of outstanding service, which somehow excused these derelictions, and recommended dismissal of all charges. On January 28, 1971, almost three months to the day after receiving General Evans' report, General Seaman dismissed the charges, at the same time—above and beyond General Evans' recommendations—issuing General Koster a letter of censure. Why it took him so long to make up his mind has never been explained, but obviously it was a tough decision and must have given him a great deal of mental anguish.

In his letter of censure, General Seaman emphasized General Koster's failure to report the twenty or more civilian casualties known to him and his failure to conduct a full and adequate investigation despite the extensive information available to him indicating that something had gone amiss in the My Lai operation. These were exactly the reasons I felt the matter should have been adjudicated in a duly appointed court martial, which would have served the best interests of General Koster, the Army, and the nation.

Many field-grade officers (majors, lieutenant colonels, and colonels) have asked why the top group got off with dismissal of charges while many of the lower-grade officers were subjected to courts martial, even though they were acquitted. To say that, in the sound judgment of the general officer rendering the decision, further judicial proceedings were not warranted is not acceptable to them. They are concerned about the future of the Army and they want a better answer.

Other knowledgeable people were also distressed by the dismissal action. Following are extracts from what Bob MacCrate had to say to *The New York Times* after the dismissal of charges against General Koster were announced:

> I cannot comment on the evidence in view of the legal proceedings which are still pending, but I am shocked by the action of the Commanding General of the First Army in dismissing at this time the charges against Major General Koster in advance of the disposition of the charges against officers within his former command. . . .
>
> I believe that the Commanding General of the First Army has effectively cut off the orderly progress of inquiry up the chain of command in acting at this time as he has. In my opinion, he has done a serious disservice to the Army. What is involved is a failure to recognize the Army's responsibility to the public at large and a failure to affirm the importance to the Army itself of acting in accordance with the rules of international law, the law of war and the principles of our own constitution.

Jerry Walsh was equally distressed; he called it a "whitewash of the top man" and told a reporter from the *Kansas City Star:* "The public's faith in the Army's ability and willingness to discipline itself will certainly be impaired by this result. General officers are given great power and responsibility. They should be held strictly to account when they fail."

Congressman Samual S. Stratton, one of the four members of the HASC investigation subcommittee, was even more vociferous in his condemnation of the Army's action. In a news release dated January 29, 1971, he said: "The decision of the Army to drop the charges against Major General Koster in the My Lai case is in my opinion a grave miscarriage of military justice. To drop the charges against the top officer responsible in this situation raises once again the whole question of military whitewash."

On February 4, 1971, Congressman Stratton made a long and extensively documented speech on the floor of the House in which he was vehement in his charges against the Army in the handling of the Koster case. Some of his comments, from the transcript, were:

> Dropping charges against the highest ranking officer involved, without any public trial or even discussion of the case against him, and doing so at a time when very grave charges involving the same incident against a junior officer in his command [Calley] are still in the process of trial, can only result in serious damage to the reputation of the U.S. Army, to the United States, and to the effectiveness of the processes and procedures of military justice in dealing with matters which involve profound national and international concerns.
>
> The dismissal of these charges is not only bad, but it has been carried out in a manner that purports to absolve the top military and civilian leadership of the Pentagon of all responsibility. . . .

I just cannot honestly believe that General Seaman made the decision to drop the charges against General Koster on his own and without any reference to the Pentagon. The precise reverse is probably true. The Pentagon must have decided to let General Koster off the hook, even while subordinates were still being tried on far more serious charges, probably because they feared that a full, public airing of the charges against Koster and of his incredible mismanagement of his command would make the Army look very, very bad.

Congressman Stratton went on to recommend:

- Reinstatement of charges against General Koster and trial by court martial.
- Release of the full records of the HASC subcommittee and the Army Inquiry.
- That if General Koster were not brought to trial he should be examined in open session by the HASC investigation subcommittee.
- That, in the future, approval by the Secretary of the Army should be required for dismissal of charges in cases of more than local interest.
- That civilian judges should be used as a tribunal under the federal court system to ajudicate cases comparable to that of My Lai.

Regarding Congressman Stratton's charge that the top Army command, and not General Seaman, made the decision to dismiss the charges against General Koster, I doubt very much that this was the case, and if it were I had no knowledge of it. General Westmoreland was very sensitive on the matter of command influence and, knowing the moral code of Secretary Resor, I do not believe he would have had any part of it either. Hence, in my view, had there been any collusion within what Congressman Stratton referred to as the West Point Protective Association, it was without their knowledge or approval.

Bob MacCrate, Jerry Walsh, and Congressman Stratton were not the only ones who objected to the dismissal of charges against General Koster. There were numerous articles and editorials in newspapers and magazines throughout the country, the essence of which was that they simply could not understand this decision.

The Article 32 investigation of the charges against Colonel Henderson was conducted by then Brigadier General Ira A. Hunt Jr. His investigation took almost six months to complete, nearly twice as long as the investigation of General Koster, and was very detailed; General Hunt interviewed a vast number of witnesses and compiled over three thousand pages of testimony. He certainly knew as much, and perhaps even more, about Colonel Henderson's actions relating to My Lai than did we of the Inquiry, and fully recognized the deficiencies in the colonel's performance, but felt that justice could best be served by action under Article 15 of the Unified Code of Military Justice[1] rather than by a general court martial. General Hunt felt that because charges had been dismissed against other senior officers it would be almost impossible to get a conviction in a general court martial. General Seaman, however, decided otherwise and, with the deletion of certain specifications, on February 25, 1971, charges were preferred against Colonel Henderson on these grounds:

- Dereliction of duty in failing to conduct a proper investigation.
- Disobedience of a regulation requiring the reporting of alleged war crimes.
- Making a false official statement and false swearing before the Inquiry.

Lieutenant General Claire E. Hutchin Jr. replaced General Seaman as commander of the First Army on February 28 and a few days later reviewed the charges against Colonel Henderson with General Hunt and the Chief of Staff, Major General Richard G. Ciccolella, both of whom presented strong arguments in favor of the Article 15 penalties. But General Hutchin sustained General Seaman's decision, and the general court martial charges remained in effect.

Colonel Henderson's trial began on August 23, 1971. His defense team was headed by the well-known and capable civilian defense lawyer, Henry B. Rothblatt, and Lieutenant Colonel Frank J. Dorsey; the prosecution was headed by a competent but comparatively young Judge Advocate General officer, Major Carroll S. Tichenor. During the trial the charge of false swearing was dropped. On December 17, 1971, Major General Charles M. Mount Jr., president of the seven-officer court (two generals and five colonels) and the only member of the panel to have served a regular tour of duty in South Vietnam, announced the verdict—not guilty of all charges and specifications. I am not aware of all the factors that influenced the court in its decision; specifically, I do not know to what extent dismissal of charges against other senior officers might have affected it. The fact remains that Colonel Henderson was tried, and I assume fairly and impartially so. However, from what I know of his performance and on the basis of what I would have expected of an officer of his grade and experience, I cannot agree with the verdict. If his actions are judged as acceptable standards for an officer in his position, the Army is indeed in deep trouble.

To complete the discussion of the military judicial action, charges were preferred against thirteen officers and enlisted men for having committed war crimes or crimes against humanity as cited by the Law of War. The decision in each case was as follows:

1. Article 15 specified "nonjudicial punishment" of officers by means of the following actions, in addition to admonition or reprimand: arrest in quarters for not more than thirty days, restriction to a specified area for not more than sixty days, and/or forfeiture of half of a month's pay for two months.

Officers

Captain Eugene M. Kotouc
Court martial; not guilty.

Captain Ernest L. Medina
Court martial; not guilty.

1st Lieutenant William L. Calley Jr.
Court martial; guilty—life imprisonment. Sentence was subsequently reduced to twenty years by the reviewing authority, and then to ten years by the Secretary of the Army. Lieutenant Calley was later released on parole.

1st Lieutenant Thomas K. Willingham
Charges dismissed.

Enlisted Men

Sergeant Kenneth L. Hodges*

Sergeant Charles E. Hutton**

Sergeant David Mitchell
Court martial; not guilty.

Sergeant Escquiel Torres*
Charges dismissed before trial.

Specialist-4 William F. Doherty**
Charges dismissed.

Specialist-4 Robert W. T'Souvas**
Charges dismissed before trial.

Corporal Kenneth Schiel*
Charges dismissed.

Private Max Hutson*
Charges dismissed before trial.

Private Gerald A. Smith**
Charges dismissed before trial.

I have often been asked whether or not I think Lieutenant Calley was a scapegoat. On the one hand, I think it most unfortunate that, of the twenty-five men who were charged with committing war crimes or related acts, he was the only one tried by court martial and found guilty. On the other hand,

---

*Discharged at the convenience of the government (under honorable conditions) and barred from re-enlistment by administrative action of the Secretary of the Army.
**Barred from re-enlistment by administrative action of the Secretary of the Army.

I think he was fortunate to get out of it with his life. He was in command of his platoon and was fully aware of what they were doing. Above and beyond that, he personally participated in the killing of noncombatants: he was convicted of killing at least twenty-two civilians but his platoon may have killed as many as 150 to 200 innocent women, children, and old men. So I don't consider him a scapegoat. On the contrary, I think the publicity given him by the news media and the notoriety he has gained are all wrong. He is certainly no hero as far as I am concerned.

chapter 20

Factors Contributing to the Tragedy

In drafting the initial outline for the final report I included a chapter entitled "Why My Lai?" When the writers got down to working on it, however, they encountered innumerable difficulties and were in favor of deleting it. But I felt strongly that if we were going to include the details of the operation we should provide some explanation of why it had developed into a massacre.

The senior panel members discussed this at length. There was no single reason for the incident, we realized—there were several. To complicate it further, what may have influenced one man to commit atrocities had had no effect on another. There seemed to be no pattern. In fact, some of the soldiers who had participated in the operation had steadfastly refused to become involved in atrocities of any form, be it burning, destruction of crops or animals, rape, or the killing of noncombatants.

Bob MacCrate put up a sound argument for not including the chapter in the report because he felt that I would be putting myself on a pedestal that could easily be knocked from under me. When the Army released the report many persons, both civilian and military, would have access to it, and if they found our rationale faulty it would tend to invalidate the entire report. While I could agree with his logic, I still wanted to include some kind of explanation in the report.

We started making a list of the things that might have influenced the various soldiers, and after considerable give-and-take finally narrowed it down to what we felt were the principal causes. We decided to include these in the report not only to highlight the deficiencies in the My Lai operation but also to indicate some of the differences between this operation and those of other units in South Vietnam. Also, we wanted to point out problems of command and control that existed within the Americal Division, problems that would require vigorous corrective action by the Army in order to prevent repetition of such an incident in the future.

Lack of Proper Training

Neither units nor individual members of Task Force Barker and the 11th Brigade received the proper training in the Law of War (Hague and Geneva conventions), the safeguarding of noncombatants, or the Rules of Engagement. This was due to many factors—the decision to ship the brigade to South Vietnam earlier than had been planned, the large turnover of personnel shortly before the overseas movement, the shortened orientation period in South Vietnam, and the continuing arrival of new troops. While some men felt they had received adequate training, others could not remember having had any training at all in these matters. Undoubtedly part of the problem was rooted in the lackadaisical manner in which this training was handled. Several of the men testified that they were given MACV's "Nine Rules" and other pocket cards, but since there had been no accompanying instructions they had put the cards in their pockets unread and never had any idea of their contents.[1] This, combined with the failure to disseminate division, brigade, and task force policies down to the individual soldier, created a significant void in many of the soldiers' minds as to what was expected of them.

Even accepting these training deficiencies as an important factor in the My Lai operation, however, the members of the Inquiry felt there were some things a soldier did not have to be told were wrong—such as rounding up women and children and then mowing them down, shooting babies out of mothers' arms, and raping.

Attitude Toward Vietnamese

The most disturbing factor we encountered was the low regard in which some of the men held the Vietnamese, especially rural or farming people. This attitude appeared to have been particularly strong in Charlie Company, some of whose men viewed the Vietnamese with contempt, considering them subhuman, on the level of dogs. Personally, I had great respect for the Vietnamese rice farmer or peasant; men and women alike worked in the fields from morning until night in all kinds of weather, often at the mercy of piastre-pinching landlords, and had little to show for it but cal-

1. Some panel members thought the MACV policy of requiring soldiers to carry a variety of cards was nothing short of ludicrous. They might have served as reminders, but they were no substitute for unit instruction. In any case, after a couple of monsoon rains they became mangled and useless.

louses, wrinkles, and bent backs.

Some of the men never referred to Vietnamese as anything but "gooks," "dinks," or "slopes." During my time in Vietnam, I had never heard these terms used so universally, and I think I lived fairly close to the troops. To be sure, one heard them from time to time, as we did in Burma and China in World War II, but they were not used in hatred.

Undoubtedly, this attitude was partly the result of the mines and booby traps that had killed or maimed so many men in their units. Many of the men thought these devices had been laid by the women, children, and old men or that if Vietnamese civilians had not actually planted them they at least knew where the devices were, but never warned the American troops. Others thought some of the innocent-appearing youngsters tending the water buffalo in the fields served as scouts who warned of approaching U.S. forces.

Also, as in all units of any size in any army, there was a sprinkling of toughs—in Task Force Barker they were almost gangsters. In the absence of effective leadership by junior officers and NCOs some of the lower-ranking enlisted men probably followed along with these hoodlums.

Attempting to follow this line of analysis, we thought that perhaps the units had included an unusual number of men of inferior quality. When we thought only Charlie Company had been involved in the incident, we had requested the deputy chief of staff for personnel to make an analysis of the men in that company. The result was a fact sheet that in the main concluded that the men in Charlie Company were about average as compared with other units of the Army;[2] 70 per cent were high school graduates and nineteen had some college credits. Later, we asked for a comparable analysis for Bravo Company, and its conclusions were about the same as those for Charlie Company.[3] It seems to follow that if these men were average American soldiers, and if other units with the same kind of men did not commit atrocities of this order, there must have been other overriding causes.

It would not be true to say that all the men in Task Force Barker held the Vietnamese in low regard. Quite a few of them, even in Charlie Company, liked the Vietnamese people. They picked up some of the language, used their own money to buy gifts for children, and gave donations to orphanages, schools, and churches. But on the whole, we concluded that the attitude of at least some of the men contributed to the atrocities that occurred at My Lai-4 and My Khe-4.

2. Document 20–1. Fact Sheet on Men in Charlie Company. See page 287.
3. Document 20–2. Fact Sheet on Men in Bravo Company. See page 289.

Permissive Attitude

The Americal Division and the 11th Brigade had strong, well-designed policies covering the handling of prisoners, the treatment of Vietnamese civilians, and the protection of their property. However, it was clear that there had been breakdowns in communicating and enforcing those policies. In fact, there was evidence that well before the My Lai operation there had been instances of mistreatment, rape, and some unnecessary killings in Task Force Barker, and possibly in other units of the brigade. We thought that perhaps because we had talked to so many soldiers of Charlie Company it seemed more prevalent in that unit than in others, but we had talked with about half the members of Bravo Company and had found no comparable permissiveness. This may be credited to Captain Michles, who was reported to have been scrupulous in the handling and treatment of civilians.

Colonel Henderson had assumed command of the brigade only the day before the My Lai operation, so he could not be blamed for the permissive attitude within the command. It had developed over a considerable period of time, and it must be assumed that it began during the tenure of his predecessor, Brigadier General Andy Lipscomb. But no matter how or when it started, the fact is that it existed.

The permissiveness did not cease within the task force with the My Lai operation. Indications were that incidents continued to occur at about the same level until the task force was disbanded. One new platoon sergeant testified that he had simply not been able take it and had asked to be transferred.

Leadership

It appeared to the Inquiry that at all levels, from division down to platoon, leadership or the lack of it was perhaps the principal causative factor in the tragic events before, during, and after the My Lai operation. Some examples were failure to follow established division policy and lack of enforcement of that policy; failure to control the situation on the ground along with a lack of personal checking to determine the true nature of the operation; failure to issue appropriate and positive instructions for an investigation; lack of follow-up on leads indicating that a massacre had occurred; and many others.

There were numerous indications that on the day of the incident the commanders did not have control of the situation. This was due in part to poor communication equipment in Lieutenant Colonel Barker's command helicopter, in the task force operations center, and elsewhere, but it was also due to the way some of the officers commanded. Barker, for example, habitually issued mission type of orders (telling subordinate commanders what to do without telling them how to do it), which is an excellent procedure, but he seldom personally checked to see that his orders were carried out properly, relying instead on reports from his subordinates. Perhaps the outstanding command failure on the day of the operation was that not a single commander landed his helicopter to check on the conduct and progress of the operation.

Although Barker was considered a strong and energetic commander, there was considerable evidence that he did not have a close working relationship with his subordinates; they respected him, but seldom questioned his decisions. This may explain, at least in part, why none of his commanders or staff members questioned his orders to burn houses, destroy crops and foodstuffs, and kill livestock in My Lai-4, all of which they knew to be illegal and contrary to division policy.

At company level, Captain Medina was a strong, effective leader who took good care of his men and was generally held in high regard by them. Since he was older than most of his contemporaries, in his early thirties, and had previous experience as a noncommissioned officer, he was thought of as the "old man" by many of his men, and was looked upon with awe and, in some instances, almost fear. Nobody questioned his authority or his judgment. This may well have been one of the more important contributing factors to the events in My Lai-4.

But although Medina was a strong leader, none of his platoon leaders were. Like almost all other platoon leaders in South Vietnam, they were young and inexperienced. The evidence indicated that they wanted to be "nice guys" or "buddies" with their men and did not take immediate, positive action to correct wrongdoings. In fact, there was evidence that before the My Lai operation one or more had joined some of their men in raping girls and women in the villages they entered. Their noncommissioned officers were likewise inexperienced in combat. But, although contributory to the tragic events of My Lai, the lack of leadership at platoon and squad levels cannot be accepted as an excuse. Every other U.S. unit in South Vietnam also had to make do with inexperienced junior officers and NCOs, yet they did not engage in such manifestly illegal operations.

Captain Michles was also an excellent, aggressive leader but his methods in exercising leadership were quite different from Captain Medina's. He was genuinely liked and admired by his men and was constantly looking after their needs. Most of the men in his company who testified said he had good rapport with everyone and was easy to approach with any problem. His platoon leaders were reported to be about average, neither especially strong nor weak, but they, along with the noncommissioned officers, had had little combat experience.

During the training of the 11th Brigade in Hawaii and in operations in South Vietnam, there was strong competition between Medina and Michles to have the best company in the brigade. This desire to excel was present, too, in the platoons and squads, and probably contributed to the making of the tragedy.

Psychological Factors

If there was any one factor as important as the failures in leadership in explaining the My Lai incident, it would probably be the series of events that created extraordinary tension in the minds of many of the participants. "Fear," "apprehension," and "keyed up" were terms frequently used in the testimony of enlisted men.

Charlie Company in particular had suffered numerous casualties from mines and booby traps—a total of twenty in the Son My Village area—yet they had not been able to establish contact with any enemy force. Within the company there was a feeling of apprehension and frustration. These attitudes and emotions were heightened just before the My Lai operation by a memorial service for Staff Sergeant Cox, who had been killed by a booby trap. Captain Medina's reference to "revenge" may have added further emotional stress.

Casualties from booby traps in Bravo Company's 2nd Platoon early on the morning of the 16th possibly contributed to the action of the 1st Platoon in My Khe-4. However, the timing and the manner in which the operation developed would make this a matter of conjecture. Some of those who testified thought the effects from mines and booby traps were the main reason for the atrocities committed by the task force.[4]

Another psychological factor was the "failure to do battle" with the 48th Local Force Battalion, as Lieutenant Colonel Barker put it. Both General Lipscomb and Colonel Henderson had urged the task force to be more aggressive and close rapidly with the enemy. Barker's aggressive nature and the competition between the company commanders to achieve the highest body count put continual pressure on the troops. Hence, their repeated failure to engage the enemy in combat affected the morale of the troops and

4. The tension created because of enemy mines and booby traps can be frightening. It requires strong leadership to keep things under control when bodies are blown apart, vehicles ripped to pieces, and even fifty-ton tanks are knocked a distance of fifty or sixty feet. The 173rd Airborne Brigade operating in Bon Son District, Binh Dinh Province, just south of Quang Ngai, was in such an area. Some officers suggested terminating operations there but it was decided not to because that would have been conceding the area to the enemy. Brigadier General Jack Barnes, the commander, and his deputy, Colonel Ross Franklin, held frequent meetings with their subordinate commanders to find ways of solving the problem, some of which included the use of native scouts, additional minesweepers, and drag lines to be cast ahead and drawn in to catch trip wires, thus exploding the mines. This improved operations but some casualties continued. Eventually, with the approval of the province chief, Rome plows were used to level the area outside the villages, in the process of which numerous mines were exploded. In addition, the population was screened by the Vietnamese authorities and some people were moved to areas of closer government control. It was a tough area in which to operate, but patience and effective leadership eventually brought it under reasonably good control.

added to their frustrations. As evidenced by the orders issued by Barker and Medina, the Son My operation was to provide the opportunity to overcome past failures to engage the enemy and to wipe out the 48th Local Force Battalion.

There was some evidence that a few of the men had stayed up drinking the night before the operation, and a couple of men were reported to have been smoking marijuana. However, after checking with numerous witnesses, we could find no substantial evidence that either marijuana or alcohol had played any significant role in the events of My Lai.

Organizational Problems

Organizational problems existed at every level, from company through task force and brigade up to the American Division headquarters. Such problems could be found in every major U.S. unit in South Vietnam, however, so although they undoubtedly contributed to the incident they cannot be cited as the principal causative factor. The solutions to most organizational problems are strong leadership, close supervision of operations, and enforcement of appropriate policies and directives.

The problems at company level were typical of those encountered throughout South Vietnam, principally shortages and frequent rotation of personnel, resulting in platoons having two squads instead of the customary three and other ad hoc arrangements. Another problem was that the task force was a temporary groupment and the companies tended to feel allegiance to their parent battalions.

Task Force Barker had such a small staff, composed of personnel from various elements of the brigade staff, that it could hardly function properly, particularly in such matters as development of intelligence, planning and supervision of operations, and even routine administration. In addition, it was reported that Lieutenant Colonel Barker often served as his own intelligence and operations officer, thus sometimes leaving those staff elements a bit in the dark. Of all of the organizational problems, those found in the task force played the most prominent part in the My Lai incident.

Nature of the Enemy

All local-force guerrilla units in South Vietnam were formidable opponents who lived and fought in their home areas and knew every path and trail, every bunker, tunnel, and hideout. Women and children often cooperated with them by giving advance warning of approaching U.S., South Vietnamese, or South Korean forces, hiding weapons, dragging away the dead, and planting mines and booby traps. Some of these units were better than others; the 48th Local Force Battalion in Son Tinh District was one of the best.

Another characteristic of local-force units was their ability to disappear underground in caves and tunnels, the entrances to which were sometimes under water. Also, when they were under pressure they could hide their weapons quickly, shed their black-pajama type of uniforms, and simply melt into the population. Hence, it was difficult for opposing forces, and particularly Americans, to distinguish combatants from noncombatants. In such traditional Communist strongholds and VC-dominated areas as Son My Village, it could be fairly well assumed that every male of military age was a VC of some form or another. The VC hold on the population was so strong that anyone who did not cooperate was killed, often dying a horrible death in a public execution. However, even those suspected of being VC should have been given appropriate treatment as prisoners of war as specified in the Geneva and Hague conventions. Most certainly they should not have been shot, without proper investigation and trial. Additionally, anyone with any appreciation of right from wrong should have known that babies and toddlers were not VC or VC sympathizers.

Together with other factors, it seems evident that the nature of the enemy, his unique capabilities, and the tactics he employed played a most significant part in the My Lai incident and subsequent events.

Plans and Orders

The operation was conceived and prepared by Lieutenant Colonel Barker. General Koster and Colonel Henderson were familiar with the operational concept, but neither of them issued any restraints about killing or wounding civilians or any instructions covering the handling of prisoners and noncombatants.

The details of the orders issued by Barker and his staff have already been covered. Those aspects that most greatly influenced the fatal outcome of the operation were:

- It was based upon false intelligence with respect to both the VC and the civilian population; many of the men felt they were going to be outnumbered two to one by the enemy.
- Artillery and gunship fire was placed on the western part of My Lai-4 without permission of higher authority.
- The use of the term search and destroy.
- Illegal instructions were given to kill livestock, burn houses, and destroy foodstuffs.
- No instructions were given about how to handle civilians.

As Barker's orders were passed down the chain of command, they were amplified and expanded upon, with the result that a large number of soldiers gained the impression that only the enemy would be left in My Lai-4 and that everyone encountered was to be killed.

Attitude of Vietnamese Government Officials

Local Vietnamese authorities, both civilian and military, were familiar with the long Communist history of the area and considered all its inhabitants to be VC or VC sympathizers. For all practical purposes, they looked upon the area as a free-fire zone, whereas it was really a specified-strike zone and required their approval for American units to operate in the area or fire artillery into it. Because of their attitude, any such request was given almost automatic approval. These facts were known by the U.S. units but they exercised little caution to reduce the noncombatant casualties that could result from such action.

The Inquiry recognized that it had neither the time nor the talent to do an in-depth study of why the My Lai tragedy occurred. It would be interesting, and it would be a great service to the military and to the country, if some qualified group of researchers could review the testimony in detail, talk with some of the men who participated in the incident, and develop a more definitive rationale. Knowing the "why" might help prevent any future such occurrence.

chapter 21

The Army's Responses to Recommendations

T he Army was stunned and greatly disturbed by the My Lai incident and the magnitude of its tragic results, and it recognized that many policy, training, and institutional changes were in order. The Inquiry's report certainly did not bring about all the necessary modifications. In many respects, however, it served as a catalyst for the Army to look at itself—to study its organization and procedures, isolate the weak spots, and take corrective action.

One of the principal recommendations of the Inquiry concerned the adequacy of policies, directives, and training as they related to the Geneva Convention. The Army responded immediately by initiating a survey which revealed that ignorance of certain aspects of the Rules of Land Warfare was not confined to Task Force Barker; in fact, it was widespread throughout the entire Army. The existing directives were satisfactory with regard to intent but were not specific enough and, most importantly, were not adequately enforced.

Based upon the results of the survey, the Army revised and greatly expanded its policy directives, with special attention given to the individual soldier's responsibilities for reporting war crimes, the procedure to follow when he was given an illegal order, and what to do when his commander participated in or sanctioned a war crime. A new Army regulation, 350–216, dated May 28, 1970 (only a little over two months after the submission of the Inquiry report), also went into considerable detail about the handling of prisoners of war and noncombatants. In addressing the scope of training, the new regulation was greatly expanded in such areas as protection of property, Rules of Engagement, treatment of civilians, and reporting procedures. These had been covered by previous regulations but they had been ambiguous and not sufficiently detailed.

In support of its new regulation the Army also published a revised subject schedule for training. It provides for two hours of mandatory annual training in the Geneva and Hague conventions to be given by a qualified Judge Advocate General officer and an experienced combat officer. A separate section is devoted to a refresher course to be given senior officers to make sure that their soldiers are familiar with and comply with the Law of War. Subsequently, the Chaplains' School added instruction covering chaplains' responsibility to report war crimes.

The most important aspect of the new instruction is that it is brought down to the soldier's level. Previous instruction materials were so condensed, and written in such legalistic terms, that they were both boring and difficult to comprehend. The revised materials use illustrations and give specific examples of illegal orders and activities and what a soldier should do to report such actions. This instruction is augmented by training films; the Army has released three such films, covering a variety of battlefield situations. Still another part of the instruction is the use of small-group discussions to get the soldier thinking and talking about his responsibilities and the actions he should take. Taken together, these techniques make a most interesting and effective period of instruction—provided, of course, that it is properly presented.

In sum, the Army responded swiftly to improve its policy directives and training with respect to the Law of War and the conventions. The problem in the future will be one of enforcement.

In Annex A of its report, the Inquiry appended a list of seven peripheral issues on which it made recommendations. These may not have been the sole contributing factor to the actions taken by the Army, but I believe it is safe to say they were a major factor. A brief synopsis of each recommendation follows.

Records Management and Disposition. The Inquiry had found that files of records and documents were incomplete and sometimes had been destroyed instead of being sent to permanent storage areas. It recommended that steps be taken to maintain the files properly and that regulations pertaining to documents should be enforced. A survey was initiated by the Office of the Army Adjutant General in March 1970, which found that the regulations were satisfactory but were not being executed properly. Within South Vietnam, General Abrams, then MACV commander, froze all records in place until the problem could be reviewed. The resulting action was a rigorous program to increase care in the maintenance of records and an orderly evacuation process to the proper archives in the United States. Similar procedures were used in the evacuation of records from Laos, Cambodia, and Thailand.

Aviation Records. The Inquiry recommended that operational records of aviation personnel and units be evacuated to appropriate archives rather than being destroyed. The army felt that the benefits to be gained were not justifiable in view of the costs involved, so existing policies remained in effect.

Use of Personal Cameras by Army Photographers. The Inquiry recommended that comprehensive policies be established regarding ownership and unauthorized release of pictures taken by Army photographers while on duty. The Army acted upon this recommendation even before the report was submitted. In a letter of instruction dated March 12, 1970, the assistant chief of staff for communications and electronics stated that when "personally owned equipment or supplies . . . are used during an official assignment, *all* photographic material exposed while on that assignment will be the property of the United States Army." Subsequent regulations relating to Army photographers prohibit engaging in photography for one's personal benefit and require that all film shot on an Army assignment must be turned in to the proper Army authorities whether the photographs were taken with the photographer's own camera or not.

Use of Smoke Grenades. The Inquiry felt that the haphazard use of varied-colored smoke grenades had caused some of the confusion at My Lai between aviation and ground units and recommended that it be clarified. The Army felt that its existing policies, permitting the local commander to establish procedures based upon his own situation and supply, were sufficient. However, instructions were issued to check the adequacy of training in the Army school system, and courses of instruction on the use of smoke grenades as signaling devices were initiated at the intelligence and signal schools.

Selection and Training of Liaison Officers. The Inquiry had recommended that more stringent training be given to liaison officers. In effect, the Army took no action on this recommendation. An Army study noted that liaison officers were not provided for by tables of organization and the situations under which they were employed were so varied that it was not feasible to prepare a course of instruction applicable to all situations. I was not consulted on this matter, but am still of the opinion that some instruction is needed in officer training to insure the proper selection and use of such personnel. Too often I have seen second-rate officers designated as liaison officers and given little, if any, instruction on what to do and how to report it, as was the case during the My Lai incident. Appropriate instruction would enable the Army to make better use of its officers.

Personnel Turbulence. The Inquiry was concerned about the twelve-month tour of duty in Vietnam, the transfer of personnel from one unit to another under the "infusion program," and men coming and going on R&R, all of which played havoc with the effectiveness of the 11th Brigade and, to a lesser extent, the Americal Division and all other major units in South Vietnam. Studies were being conducted at the time on these problems, but except for some emoluments offered to induce extensions of service in South Vietnam, no real changes were made in the programs—it was too late in the war. In any case, it is a good lesson to remember in the event of another conflict so that sound personnel policies can be established at the outset. It is a very complex problem.

Utilization of First Sergeants. The Inquiry recommended that greater use be made of first sergeants in the field. This recommendation stemmed from my experience in South Vietnam during which first sergeants, as the senior noncommissioned officers in a company, were required to spend most of their time with their unit in the field rather than at the base camp. It paid handsome dividends in unit morale and effectiveness. This was not the policy during the My Lai operation. The Army responded by placing greater emphasis on the use of first sergeants as instructors within the Army school system. More importantly, as a side effect, the Army has made a strenuous effort to improve the quality and stature of all senior noncommissioned officers, the backbone of which is a senior noncommissioned officer school created to serve that purpose.

During the Inquiry the question arose as to the propriety of General Westmoreland—the senior U.S. commander in the Vietnam at the time of the My Lai incident and the Army Chief of Staff—being a signatory to the Inquiry directive. Suppose, for example, that during the Inquiry we had heard testimony alleging that by some means or other General Westmoreland (or someone in his headquarters in Vietnam) had become aware that a sizable number of civilian noncombatants had been killed during the operation of March 16, 1968. Under the circumstances, I would have felt obliged to have him appear as a witness under oath, but I certainly would have discussed it with Secretary Resor before calling him.

Fortunately, the Inquiry was not put to the test. At the conclusion, having heard all the testimony, reviewed all the pertinent documents, and checked all the unit logs, it was the unanimous opinion of the panel members that word of civilians being killed and of atrocities or war crimes being committed at My Lai-4 had never reached General Westmoreland's MACV headquarters. Neither did such word reach U.S. Army, Vietnam, headquarters nor the Third Marine Amphibious Force, which was immediately superior to the Americal Division. The only information these headquarters received was in the daily operation report to the effect that Task Force Barker had killed 128 Viet Cong and captured three weapons while suffering two killed and eleven wounded. Knowledge of civilian casualties was confined within the Americal Division and possibly the U.S. advisory elements of Quang Ngai Province and the 2nd ARVN Division.

Although it was not necessary to have General Westmoreland called as a witness, the possibility raised some question as to the propriety, organization, and structure of the Inquiry. Perhaps it would have been better had the directive been signed only by Secretary Resor, or maybe there is an even better solution. In any case, it should be considered in the extreme possibility that such a situation could arise again in the future.

On July 9, 1970, F. Edward Hébert, Chairman of the My Lai Incident Subcommittee, submitted the subcommittee's report to L. Mendel Rivers, chairman of the House Armed Services Committee. It was released to the public on July 15. The testimony, documents, and other materials relating to the report were not released to the public until April 13, 1976.

In the main the subcommittee report was exceedingly well done, short and to the point, only fifty-three pages long. Generally, the subcommittee's findings were consistent with those of the Inquiry. Of course, as has already been discussed, the subcommittee took the Army to task for lack of cooperation and chastised us for preparing additional charges for which the subcommittee thought there was insufficient evidence.

One of the subcommittee findings stated, in part: "There is also testimony that the Third Marine Amphibious Force . . . received sufficient information about this incident to have reported it to the Military Assistance Command." The Inquiry questioned the commanding general of III MAF, his deputy, the operations officer, and one assistant. None of them had any information concerning the possible killing of noncombatants in the Task Force Barker operation. Subsequently, I talked with John F. Lally, who had served as assistant counsel to the subcommittee. After checking the testimony, he advised me that the finding was based solely upon the testimony of General Koster. In his testimony before the Inquiry, General Koster had been quite vague on this score—"I seemed to remember mentioning it to General Cushman"—and hence I have strong doubts as to the validity of this finding.

One part of the subcommittee report I fail to understand is why it made such an issue of Warrant Officer Thompson's confrontation with ground troops at My Lai and his subsequent awards and decorations: approximately one-fourth of the report is devoted to Thompson's verbatim testimony. In reading the quotes from his testimony, it appears to be more of an inquisition than an investigation; they had him so confused he did not know which way to turn. The only plausible reason I can offer is that they were misdirected in their efforts by the subcommittee staff.

What I found equally incomprehensible is that the report makes only scant reference to the heroic actions of Thompson and his crew; nothing is said about the dangers and skill involved in their marking the wounded civilians for medical assistance, rounding up the two VC suspects, locating the mortar site, investigating the situation at the ditch, rescuing approximately fifteen women and children from a shelter, and finally returning to the ditch to retrieve a wounded child and fly him to the hospital. Moreover, Thompson reported his observations and actions to his commanding officer and later to a chaplain. Of all those who participated in the operation, he was the only American who cared enough to take action to protect the Vietnamese noncombatants and to try to stop the wanton killing and destruction of property. Instead of being castigated, in my view he should have been highly commended. If there was a hero of My Lai, he was it.

As to the awards and decorations, Thompson felt strongly about his door gunners, who had given him such effective support, and wanted to make sure that they were properly recognized. However, as reported by the subcommittee, he was in error when in his supporting statements for their awards he said that the rescue of the women and children had taken place "between friendly forces and hostile forces engaged in a heavy firefight." There was no firefight, although the incident did take place well outside of My Lai-4 and they could have been subjected to enemy sniper fire. In doing this, Thompson unwittingly had participated in the coverup. The same criticism applies to his own award, the Distinguished Flying Cross, for which the citation said he had been "caught in intense crossfires"; this was not in the original draft but had been inked in by somebody later. Reportedly, Thompson was not happy with the award when it was presented and later threw the medal into his footlocker. If he knew what the citation said, he was wrong in accepting it and should have returned it or have had the citation corrected. Nevertheless, considering what he, Andreotta, and Colburn did at My Lai, they were most deserving of their awards, perhaps even of a higher order.

The subcommittee's recommendations were short and to the point. They included, in brief:

- Prohibition on the release of information on charges against an individual prior to court martial. (To date this has not been effected in the UCMJ.)
- A requirement that persons charged with capital-offense war crimes be given a psychological examination. (UCMJ not so revised to date.)
- Amendment of appropriate sections of the United States Code to provide trial in district courts of those charged with war crimes who are beyond the jurisdiction of the U.S. military services. (To be discussed later.)
- Insuring adequate training in the Hague and Geneva conventions and the proper reporting thereof.*
- Appointment of qualified investigators outside the chain of command for all alleged war crimes.*

*The Acting Secretary of the Army, Thaddeous R. Beal, responded to the recommendations directed at the Army. In a letter dated September 4, 1970, to Chairman Rivers, he covered each of these recommendations, describing the actions that had been taken by the Army. Generally, they were consistent with the subcommittee's recommendations, although there were certain modifications.

- A requirement that military photographers submit all photographs taken, either with a government or personally owned camera, to their superiors.*
- Insurance of proper training of military photographers.*
- Establishment of review procedures for awarding decorations, including supporting statements in affidavit form and special attention to reciprocal awards.*

On November 13, 1974, Secretary of the Army Howard W. Callaway released Volumes I and III (main body and documentation) of the Inquiry report. In the accompanying news release, Secretary Callaway stated that he had "made the decision to release Volumes I and III only after carefully weighing the public interest in obtaining a complete account of the events surrounding the My Lai incident against the possible harm to the lives and reputations of various individuals which could result from release of material contained in the Report."

On March 17, 1975, Secretary Callaway, after much deliberation, made public Volumes II and IV (testimony and CID statements used by the Inquiry) of the report. All names had been deleted and an alphabetical code had been provided with which to identify the participants. As Secretary Callaway explained in a memorandum accompanying the volumes:

> Those individuals who have previously been identified in connection with the My Lai incident or the Peers Inquiry are identified in the code key, while the identity of those not previously identified will be protected.
>
> This coding was necessary because Volumes II and IV consist of raw investigatory material including hearsay, impressions, suppositions and mere rumors offered by witnesses. This information could possibly result in damage to the lives, careers and reputations of those individuals, should they be identified, against whom allegations were made, many of whom may be completely innocent of any wrongdoing. Other information, such as unit assignments or locations, which might identify personnel mentioned in the report, has also been deleted in some cases.

Secretary Callaway's decision to release the report in its entirety was a bold one in view of the resistance he was receiving from the Department of Defense, prompted by the White House. Unfortunately, the approximately five-year delay in its release contributed to the impression that the earlier coverup was being extended to the detailed examination contained in the report. There is, of course, the difficult problem of protecting the rights of those involved in criminal proceedings while at the same time, from an institutional viewpoint, assuring the public that action is being taken to correct prior omissions. However, after the completion of Colonel Henderson's trial in December 1971 the only remaining litigation was the review of Lieutenant Calley's sentence by higher military appeal boards, which should not have been affected by release of the report. From that point of view, it could have been released much earlier, but then there was the problem of Watergate, which served to put the My Lai incident and the release of the report well into the background.

The coding process caused me untold difficulty and endless hours in trying to decipher the testimony. It was further complicated by the fact that out of the 403 witnesses the key code identified only 123. Under the circumstances, each page was like a coded message. Testimony such as HN talking to PA with WZ, CZ, and YP also in the room, or that FA, BP, and XY were aboard MV's helicopter, were especially laborious to decipher. Reportedly, at some future date the Army will release the identity of 290 other witnesses but it will still be difficult to read the testimony.

The coding also had its humorous side. I was told by one of the officers responsible for releasing the report that two reporters from one of the leading national newspapers came to the Pentagon to review the testimony, but after working a full day they called their home office to say they couldn't make heads or tails of it. They were told to keep on reading, but after another day of no progress were finally allowed to return home.

chapter 22

Some Final Thoughts

Bob MacCrate suggested several times during the Inquiry that we try to inject my philosophy of command and leadership into the report, but try as we may, there was simply no place for such a dissertation. When we had completed the draft of the report, I asked General Westmoreland if he would like to have my thoughts on the matter as they related to My Lai, and he said he would. Accordingly, with some editing assistance, I prepared and submitted the following memorandum to him.

18 March 1970

MEMORANDUM FOR: Chief of Staff, US Army
SUBJECT: The Son My Incident

1. The recently completed Inquiry of the Son My incident has served to reinforce several of my views regarding the moral and ethical standards required of US Army officers and noncommissioned officers. Accordingly, I feel it appropriate to provide you with a summary of such views while they are still fresh in my mind and before they become diffused in the aftermath of the formal findings previously forwarded to you. The summary of such views is inclosed herewith.

2. In stating these views, it is not my intent to prescribe the overall character and qualities required of an officer or noncommissioned officer. Rather it is to focus on some of the unique requirements placed upon an individual chosen to serve in a position of responsibility in a counterinsurgency environment such as existed in South Vietnam at the time of the Son My incident.

3. I have no doubt that these views influenced the judgments, findings and the recommendations contained in the formal report of investigation. They are provided to you for whatever use you may deem appropriate.

W. R. Peers
Lieutenant General, USA

Leadership Requirements in a
Counterinsurgency Environment

1. Throughout the Vietnam war, Headquarters MACV has consistently placed great emphasis on the other side of the war—the Pacification Program—the battle for the hearts and minds of the people. In addition to the directives on this broad subject and the discussions at the various senior commanders' conferences, the matters of soldierly conduct and the proper treatment of Vietnamese civilians have been topics continually emphasized by senior military and civilian officials during their visits to the forces in the field. This guidance has provided direction to the actions of all US subordinate commands and agencies within South Vietnam and is of sufficient clarity, quality, and strength as to preclude any doubt as to what was and is intended of our conduct toward the Vietnamese people.

2. The application of this guidance may have been more forceful and direct on the part of some commanders than in the case of others. Based on my knowledge of the war in South Vietnam, however, most senior combat commanders have adopted extremely high standards and criteria in transmitting such guidance to their subordinate commanders and in overseeing the results of that guidance.

3. My interpretation of the guidance noted above, my views concerning the attitudes and moral standards required of personnel in the US Army, and my exposure to the events of Son My, have all served to temper the feelings expressed below:

a. Commanders at all echelons are responsible for the actions and the welfare of all of the men under them. A commander cannot delegate such responsibility to his subordinates nor can he shrug it off by indicating a lack of knowledge. It is his duty to ferret out potential and actual trouble areas and to be on the spot to take corrective action. Obviously, he cannot do this alone. Instead, he must have an effective system of command and control so that his desires and concerns are communicated and reflected throughout his command.

b. There can be no vacillation with the truth. Statements and reports, whether in combat or garrison, must be precise, factual, and complete, with no shading of the unpleasant or unflattering aspects of such reports. Officers who fail to adhere to this practice violate their commission.

c. All officers, irrespective of their position, are responsible for taking corrective action on the spot when they see something wrong. Whether the officer is a commander or a staff officer, and whether the violator belongs to his unit or another makes no difference. If the officer does not take corrective action at once, he fails completely in his responsibilities.

d. Because men's lives are at stake in combat, there can be no acceptance of mediocre leadership nor mediocrity in performance of other duties relating to the support of combat. Failures in leadership or in the performance of duty in combat are due cause for and should demand the removal or reassignment of the officers concerned to positions of lesser responsibility.

e. Directives and regulations, no matter how well prepared and intended, are only pieces of paper unless they are enforced aggressively and firmly throughout the chain of command. To be effective, a commander must make his presence felt by insuring that the information and guidance contained in directives are communicated to the appropriate unit level and members of his command.

f. The Army General and Special Staff System is designed to assist commanders in the conduct and administration of their operations. On the one hand, a commander who fails to effectively utilize the talents and experience of his staff will not be able to achieve the full potential of his command. On the other hand, assignment to a staff position carries with it the responsibility to assist and advise the commander in the planning and execution of functions affecting the entire command. Hence, within his area of interest, a staff officer shares part of the responsibilities with those of the commander.

g. Leadership is most effective when it is conducted on a person-to-person, face-to-face basis; it cannot effectively be exercised over a telephone, radio, or any other form of electronic communication. To be effective a combat leader frequently must be on the ground with his men to know firsthand the situation that exists.

h. Senior noncommissioned officers provide the link between the commander and the enlisted personnel of a unit. They serve as a sounding board, and an informal but highly effective communications means for providing information and suggestions to the commander. They are the prime means for determining the condition and well-being of the men, and to alert him to any trouble spots which may arise. To be effective, commanders must utilize their capabilities to the fullest.

i. A commander must be constantly alert to changes in the attitude and temperament of his men and the units to which they belong. Ground combat in a counterinsurgency environment may develop frustrations and bitterness which manifest themselves in acts quite apart from that which would normally be expected. Accordingly, commanders must be quick to spot such changes and to take appropriate corrective action. Any indications of an attitudinal change from one of physical toughness in combat to senseless brutality requires immediate remedial action by the commander concerned.

j. An effective combat commander must from time to time require troops to do things which at the moment may be against their will. For example, after a full day's operation, to dig in at night and build overhead cover can be sheer drudgery. Popularity of the leader does not necessarily accrue from requiring troops in the jungle to properly care for themselves and their equipment, or continually maintain their security. Forcing unpleasant duties on men, in their own and their unit's best interest, is an accepted part of combat leadership. It is a difficult and encompassing job, requiring discrimination between what is necessary and right and that which is patently illegal.

k. In the heat of battle, some officers and men tend to lose sight of the more fundamental issues upon which the war is being waged. Along with the attitudinal changes described above, this can lead to winning a battle or two but losing a war. It is an inherent and paramount responsibility of the commander to insure that his officers and men understand, are constantly reminded of, and put into practice the principles of discriminate and tightly controlled application of firepower; genuine and practical concern for private property no matter how valueless or insignificant it may appear; humane treatment and care of refugees, noncombatants, and wounded (whether friendly or enemy); and the judicious safeguarding and processing of suspects and prisoners of war.

1. An officer's highest loyalty is to the Army and the nation. On those rare occasions when people around him engage in activities clearly wrong and immoral, he is required by virtue of his being an officer to take whatever remedial action is required, regardless of the personal consequences.

4. The combat commander at any level who fails to keep these considerations uppermost in his mind and in the minds of the men who serve under him, invites disaster. In my view, the validity of these considerations and their importance to us, as soldiers, are borne out in a review of the events of Son My.

In submitting the memorandum, I wanted to provide General Westmoreland with an insight into my views of command and leadership so that he would better understand the report, its findings, and its recommendations. General Westmoreland took the issue further, and sent the memorandum to Lieutenant General Kerwin, deputy chief of staff for personnel, with instructions to study it and submit recommendations based upon it. The results are described in this extract from an Army paper prepared by Major Jerry M. Sollinger of the Office of the Chief of Staff:

Perhaps one of the most significant effects of the Peers Inquiry and a separate memorandum from LTG Peers to General Westmoreland was the direction from the Chief of Staff to the Army War College to study the moral and ethical climate of the U.S. Army. The study, in essence, examined the Army's professionalism. The findings of this study surprised and, in some cases, shocked many of the Army's senior leaders. In general, it discovered that the majority of the Officer Corps perceived a stark dichotomy between the appearance and reality of the adherence of senior officers to the traditional standards of professionalism, which the words duty, honor and country sum up. Instead, these officers saw a system that rewarded selfishness, incompetence and dishonesty. Commanders sought transitory, ephemeral gains at the expense of enduring benefits and replaced substance with statistics. Furthermore, senior commanders, as a result of their isolation (sometimes self-imposed) and absence of communication with subordinates, lacked any solid foundation from which to initiate necessary corrective action. The study made recommendations in nine major areas that embraced 33 subsidiary proposals, many of which suggested fundamental and revolutionary changes. Of these, some 16 have been implemented, either wholly or in part. As in the case of the records-management issue, it cannot be said that the Peers Inquiry directly and solely caused the actions taken in response to this study. Instead, it served to direct attention to a problem and lend emphasis to the pursuit of solutions. In that sense the Inquiry played a crucial if not direct role.

Some of the reforms instituted as a result of the Army War College study were:

- Wide dissemination of its findings to senior officers, major commands, and institutions of the Army school system.
- Initiation of courses, seminars, and electives at the Army War College, the Command and General Staff College, and the Military Academy on such matters as leadership, command, communications, and ethics
- Replacement of the time-consuming, statistically oriented command maintenance inspections with assistance teams.
- Revision of the rating system of technical inspections from a highly competitive sliding scale to a simple "satisfactory—unsatisfactory" basis.
- Greater emphasis on personnel counseling at all levels, augmented by such publications as "Leadership Counseling" and "Commanders Guide to the Retention of Junior Officers."
- Passage of a written examination has become a prerequisite in some of the Army schools, but has not been adopted as yet by the Command and General Staff College.
- Eligibility for command positions in the grades of lieutenant colonel and colonel is now determined by a centralized command selection board.
- Command assignments in other than short-tour areas has been stabilized at eighteen months.
- Revision of the Officer Evaluation Report system, with additional modifications being studied.
- Revision of promotion policies to require increased time in grade, and modification of the requirements of the former rigid career pattern system.
- Development of alternate career specialties to improve utilization and job satisfaction.

To me, the most satisfying action the Army has taken is in the areas of professional ethics, honesty, and integrity. The need for such action was brought into sharp focus by the My Lai incident and was further highlighted by the misdeeds of certain senior officers and noncommissioned officers in positions of trust, which created grave doubts in the minds of many people as to the trustworthiness of the officer and noncommissioned officer corps. Today these subjects are included in the curriculum at all levels of the Army school system and within the training command. The students are keenly interested and eager to ask questions and discuss their point of view. They want to know why these things happened, what was wrong with the system, and what they as individuals can do to improve it. This is a good sign. These men and women will be the future leaders of the Army, so it is especially important that they not only understand the meaning and philosophy of such principles but that they apply them in practice.

Although at the top level the Army has made a conscientious and concerted effort to correct its moral ills, signs of internal disorder linger on. For example, the following is part of a letter from an Army colonel for whom I have great regard, both morally and professionally. Granted, it represents the views of only one man, but it is an honest and straightforward appraisal and merits close scrutiny.

> We may be able to produce a great deal of paper—studies and directives—but I fail to see any substantive moves to restore integrity. We still have colonels and generals who are guided not by what is best for our country or our Army, but what is best for me. And rather than their number diminishing, I find the number increasing by an alarming rate. The new Officer Personnel Management System has done more to hurt integrity in the officer corps than any other dozen actions. Before, it was only the senior officers (and a few opportunists in the lower grades) who worried more about their own advancement than they did about the Army. Now everyone is on the bandwagon. It is a case of "every man for himself"— and the Army has caused it. We have so instilled the philosophy of "career management" in our officers that everyone considers this factor as one of primary importance. Among our enlisted men it is even worse—and more to the discredit of our leadership. Among our troops there is a growing belief that "no one cares." At least not to the extent that any of our senior commanders are willing to stand up and be counted.

I asked some other knowledgeable senior officers about the time spent and the quality of instruction regarding professional ethics and morality. The answer was quite surprising. Essentially, it was that so much time had to be devoted to "hands on" kinds of training (weapons, vehicles, armor, communication equipment, etc.) that there was little time to teach such subjects, so they had to be pieced in between other periods of instruction. In my view such training should be given a higher order of priority.

In citing the above problems, it is not my intent to be overly critical. In fact, the Army is in better condition in this regard than I have seen it for many years. Yet it would be foolhardy to think that such institutional problems do not exist. Instead they should be identified, isolated, and corrected. This is the very essence of the military profession.

The American people showed little sympathy to those of our World War II enemies who committed war crimes, yet our system of military justice was more than lenient to those responsible for the My Lai incident even though our country, as a signatory to the Geneva Convention, was obligated to punish those guilty of war crimes. In effect two standards were created —one for the enemy and one for ourselves. Within that context there are two things about the My Lai episode that greatly concern me:

- The failure of the military judicial system to effectively prosecute those persons suspected of either committing war crimes or of failing to report or investigate such crimes.
- The fact that an estimated twenty-five to fifty persons suspected of committing war crimes at My Lai had been separated from military service and were thus outside the jurisdiction of military law, and their cases were never adjudicated by any form of civilian court.

The problem for the future is to insure that such a situation does not recur.

As I see it, the chances of another tragedy of the magnitude of My Lai are quite remote. Moreover, if it did occur, the odds against it not being reported through military channels, not being properly investigated, and remaining hidden for over a year would be on the order of thousands to one. However, it happened at My Lai and conceivably it could happen again. That is what must be guarded against, and we must be able to guarantee that those responsible are properly punished.

One line of thinking, to which I fully subscribe, holds that the responsibility for the failure or inadequacy of the Army's investigative and judicial system cannot be blamed exclusively on the Army as an institution. It is Congress that ultimately determines the shape, substance, character, capabilities, and limitations of our system of military justice. Over the past dozen years or so, the thrust of congressional action has been to reduce the scope of military institutional authority, and hence Congress must also share a large portion of the blame for the inadequacies of the Inquiry and related judicial actions, which were part of the total story.

Quite obviously, the shortcomings of our overall judicial system need to be remedied. The burden of defining those remedies must be borne by our military lawyers, but only Congress can bring them into being. The work of the My Lai Inquiry and the efforts to bring the responsible parties to trial serve as tangible evidence of our desire to avoid application of dual standards. The fact that the end results were not what we thought they should be is a result of the previously cited weaknesses and not of any ulterior motive on the part of the Army or of national policy.

From my discussions with General Westmoreland I believe he concurs with this thesis. He perceives that the Army system prevailed—it was the system of military justice that failed. Legalistically, he is correct, and he did all that he could under the circumstances. However, it is difficult for the American public to separate the Army system from military justice. To them it is all the same, and the Army is responsible.

Wherever the blame may lie, the fact is that military justice did not make sure that those responsible for My Lai and its coverup were properly punished. Charges were dismissed on eleven of the twelve cases referred to First Army for possible trial by court martial. Only one, Colonel Henderson, was brought to trial, and he was acquitted. And of the thirteen men suspected of having committed war crimes, charges were dismissed in eight cases, five were tried by court martial, and only Lieutenant Calley was found guilty. I feel that these results are totally inequitable when compared to the tragedy that occurred at My Lai.

Even though the Army is not blameless for the failures of its system of military justice, there is one aspect of the aftermath of the My Lai tragedy for which it cannot be held responsible. To appreciate fully what occurred during the judicial process one must look at the situation that existed in the country at the time. The American people were still in the throes of the anti-Vietnam War turmoil. Street marches, demonstrations, and rallies by anti-war groups were in full swing, including those generated by Vietnam veterans who opposed the war. Meanwhile, the majority of Americans remained passively silent. The Nixon Administration was trying to find ways to disengage from South Vietnam and still leave a government and military establishment there capable of providing its own self-defense. In view of this turmoil the Administration did not want to take any action that would add fuel to the flames of the various anti-war groups, nor did it wish to alienate some of its supporters who could not have been expected to have any sympathy for war-crimes prosecutions.

In this context, it was embarrassing and unwelcome news for the American people and the Administration to learn officially from our report that on March 16, 1968, a large number of women, children, and old men, possibly in excess of four hundred, had been ruthlessly killed at My Lai, that several rapes, extensive destruction of property, and killing of livestock had also occurred, and that senior Army officers were charged with concealing what had happened. It was clear to all that the forthcoming prosecutions would provide further unwelcome publicity, and that the Administration[1] just wished the whole thing would go away.

The Administration was quite correct, initially, in saying little and allowing the prosecutions to proceed, but when President Nixon did speak out —after the conviction of Lieutenant Calley—he missed an opportunity to provide real leadership and instead catered to the public outcry by saying he would personally review Calley's conviction. As Commander in Chief he was certainly entitled to make such a review, but the purpose—and effect —of his statement was to appease those misguided people who either viewed Calley as an innocent scapegoat or opposed the whole idea of war-crimes prosecutions of Americans. Instead of treating the public clamor over Calley's conviction as a short-term political problem to be "defused" by promising to review the matter, the President could well have taken the occasion

---

1. It should be understood that my references to "the Administration" do not include Secretary Resor, who fully appreciated the importance to the Army and to the country of bringing the My Lai offenders to account and who did everything within his power to achieve that result.

to remind the American people of this country's obligations to punish those who commit war crimes, of the overwhelming evidence of Calley's guilt as adduced at the trial, and of the fact that he had been found guilty after a long trial, not by anti-military war protestors but by a panel of his peers. I believe the vast majority of Americans would have understood and accepted such an explanation, and it might have changed the atmosphere in which the subsequent courts martial were held. But it was not forthcoming.

I have already said that I believed the action of General Seaman in dropping all charges against General Koster and General Young seriously undermined the subsequent prosecutions of the more junior officers. When the President thereafter appeared to sympathize with those protesting Lieutenant Calley's conviction, the difficulties of obtaining convictions against Captain Medina, Colonel Henderson, and others became almost insurmountable. Thus the failures of leadership that characterized nearly every aspect of the My Lai incident itself had their counterpart at the highest level during the attempt to prosecute those responsible.

A number of suggested changes in the laws relating to the prosecution of war crimes have been made in response to the failure to adequately punish those responsible for the atrocities committed at My Lai. The House Armed Services Committee recommended turning over the cases of persons outside of military jurisdiction to the federal courts. Congressman Stratton recommended the creation of a civilian tribunal to adjudge such cases. And others have suggested vesting jurisdiction of all war crimes prosecutions in the U.S. District Court for the District of Columbia, with the Department of Justice being responsible for investigation and prosecution.

Although I strongly support legislative action to insure that all those who commit war crimes and related acts are brought to justice, I do not favor giving total responsibility to the U.S. civil court system or any comparable civilian body. I have great faith in the military profession and the morality and integrity inherent within it. Moreover, I believe that military men are best equipped to investigate, analyze, and adjudicate situations such as My Lai that may develop within their own ranks. War crimes are likely to occur, if at all, in combat areas outside the United States, during the course of combat operations. Our inquiry demonstrated that in order to investigate such charges adequately the investigators must have intimate knowledge of military operations, procedures, and records as well as access to personnel, communications, transport, and many other specialized skills and services found only in the military. It is inconceivable to me that allegation of war crimes could be more efficiently investigated by the Department of Justice than by the military services themselves, and I would certainly question whether our report could have been duplicated by any civilian agency within the time limitation imposed on us.

If, despite these considerations, it is argued that a civilian agency would be more appropriate because it would be more vigorous in its pursuit of suspected war criminals, I would strongly disagree, based again upon the My Lai experience. I understand from good authority that the Defense Department sent a legal memorandum to the Department of Justice outlining the basis upon which prosecutions could be brought against some of the men involved in the My Lai incident who were beyond the scope of military justice because they had left military service. This suggestion was quietly shelved and no action was taken. Given the Administration's apparent distaste for everything about the My Lai prosecutions, and considering also the extent to which Department of Justice investigations were stopped or limited for political purposes during the Watergate disclosures, I would have little confidence that a Department of Justice investigation and prosecution of the My Lai incident would have improved on the Army's performance.

Accordingly, while I believe that some legislation is needed to permit former military personnel to be tried in civilian courts, the prosecution of military personnel should be left to the military. However, the procedures should be made more responsive and effective. There are three possible alternatives:

First, to employ the procedures used in the My Lai Inquiry and subsequent court action. Its weakness is that it lacks the power of court martial subpoena. U.S. courts would be used to administer justice to those outside military law.

Second, to utilize a military Court of Inquiry, which does have court martial powers of subpoena and can require civilians to appear as witnesses. However, a Court of Inquiry is still an investigative body and cannot assure that all responsible military parties are punished. Again, U.S. courts would be used for those outside military jurisdiction.

A third solution, and the one I would favor, would be to revise the Uniform Code of Military Justice to incorporate a military tribunal. The tribunal, as I see it, would be composed of an appropriate number of highly qualified combat arms and legal officers and would have the powers of a court martial to subpoena civilian witnesses. It would have not only the investigative powers of a Court of Inquiry but also the authority to pass sentence upon those individuals remaining under military jurisdiction— subject, of course, to review by higher authorities. All proceedings would be in open session except those involving classified matters related to national security. It is recognized that in-depth study will be required to develop the organizational and operational procedures of such a tribunal and to obtain executive and congressional approval. However, such a process would insure the application of military justice by a group of officers who would be knowledgeable about both the tactical and legal aspects of the incident.

As for those who are suspected of having committed war crimes but who, because they are no longer in military service, are no longer subject to military law, they too must be brought to trial. There is no statute of limitations for war crimes, and persons suspected of such acts should be tried, regardless of their status, military or civilian. Section 803(a), Title 10, of the United States Code should be amended to provide for such trials. This kind of procedure was recommended by the House My Lai Investigating Subcommittee, and it would fill the gap remaining above and beyond the authority of the military tribunal.

The full and true story of the My Lai incident has not yet been told— not in the Inquiry report, the House Armed Services subcommittee report, this or any other book, or all of them together. The account of the actual operations of both Charlie and Bravo companies as related in the Inquiry report is reasonably accurate, but more is needed to fill in a few of the gaps and develop definitive noncombatant casualty figures. With respect to reports, investigations, and suppression of information, there were numerous gaps and inconsistencies in the testimony before the Inquiry. In order to complete the picture, some persons who did not tell us everything they knew, ceased giving testimony, or refused to testify will have to come forth with the details. This, of course, is a matter of personal integrity which only they can decide.

Documents

chapter 1

1-1. Directive for Investigation (November 26, 1969)

26 November 1969

MEMORANDUM FOR: Lieutenant General William R. Peers 218–34–
7471
SUBJECT: Directive for Investigation

Confirming oral instructions given you on 24 November 1969, you are directed to explore the nature and the scope of the original U.S. Army investigation(s) of the alleged My Lai (4) incident which occurred 16 March 1968 in Quang Ngai Province, Republic of Vietnam. Your investigation will include a determination of the adequacy of the investigation(s) or inquiries on this subject, their subsequent reviews and reports within the chain of command, and possible suppression or withholding of information by persons involved in the incident.

Your investigation will be concerned with the time period beginning March 1968 until Mr. Ronald L. Ridenhour sent his letter, dated 29 March 1969, to the Secretary of Defense and others. The scope of your investigation does not include, nor will it interfere with, ongoing criminal investigations in progress.

The procedures contained in AR 15–6 are authorized for such use as may be required.

You are authorized to select and use on a full-time basis officer and civilian members of the Army whom you deem necessary for the conduct of the investigation. Your deputy is designated as Mr. Bland West, Assistant General Counsel, Department of the Army. Should you require other assistance, please let us know.

You will inform us at an early date of the expected completion date of your report.

W. C. Westmoreland   Stanley R. Resor
General, U.S. Army   Secretary of the Army
Chief of Staff

1–2. Memorandum on Concept, Organization, and Schedule of Inquiry (November 30, 1969)

30 November 1969

MEMORANDUM FOR: Secretary of the Army Chief of Staff, United States Army

SUBJECT: Investigation of the Adequacy of the Preliminary Inquiries into the My Lai (4) Case

1. This responds to your request in Referral Slip No. 58313, 26 November 1969, for a memorandum outlining the concept of the subject investigation, the organization of the investigative team, and an estimated completion date of the report of investigation.

2. *Concept of Investigation.*

The above reference assigns me the mission of determining the adequacy of the original inquiries into the My Lai (4) incident of 16 March 1968, the propriety of the command actions based thereon, and whether there was any improper suppression of information by persons in the chain of command or otherwise responsible for reporting the incident to superior authority. I have organized a team of investigative assistants and propose to accomplish the mission by reviewing the facts available to date for background purposes, collecting pertinent official records of the units in Vietnam involved in the assault on My Lai (4), locating and interrogating all witnesses known to have information bearing on the mission, and by preparing a report on the results of such investigation, including appropriate findings and recommendations.

3. *Organization.*

I will be assisted in the investigation by the following personnel:

Mr. Bland West, OGC (Deputy)
Colonel W. V. Wilson, OTIG
Colonel Robert E. Miller, OTJAG
Major E. F. Zychowski, OPMG
Mr. James S. Stokes IV, OGC
Major Clyde Lynn, Recorder
Four Court Reporters not yet named
Lieutenant Colonel J. H. Breen, Executive
Two or more clerk/stenos

Points of contact have been established with OCINFO, OCACSI, TAG and Headquarters USMC. Others will be arranged as required.

4. *Tentative Schedule of Activities.*

It is planned that the organization and administration will be finalized on 1 Dec 69 at which time personnel immediately associated with the investigation will be sworn in. The interrogation of witnesses will begin on 2 Dec 69. There being thirty to forty witnesses, the interrogations will probably go on for at least two weeks. Thereafter, a visit will be made to Vietnam to review records, reports, files and other pertinent documents. Upon return to the States additional testimony will be taken as required and the report drafted and finalized. The estimated date of completion is 10 Jan 70.

5. It is recommended that:

a. The investigation be given an official title to establish its separate identity and to facilitate communications.

b. Information as to its title and purpose be disseminated to appropriate military commands with instructions to provide requisite assistance.

> W. R. Peers
> Lieutenant General, USA

chapter 4

4-1. Extracts from MACV Directive 20-4

DIRECTIVE   27 April 1967
NUMBER 20-4   (MACJA)

Inspections and Investigations
WAR CRIMES

1. *Purpose.* To provide uniform procedures for the collection and perpetuation of evidence relative to war crimes incidents and to designate the agencies responsible for the conduct of investigations for alleged or apparent violations of the Geneva Conventions of 12 August 1949 For the Protection of War Victims.

2. *Scope.* This directive is applicable to all alleged or apparent war crimes violations of the subject Geneva Conventions, inflicted by hostile forces upon US military or civilian personnel assigned in Vietnam, or by US military personnel upon hostile military or civilian personnel.

3. *Definition.*

a. War Crimes. War crimes are violations of the law of war (see DA

Field Manual 27–10, The Law of Land Warfare, July 1956).

b. A "grave breach" of the Geneva Conventions constitutes a war crime. Some examples of "grave breaches" are as follows (when committed against persons taking no active part in the hostilities, including members of armed forces who have laid down their arms and those placed *hors de combat* by sickness, wounds, detention, or any cause): Willful killing, torture or inhuman treatment, willfully causing great suffering or serious injury to body or health.

* * *

5. *Responsibilities.*

a. It is the responsibility of all military personnel having knowledge or receiving a report of an incident or of an act thought to be a war crime to make such incident known to his commanding officer as soon as practicable. Personnel performing investigative, intelligence, police, photographic, grave registration, or medical functions, as well as those in contact with the enemy, will, in the normal course of their duty, make every effort to detect the commission of war crimes and will report the essential facts to their commanding officer. Persons discovering war crimes will take all reasonable action under the circumstances to preserve physical evidence, to note identity of witnesses present, and to record (by photograph, sketch, or descriptive notes) the circumstances and surroundings.

b. Commanders and MACV staff sections receiving reports of probable war crimes will, in addition to any other required reports, report the facts as soon as practicable to the Staff Judge Advocate, USMACV, and will make pertinent collateral information available to the appointing authority and investigating officers.

* * *

d. Appointing Authority:

(1) Will appoint an investigating officer and, if appropriate, designate a qualified criminal investigator or CIC agent as technical assistant. Upon receipt of notification of an alleged or apparent war crime concerning a member of his command, one of the following appointing authorities will, with all dispatch, appoint an investigating officer to prepare and transmit to him a report of investigation.

* * *

(3) When the completed Report of Investigation (ROI) has been submitted to the appointing authority by the Investigating officer, the appointing authority will receive, review, and approve the report. Two copies of the ROI and physical evidence will be transmitted to COMUSMACV, Attn: SJA.

4–2. MACV Message, "Mistreatment of Detainees and PW"

12 February 1968

FROM: COMUSMACV
TO: VMAC

Subj: Mistreatment of Detainees and PW (U)   From MACJ15

1. (C) Extensive press coverage of recent combat operations in Vietnam has afforded a fertile field for sensational photographs and war stories. Reports and photographs show flagrant disregard for human life, inhumane treatment and brutality in handling of detainees and PW. These press stories have served to focus unfavorable world attention on the treatment of detainees and prisoners of war by both ARVN and FWMAF.

2. (C) These actions will not be condoned.

3. (U) Vigorous and immediate command action is essential to insure that all personnel are familiar with and observe strictly:

a. FM 27–10, Law of Land Warfare

b. UCMJ, Article 93

c. Geneva Convention relative to treatment of PW (Articles 12 through 20 and 121)

d. Geneva Convention for Amelioration of Condition of wounded and sick armed forces in the field, Articles 12, 17 and 50.

e. MACV Directives 20–4, 27–5 and 190–3

4. (C) In addition, US Advisors will themselves adhere strictly to these provisions and make every effort to influence their counterparts to observe humane principles and the Geneva Conventions. Advisors must not become involved with war crimes and atrocities and shall advise their counterparts that they are required to report these incidents to higher headquarters. Advisors will use all influence to stop and prevent any maltreatment, war crimes or atrocities and will inform the senior in the chain of command of all details surrounding such incidents as quickly as possible.

5. (C) All known, suspected or alleged war crimes or atrocities committed by or against US personnel will be investigated IAW MACV Directive 20–4.

4-3. MACV Pocket Card, "Nine Rules"

NINE RULES
for Personnel of US Military
Assistance Command, Vietnam

The Vietnamese have paid a heavy price in suffering for their long fight against the communists. We military men are in Vietnam now because their government has asked us to help its soldiers and people in winning their struggle. The Viet Cong will attempt to turn the Vietnamese people against you. You can defeat them at every turn by the strength, understanding, and generosity you display with the people. Here are nine simple rules:

1. Remember we are guests here: We make no demands and seek no special treatment.
2. Join with the people! Understand their life, use phrases from their language and honor their customs and laws.
3. Treat women with politeness and respect.
4. Make personal friends among the soldiers and common people.
5. Always give the Vietnamese the right of way.
6. Be alert to security and ready to react with your military skill.
7. Don't attract attention by loud, rude or unusual behavior.
8. Avoid separating yourself from the people by a display of wealth or privilege.
9. Above all else you are members of the US Military Forces on a difficult mission, responsible for all your official and personal actions. Reflect honor upon yourself and the United States of America.

DISTRIBUTION—1 to each member of the United States Armed Forces in Vietnam (September 1967)

4-4. MACV Pocket Card, "The Enemy in Your Hands"

THE ENEMY IN YOUR HANDS

As a member of the US Military Forces, you will comply with the Geneva Prisoner of War Conventions of 1949 to which your country adheres. Under these Conventions:

You can and will:
Disarm your prisoner
Immediately search him thoroughly
Require him to be silent
Segregate him from other prisoners
Guard him carefully
Take him to the place designated by your commander

You cannot and must not:
Mistreat your prisoner
Humiliate or degrade him
Take any of his personal effects which do not have significant military value
Refuse him medical treatment if required and available

ALWAYS TREAT YOUR PRISONER HUMANELY

KEY PHRASES

English	*Vietnamese*
Halt	Dúng lai
Lay down your gun	Buông súng xuõng
Put up your hands	Dua tay lên
Keep your hands on your head	Dua tay lên däu
I will search you	Tôi Khám ông
Do not talk	Dùng nói chuyện
Walk there	Lại dăng kia
Turn Right	Xây bên phải
Turn Left	Xây bên trái

"The courage and skill of our men in battle will be matched by their magnanimity when the battle ends. And all American military action in Vietnam will stop as soon as aggression by others in stopped."

21 August 1965   Lyndon B. Johnson

THE ENEMY IN YOUR HANDS

1. *Handle him firmly, promptly, but humanely.*

The captive in your hands must be *disarmed, searched,* secured and watched. But he must also be treated at all times as a human being. He must not be tortured, killed, mutilated, or degraded, even if he refuses to talk. If the captive is a woman, treat her with all respect due her sex.

2. *Take the captive quickly to security.*

As soon as possible evacuate the captive to a place of safety and interrogation designated by your commander. Military documents taken from the captive are also sent to the interrogators, but the captive will keep his person equipment except weapons.

3. *Mistreatment of any captive is a criminal offense. Every soldier is personally responsible for the enemy in his hands.*

It is both dishonorable and foolish to mistreat a captive. It is also a
punishable offense. Not even a beaten enemy will surrender if he knows his
captors will torture or kill him. He will resist and make his capture more
costly. Fair treatment of captives encourages the enemy to surrender.

4. *Treat the sick and wounded captive as best you can.*

The captive saved may be an intelligence source. In any case he is a
human being and must be treated like one. The soldier who ignores the sick
and wounded degrades his uniform.

5. *All persons in your hands, whether suspects, civilians, or combat captives,
must be protected against violence, insults, curiosity, and reprisals of any
kind.*

Leave punishment to the courts and judges. The soldier shows his
strength by his fairness, and humanity to the persons in his hands.

(September 1967)

4–5. MACV Pocket Card, "Guidance for Commanders in Vietnam"

GUIDANCE FOR COMMANDERS IN VIETNAM
by General W. C. Westmoreland, COMUSMACV

1. Make the welfare of your men your primary concern with special attention to mess, mail, and medical care.
2. Give priority emphasis to matter of intelligence, counter-intelligence,
and timely and accurate reporting.
3. Gear your command for sustained operations: keep constant pressure on
the enemy.
4. React rapidly with all force available to opportunities to destroy the
enemy; disrupt enemy bases, capturing or destroying his supply caches.
5. Open up methodically and use roads, waterways, and the railroad; be
alert and prepared to ambush the ambusher.
6. Harass enemy lines of communication by raids and ambushes.
7. Use your firepower with care and discrimination, particularly in populated areas.
8. Capitalize on psywar opportunities.
9. Assist in "revolutionary development" with emphasis on priority areas
and on civic action wherever feasible.
10. Encourage and help Vietnamese military and paramilitary units; in-

volve them in your operations at every opportunity.

11. Be smarter and more skillful than the enemy; stimulate professionalism, alterness and tactical ingenuity; seize every opportunity to enhance training of men and units.

12. Keep your officers and men well informed, aware of the nine rules for personnel of MACV, and mindful of the techniques of communist insurgency and the role of free world forces in Vietnam.

13. Maintain an alert "open door" policy on complaints and a sensitivity to detection and correction of malpractices.

14. Recognize bravery and outstanding work.

15. Inspect frequently units two echelons below your level to insure compliance with the foregoing.

chapter 6

6–1. Purpose of the Inquiry as Read by Witnesses

This investigation was directed jointly by the Secretary of the Army and the Chief of Staff, United States Army, for the purpose of determining facts and making findings and recommendations concerning:

1. the adequacy of prior investigations and inquiries into, and subsequent reviews and reports within the chain of command, of what is now commonly referred to as the My Lai incident of 16 March 1968;

2. possible suppression or withholding of information by any person who had a duty to report and to furnish information concerning this incident.

This investigation is not being conducted to investigate all facts and circumstances of what happened at My Lai. It is directed to those specific purposes just stated. GEN Peers has had made available to him and has reviewed prior official statements obtained in other official investigations of the My Lai incident.

Your testimony will be taken under oath. A verbatim transcript will be prepared. A tape recording is being made in addition to the verbatim notes being taken by the reporter.

Although the general classification of the report will be *confidential,* it is possible that testimony, or parts of it, may later become a matter of public knowledge.

There are several persons in the room who may ask you questions. These individuals are assistants and they are authorized to ask questions. However, GEN Peers has the responsibility of weighing the evidence and making the findings and recommendations.

You are requested not to discuss your testimony with others except in the performance of duty or as you may be required so to do before a competent judicial, legislative, or administrative body. You are cautioned that, if you are subject to the order issued by the military judge in the general court-martial case of *United States* v. *Calley,* your appearance here in no way changes the applicability and effect of that order.

You may be requested to appear before a Special Subcommittee of the House Armed Services Committee. This Committee is looking into the entire incident of My Lai and your appearance and instructions before the Peers Inquiry in no way restricts your appearance before the House Armed Services Committee. You will be notified prior to your departure if you are to appear before the Committee.

chapter 7

7–1. Lt. Col. Barker's Combat Action Report (March 28, 1968)

28 March 1968

Headquarters, Task Force Barker, Americal Division 28 March 1968
SUBJECT: Combat Action Report (RCS AVDF-GC1)
TO: Commanding Officer
    11th Infantry Brigade
    ATTN: XIOP
    APO 96217

1. *Type of Operation:* Helicopter Assault.
2. *Dates of Operation:* 160730 to 161800 Mar 68.
3. *Location:* My Lai, RVN, BS 728795.
4. *Command Headquarters:* Task Force Barker, 11th Infantry Brigade.
5. *Reporting Officers:*
    LTC Frank A. Barker, Jr., CO, Task Force Barker
    CPT Ernest Medina, CO, Co C, 1/20 Inf
    CPT Earl Nichols, CO, Co B, 4/3 Inf
    CPT William Rigg, CO, Co A, 3/1 Inf

6. *Task Organizations:*
   Headquarters, Task Force Barker
   Company A, 3d Battalion, 1st Infantry
   Company B, 4th Battalion, 3d Infantry
   Company C, 1st Battalion, 20th Infantry
7. *Supporting Forces:*
   Btry D, 6th Battalion, 11th Arty (105 How).
   174th Avn Co (Recon Acft and gunships), timely and effective.
   Co B (Aero scout), 123d Avn Bn, timely and effective.
   Coastal Surveillance Force, USN (Swift Boat), timely and effective.

8. *Intelligence:* Enemy forces in the area of operation were estimated to be one local force battalion located in the vicinity of My Lai, BS 728795 as shown in Inclosure 1. This information was based upon previous combat operations in this area, visual reconnaissance, and PW and agent reports. During the operation it was estimated that only two local force companies supported by two to three local guerrilla platoons opposed the friendly forces. The area of operation consisted of six hamlets to varying degree of ruin, each separated by rice paddies which were bounded by a series of hedge rows and tree lines. The area was also honeycombed with tunnels and bunkers. The many hedge rows offered the enemy considerable cover and concealment from the attacking friendly forces. However the clear weather permitted maximum utilization of reconnaissance aircraft and helicopter gunships to seek out and destroy enemy defensive positions.

9. *Mission:* To destroy enemy forces and fortifications in a VC base camp and to capture enemy personnel, weapons and supplies.

10. *Concept of Operation:* Task Force Barker conducts a helicopter assault on 160730 Mar 68 on a VC base camp vicinity BS 728795 with Company C, 1st Battalion, 20th Infantry landing to the west and Company B, 4th Battalion, 3d Infantry landing to the southeast of the VC base camp. Company A, 3d Battalion, 1st Infantry moves by foot to blocking positions north of the base camp prior to the helicopter assault. USN Swift Boats screen the coastal area to the east of the base camp and Company B (Aero Scout) 123d Avn Bn screens to the south to block or destroy enemy forces attempting to withdraw. See Incl 1. An artillery preparation and gunship suppressive fires are planned for both landing zones. Artillery blocking fires are planned on all paths of escape which the enemy might use. Upon landing, the two rifle companies assault enemy positions making a detailed search of all buildings, bunkers and tunnels as they move.

11. *Execution:* The order was issued on 14 March 1968. Coordination with supporting arms reconnaissance and positioning of forces was conducted on 15 Mar 68. On 160726 Mar 68 a three minute artillery preparation began on the first landing zone and at 0730 hours the first lift for Co C touched down while helicopter gunships provided suppressive fires. At 0747 hours the last lift of Co C was completed. The initial preparation

resulted in 68 VC KIA's in the enemy's combat outpost positions. Co C then immediately attacked to the east receiving enemy small arms fire as they pressed forward. At 0809H a three minute artillery preparation on the second landing zone began and the first left for Co B touched down at 0815 hours. At 0827 the last lift of Co B was completed and Co B moved to the north and east receiving only light enemy resistance initially. As Co B approached the area of the VC base camp, enemy defensive fires increased. One platoon from Co B flanked the enemy positions and engaged one enemy platoon resulting in 30 enemy KIA. Throughout the day Co B and Co C received sporadic sniper fire and encountered numerous enemy booby traps. Co A in blocking positions to the north had only light contact against small enemy elements attempting to withdraw to the north. Attempts of the enemy to escape along the beach or to the south were successfully countered by the Swift Boats and the Aero Scout Company. By 1630 hours the surviving enemy elements had broken all contact with friendly forces by infiltrating with civilians leaving the area, or by going down into the extensive tunnel systems throughout the area. At 1715 hours Co C linked-up with Co B and both units went into a perimeter defense for the night in preparation for conducting search and destroy operations the next day. With the establishment of the night defensive position at 161800 March 1968 the operation was terminated.

 12. *Results:*
  a. Enemy losses:
   (1) Personnel:
    128 KIA
    11 VCS CIA
   (2) Equipment captured:
    1 M-1 rifle
    2 M-1 carbines
    10 Chicom hand grenades
    8 US M-26 hand grenades
    410 rounds small arms ammo
    4 US steel helmets with liners
    5 US canteens with covers
    7 US pistol belts
    9 sets US web equipment
    2 short wave transistor radios
    3 boxes of medical supplies
   (3) Equipment and facilities destroyed:
    16 booby traps
    1 large tunnel complex
    14 small tunnel complexes
    8 bunkers
   numerous sets of web equipment

b. Friendly losses:

2 US KHA

11 US WHA

13. *Administrative Matters:*

a. Supply. Units moved with basic loads of ammunition and three C-ration meals per man. Resupply was planned and effected by helicopter. No problem existed in resupply.

b. Maintenance. No problems encountered.

c. Medical treatment and evacuation. All casualties requiring evacuation were removed from the area by helicopters including wounded VC and some of their civilian supporters. All other casualties were treated by company aidmen.

d. Transportation. Helicopters were the primary means of transportation. No problems encountered.

e. Communications. No problems encountered.

14. *Special Equipment and Techniques:*

a. Aero Scout Company. This unit was used effectively as a reconnaissance and supporting force along the southern portion of the area of operation.

b. US Navy Swift Boats. Effective use of these craft was made to provide surveillance of the beach area and to detect enemy personnel attempting to escape in boats or along the beach.

15. *Commander Analysis:* This operation was well planned, well executed and successful. Friendly casualties were light and the enemy suffered heavily. On this operation the civilian population supporting the VC in the area numbered approximately 200. This created a problem in population control and medical care of those civilians caught in fires of the opposing forces. However, the infantry unit on the ground and helicopters were able to assist civilians in leaving the area and in caring for and/or evacuating the wounded.

16. *Recommendations:* Operations conducted in an area where large numbers of refugees might be generated should provide for civil affairs, psyops, medical, intelligence and police teams to be brought to the area as early as practicable after the arrival of combat troops. This would facilitate population control and medical care, and would permit the sorting out of VC which have mingled among the population for cover. The presence of these teams would free infantry personnel for combat operations.

Frank A. Barker, Jr.

Lt Colonel, Infantry

Commanding

7–2. Col. Henderson's Report of Investigation (April 24, 1968)

24 April 1968

SUBJECT: Report of Investigation
Commanding General
Americal Division
APO SF 96374

1. (U) An investigation has been conducted of the allegations cited in Inclosure 1. The following are the results of this investigations.

2. (C) On the day in question, 16 March 1968, Co C 1st Bn 20th Inf and Co B 4th Bn 3rd Inf as part of Task Force Barker, 11th Inf Bde, conducted a combat air assault in the vicinity of My Lai Hamlet (Son My Village) in eastern Son Tinh District. This area has long been an enemy strong hold, and Task Force Barker had met heavy enemy opposition in this area on 12 and 23 February 1968. All persons living in this area are considered to be VC or VC sympathizers by the District Chief. Artillery and gunship preparatory fires were placed on the landing zones used by the two companies. Upon landing and during their advance on the enemy positions, the attacking forces were supported by gunships from the 174th Avn Co and Co B, 23rd Avn Bn. By 1500 hours all enemy resistance had ceased and the remaining enemy forces had withdrawn. The results of this operation were 128 VC soldiers KIA. During preparatory fires and the ground action by the attacking companies 20 non-combatants caught in the battle area were killed. US Forces suffered 2 KHA and 10 WHA by booby traps and 1 man slightly wounded in the foot by small arms fire. No US soldier was killed by sniper fire as was the alleged reason for killing the civilians. Interviews with LTC Frank A. Barker, TF Commander; Maj Charles C. Calhoun, TF S3; CPT Ernest L. Medina, Co Co C, 1-20; and CPT Earl Michles, Co Co B, 4-3 revealed that at no time were any civilians gathered together and killed by US soldiers. The civilian habitants in the area began withdrawing to the southwest as soon as the operation began and within the first hour and a half all visible civilians had cleared the area of operations.

3. (C) The Son Tinh District Chief does not give the allegations any importance and he pointed out that the two hamlets where the incident is alleged to have happened are in an area controlled by the VC since 1964. COL Toan, Cmdr 2d Arvn Div reported that the making of such allegations against US Forces is a common technique of the VC propaganda machine. Inclosure

2 is a translation of an actual VC propaganda message targeted at the ARVN soldier and urging him to shoot Americans. This message was given to this headquarters by the CO, 2d ARVN Division o/a 17 April 1968 as matter of information. It makes the same allegations as made by the Son My Village Chief in addition to other claims of atrocities by American soldiers.

4. (C) It is concluded that 20 non-combatants were inadvertently killed when caught in the area of preparatory fires and in the cross fires of the US and VC forces on 16 March 1968. It is further concluded that no civilians were gathered together and shot by US soldiers. The allegation that US Forces shot and killed 450–500 civilians is obviously a Viet Cong propaganda move to discredit the United States in the eyes of the Vietnamese people in general and the ARVN soldier in particular.

5. (C) It is recommended that a counter-propaganda campaign be waged against the VC in eastern Son Tinh District.

Oran K. Henderson
COL, Infantry
Commanding

Enclosure 1 to Report of Investigation

The American Devils Divulge Their True Form

The empire building Americans invade South Vietnam with war. They say that they came to Vietnam to help the Vietnamese people and that they are our friends.

When the US Soldiers first arrived in Vietnam they tried to conceal their cruel invasion. They gave orders to the US soldiers to be good to the Vietnamese people thus employing psychological warfare. They also employed strict discipline which required US soldiers to respect the Vietnamese women and the customs of the Vietnamese people.

When the first US soldiers arrived in Vietnam they were good soldiers and they paid when they made purchases from the people. They would even pay a price in excess of the cost. When they did wrong they gave money to indemnify their deeds. They gave the people around their basecamps and in nearby hamlets medical aid. US newspapers often printed pictures of US troops embracing the Vietnamese people and giving candy to children. The American Red Cross also gave medical attention to the Vietnamese. This led a small group of ARVN's to believe that the American man was a good friend and had continued pity for the people. The Army Republic of Vietnam was happy to have allies which are such good friends and who are rich.

But, it is a play and every play must come to an end and the curtain come down. The espionage was very professional and clever. If the plan is completed it will one day become saucy, because all the people will know what they are trying to hide and what they are really doing to the Vietnamese people.

They continue to produce this play but each year they receive fewer victorious responses. Each year they are attacked by the enemy in the south and they are being defeated more every day. This play lies to the people and will soon be disclosed to them. Today the Americans cannot cover anything. Now they only kill and rape day after day. Their animalistic character has been uncovered even by the American civilians. In Saigon there are some Americans that put their penis outside of their pants and put a dollar on it to pay the girls who sell themselves. The Americans get laid in every public place. This beast in the street is not afraid of the presence of the people.

In the American basecamps when they check the people they take their money, rings, watches, and the women's ear rings. The Americans know the difference between good gold and cheap bronze. If the jewelry is of bronze they do not take it.

Since the Americans heavy loss in the spring they have become like wounded animals that are crazy and cruel. They bomb places where many people live, places which are not good choices for bombings, such as the cities within the provinces, especially in Hue, Saigon, and Bon Tre. In Hue the US newspapers reported that 70% of the homes were destroyed and 10,000 people killed or left homeless. The newspapers and radios of Europe also tell of the killing of the South Vietnamese people by the Americans. The English tell of the action where the Americans are bombing the cities of South Vietnam. The Americans will be sentenced first by the Public in Saigon. It is there where the people will lose sentiment for them because they bomb the people and all people will soon be against them. The world public objects to this bombing including the American public and that of its Allies. The American often shuts his eye and closes his ear and continues his crime.

In the operation of 15 March 1968 in Son Tinh District the American enemies went crazy. They used machine guns and every other kind of weapons to kill 500 people who had empty hands, in Tinh Khe (Son My) Village (Son Tinh District, Quang Ngai Province). There were many pregnant women some of which were only a few days from childbirth. The Americans would shoot everybody they saw. They killed people and cows, burned homes. There were some families in which all members were killed.

When the red evil Americans remove their prayer shirts they appear as barbaric men.

When the American wolves remove their sheepskin their sharp meat-eating teeth show. They drink our peoples blood with animal sentimental-ity.

Our people must choose one way to beat them until they are dead, and stop wriggling.

For the ARVN officer and soldier, by now you have seen the face of the real American. How many times have they left you alone to defend against the National Liberation Front? They do not fire artillery or mortars to help you even when you are near them. They often bomb the bodies of ARVN soldiers. They also fire artillery on the tactical elements of the ARVN soldiers.

The location of the ARVN soldier is the American target. If someone does not believe this he may examine the 39th Ranger Battalion when it was sent to Khe Sanh where its basecamp was placed between the Americans and the Liberation soldiers. They were willing to allow this battalion to die for them. This activity was not armed toward helping South Vietnam as is the National Liberation Front but was to protect the 6,000 Americans that live in Khe Sanh.

Can you accept these criminal friends who slaughter our people and turn Vietnam into red blood like that which runs in our veins?

What are you waiting for and why do not you use your US Rifles to shoot the Americans in the head—for our people, to help our country and save your life too?

> There is no time better than now
> The American Rifle is in your hands
> You must take aim at the Americans head and
> Pull the trigger

Enclosure 2 to Report of Investigation

14 April 1968

Statement

This statement is in reference to letter from the Son Tinh District Chief to the Quang Ngai Province Chief Subject: Allied Forces Gathered People of Son-My Village for Killing, dated 11 April 1968.

The Son Tinh District Chief received a letter from the Village Chief of Son-My Village containing the complaint of the killing of 450 civilians including children and women by American troops. The Village Chief alleged that an American unit operating in the area on 16 March 1968 gathered and killed these civilians with their own personal weapons. The incident took place in the hamlets of Tu-Cong and Co-Luy located in the eastern portion of Son Tinh District. According to the Village Chief the American unit gathered 400 civilians in Tu-Cong hamlet and killed them. Then moved to Co-Luy hamlet. At this location the unit gathered 90 more civilians and killed them.

The Son-My Village Chief feels that this action was taken in revenge for an American soldier killed by sniper fire in the village.

The letter was not given much importance by the District Chief but it was sent to the Quang Ngai Province Chief. Later the Son Tinh District Chief was called and directed by the 2d Division Commander, Col Toan, to investigate the incident and prepare a report. The District Chief proceeded to interview the Son-My Village Chief and got the same information that I have discussed above. The District Chief is not certain of the information received and he has to depend on the word of the Village Chief and other people living in the area.

The two hamlets where the incident is alleged to happen are in a VC controlled area since 1964.

chapter 13

13–1. Letter from Census Grievance Cadreman (March 18, 1968)

18 March 68

REPUBLIC OF VIET NAM
Letter Report

Report of results Son My Village, Tu Cung hamlet, Son Tinh District:

About 7 AM 15 Mar 68, an operation conducted by allied forces was conducted in Tu Cung hamlet.

A force composed of District VC and local guerillas (strength unknown) opposed the Allied operation.

After a fierce battle the allies killed 320 people at subhamlet Thuan Yen and Binh-Dong.

27 people were killed at My Lai. Among this number was a hamlet security chief named Le Van Gia.

At Co Luy Hamlet 80 people young and old were killed. The total civilians and guerillas killed during the last 3 days (427), including young and old.

At this time the Allied operation is continuing and the force is now located at Co Luy in Son My Village.

Presented for CSG Chief, Quong Ngai
Completed at 1600 Hrs 18 Mar 68

> CSG Cadreman
> Phong Duc_____
> (Last name not legible

13-2. Report from Son My Village Chief (March 22, 1968)

Son My 22 March 1968

Son Tinh District
Son My Village
NR *116* Admin Office

Margin notes in pen:
Thuan Yen   19
My Khe   3
Trung Binh   4
Binh Tay   3
Binh Dong   23

REPUBLIC OF VIET NAM
Administrative Council Son My Village
TO: 1LT District Chief, Son Tinh District
SUBJECT: Report of the Allied Operation of 16 March 68
Concerning the allied operation conducted 16 March 1968 at Tu Cung and Co Luy hamlets of Son My village:
Results: Allies: 1 killed, 2 WIA (at Thuan Yen subhamlet, Tu Cung hamlet).
Viet Cong: 48 killed, 52 wounded (including guerillas, cadre from subhamlet, hamlet, village and district).
Civilians: Tu Cung 480
             Co Luy 90
Total: 570 civilians
Besides persons killed, animals, property and houses were 90% destroyed.
For information of the District Chief.
                    signed

> Mr. Dinh Luyen Do
> Chairman Village
> Council
> (also Village Chief)

Translator's Note:
Subhamlets of Tu Cung Hamlet are:
Thuan Yen
Binh Tay
Binh Dong
Truong Hoa
Truong An
Above total is 52—same as number of VC reported wounded.

13-3. Lt. Tan's Letter to Province Chief (March 28, 1968)

No. 181/HC/ST/M

FROM: 1LT Tran Ngoc Tan
       Son Tinh District Chief
TO: Quang Ngai Province Chief
SUBJECT: Confirmation of Allied Troops Shooting at the Residents of Tu
       Cung Hamlet, Coordinates BS 721795

It is respectfully reported that:
On 19 March 1968, an element of the US Forces (unspecified, because this
District Headquarters had not been notified of the operation) conducted an
operation at Tu Cung Hamlet (BS 721795), Son My Village, Son Tinh
District. It was reported that when the element entered the hamlet, one of
its members was killed and some others wounded by a VC booby-trapped
mine. At this time the VC opened up fiercely from their positions in the
hamlet. Meanwhile, the US troops used intense firepower while moving in
with artillery and air support, inflicting injuries on a number of hamlet
residents because the VC mingled with the population.
Observation by this Headquarters:
The Tu Cung Hamlet and the two neighboring hamlets, e.g., My Lai (BS
737800) and Van Thien (BS 794804), in Son My Village had become insecure since 1964, so the administrative authorities of these areas had been
forced to flee to Son Long (BS 638756), leaving these hamlets under VC
control. Casualties were unavoidably caused to the hamlets residents during
the firefight, while the local administrative authorities were not present in
the area. The enemy may take advantage of this incident to undermine,
through fallacious propaganda, the prestige of the RVNAF, and frustrate
the Government's rural pacification efforts.

Respectfully yours,
1st Lt Tran Ngoc Tan

Copies to:
S2 and S3, Quang Ngai Sector HQ

13–4. Lt. Tan's Letter to Province Chief (April 11, 1968)

Son Tinh, 11 April 1968
Number 190/CT/ST

FROM: District Chief, Son Tinh
TO: Lieutenant Colonel Province Chief, Quang Ngai
SUBJECT: Allied Operation at Son My assembled and killed civilians

On 16 March 1968 an American Army unit conducted a mopping-up operation at Tu Cung and Co Luy hamlets of Son My Village, Son Tinh District. At About 10 o'clock on the above day, the American unit encountered a VC mine and received fire from Tu Cung hamlet. One American soldier was killed and a number of others wounded.

In response the operational forces attacked the village, assembled the people and shot and killed more than 400 people at Tu Cung hamlet, and 90 more people in Co Luy hamlet of Son My Village. While the VC were withdrawing from the Hamlet, 48 VC and more than 52 guerillas and self defense soldiers were wounded by helicopter gun ships.

Subsector comments.
Tu Cung and Co Luy are two areas of Son My Village that have long been held by the VC. The district forces lack the capability of entering the area. Therefore, allied units frequently conduct mop-up operations and bombing attacks freely in the area. But the basic position of the report of the Son My village committee is that although the VC cannot be held blameless for their actions in the 16 March 1968 operation, the Americans in anger killed too many civilians. Only one American was killed by the VC, however the allies killed near 500 civilians in retaliation.

Really an atrocious attitude if it cannot be called an act of insane violence. Request you intervene on behalf of the people.

Respectfully,
1st Lt Tran Ngoc Tan
District Chief

Copies to:
2nd ARVN Div Hq.
MACV Quang Ngai Sector

Major U.S. Advisor, Son Tinh Subsection
(Courtesy Copy)

13–5. VC Propaganda Broadcast, "American Evil Appears"

Broadcast   American Evil Appears
(Coordinate this broadcast with leaflets: "Let American Enemy Pay This Bloody Debt")

American imperialists make Vietnam aggressive war, but he said that he came here to "help" our people and he calls himself as our friend.

When he arrives in South Vietnam he tries to hide his bad aggressive ambition. He told his troopers to respect Vietnamese people and make good relationship with them. His psyops also give troops "commandments" whose contents are "Have to respect women and Vietnamese traditions and customs."

When American troops had just arrived in Vietnam, they tried to show themselves as "Honorable gentlemen" selling or buying fair and square, even paying higher than market prices. When they destroyed something, they paid for it with money. Then some posts allowed people to come, and doctors were sent to somewhere to give people medical aid. American press shows some pictures of Americans and Vietnamese shaking hands—Americans kiss Vietnamese people and give them candies—or Americans with Red Cross signs at their arms give medical aid to Vietnamese people . . . and they boast that this is one of familiar pictures around American troops locations.

This demagogy makes some ARVN troops believe Americans are good friends. How happy it is if we have such good and rich friends!

But any play has to end, although the actors are skillful, but they play only one act, they will become soon unskillful—and the play will become a bad one. So the demagogy will become "true," "unmask," easier than any plays.

The role can be played more beautifully if U.S. troops collect more victories every year, but they are beaten more heavily by our people year by year. So the demagogy is unmasked more easy. Now, U.S. troops can not hide anything, they have shown all bad ambition which belongs to any aggressive troops. In sweep operations, they loot people's properties, destroy everything, rape women, they have shown their animal ambition, their civilization. In Saigon one American had put his penis outside his pants, and one dollar was put on it, which he paid to a girl. U.S. troops play girls every public areas: beach, roadside . . . they do not care about people passing by. In U.S. troop locations, they search people to get piaster, gold rings, watches, ear rings, they are so cunning that they do not pick up false gold.

Due to their great defeats in the recent Spring, they are like wild wounded animal, the more they wriggle, the more bad actions are done—definitely inhuman doings. They had dropped bombs at random onto populous areas and cities such as HUE, SAIGON, BEN TRE. They confirmed that 90% of houses were destroyed in HUE City. Thousands of our people were killed or homeless. Western newspapers and radio stations also confirmed that all the damages of houses in South Vietnam cities came from American bombs and ammo because U.S. has more fire power than NLF troops. British newspapers said Americans bombed cities, especially Saigon City, it would be condemned by opinion it was too much when Americans did that. Japanese public opinion said: America would be isolated and lose appreciation when they bomb South Vietnamese cities. It would make an anti-American wave in the South Vietnam, unless the world public opinion protested, and also there was not a unanimity of Allies. Americans still close their eyes, shut their ears to perform their cruel acts.

A sweep operation was conducted on 15 Mar 68 recently in SON TINH. Crazy American enemy used light machineguns and all kinds of weapons to kill our innocent civilian people in TINH KHE Village (SON MY (V)). Most of them were women, kids, there were some just born babies and pregnant women. They shot everything they saw, they killed all domestic animals, they burned all people's houses. There were 26 families killed completely—no survivors.

The fierce devil Americans dropped down their priest covers to become barbarous, and cruel.

American wolf forgot their good sheeps' appearance. They opened mouth to eat, drink our people blood with all their animal barbarity.

Our people have only one way, it is to kill them so they can not bite around anymore.

Vietnam officers, soldier brothers, it is about time to know the true face of Americans. There were so many times they forgot you when you were bitten by NLF's troops but they have never fired any mortar round to support you. Even they are right beside you and they also dropped bombs on puppet dead bodies to suppress and sometimes they mortared right on your formation.

The position of puppet troops as their targets are so clear. Any one still doubt, just look at the 39th Ranger Battalion stationed in KHE SANH area. They used the unit as an obstacle in the front for American Marines, you already know they offered this battalion as "ready to die" but it doesn't mean the same as the meaning of "die for fatherlands" as NLF soldiers, they said that because they wanted to protect 6000 American troops there.

So it is the American civilization it is the good of friend as you see them —a murdered, killed your blood people—made a Vietnamese blood stream running as blood in our own bodies—as an allied or not?

What are you waiting for! Use right American guns to shoot right their heads in order to avenge our people, to wash out insult to our nation and save your proud and your own life.

> This time: more than ever before
> American guns are in your hands
> Point to American heads and shoot!

13–6. Maj. Pho's Memorandum to Col. Toan (April 12, 1968.)

12 April 1968

MEMO FOR: Col CG, 2d ARVN Div

SUBJECT: An American Unit Operating in East Son Tinh on 16 Mar 68, Shot and Killed More Than 400 Civilians.

In a propaganda leaflet the VC have used the operation conducted by an American unit at Son My (Son Tinh) on 15 March 1968, saying that the US unit assembled, shot and killed 500 people (including men and women, young and old). Their objective is to incite the people against the US military.

On this matter, the Son Tinh District Chief has confirmed the following:

On 16 Mar 68 US unit conducted an operation at Son My (East Son Tinh area, considered by Son Tinh subsector to be an insecure area). At 1000 hours the US unit received fire from Tu Cong hamlet and also hit a mine. One US was killed and a number wounded.

After that the US unit assaulted the hamlet, assembled the people, then shot and killed over 400 people in Tu Cong hamlet and 90 people in Co Luy hamlet.

Attached is a copy of the VC propaganda leaflet and the report of the Son Tinh District Chief.

> KBC 4.277, 12 April 1968
> Major Pham Van Pho
> G-2

Margin notes made by General (then Colonel) Toan on this document as follows:

Quang Ngai Sector Review this
investigation. If there is nothing

to it, have the District rectify report—
If it is true, link-up with the
Americal Division to have this stopped.

13–7. Col. Toan's Postal Message to Lt. Col. Khien (April 15, 1968)

FROM: G-2, Tactical Zone 12.
TO: Quang Ngai Sector

Message Number 1242/18

Reference report number 190/CK/ST, dated 11 April 1968 from Son Tinh District, Subject: Report that an American unit operation at Son My Village on 16 Mar 68 where near 500 civilians were assembled, shot and killed.

Request Sector conduct another investigation. In event report is not true, instruct Son Tinh District to rectify the above report. If correct, report to G-2, 2nd Division; this headquarters will intervene.

> KBC 4.277, 15 April 1968
> COL Nguyen Van Toan
> CG 2nd ARVN Div, 12 Tactical Zone
> Signed LTC Pham Cao Dong Chief of Staff

13–8. VC Notice, "Concerning the Crimes Committed by US Imperialists and Their Lackeys" (March 28, 1968)

[The following is a full translation of a three-page notice issued by the QUANG NGAI (P) National Liberation Front Committee, dtd 28 Mar 68.]

N O T I C E

Concerning the Crimes Committed by U S Imperialists and Their Lackeys
Who Killed more than 500 Civilians of TINH KHE (V), SON TINH (D)

The morning of 16 March 1968 was a quiet morning, just like every other morning, with the people of TINH KHE Village about to start another laborious day of production and struggle. Suddenly, artillery rounds began pouring in from NUI RAM Mountain, BINH LIEN and QUANG NGAI

Sub-Sector. XOM LANG Sub-Hamlet of TU CUNG Hamlet and XOM GO Sub-Hamlet of CO LUY Hamlet were pounded by artillery for hours. After the shelling, nine helicopters landed troops who besieged the two small sub-hamlets. The US soldiers were like wild animals, charging violently into the hamlets, killing and destroying. They formed themselves into three groups: one group was in charge of killing civilians, one group burned huts and the third group destroyed vegetation and trees and killed animals. These American troops belonged to the 3d Brigade of the 82d Division which had just come to Viet Nam and suffered a defeat in the Spring. Wherever they went, civilians were killed, houses and vegetation were destroyed and cows, buffalo, chickens and ducks were also killed.

They even killed old people and children; pregnant women were raped and killed. This was by far the most barbaric killing in human history.

At XOM LANG Sub-Hamlet of TU CUNG Hamlet, they routed all the civilians out of their bunkers and herded them, at bayonet point, into a group near a ditch in front of Mr. NHIEU's gate (Mr. NHIEU was 46 years old). About 100 civilians who squatted in a single line were killed instantly by bursts of automatic rifle fire and M79 rounds. Bodies were sprawled about, blood was all over. Among those killed were 60 year old men and newly born babies still in their mother's arms. Most of them were children from 1 to 14 years old. Badly wounded children who were screaming were shot to death.

Some entire families were massacred. Inhabitants were killed inside bunkers, in the gardens of their homes or in the alleys of the hamlet. Mr. HUONG THO, 72 years old, was beaten, his beard was cut, and he was pushed into a well and shot with automatic rifle fire until his body submerged. NGUYET, 12 years old, after being raped, was bayoneted in the vagina and rest of her body. PHAN THI MUI, 15 years old, was raped and then burned to death in a rice bowl. The entire seven members of Mr. LE LY's family were killed, including the youngest 4 year old nephew and 70 year old Mr. LY. The only survivor of the family was a married daughter who lived somewhere else and returned to the hamlet after the massacre, to cry, holding her beloved relatives' bodies in her arms. (She set up an altar at her father's burned house and prayed for her seven dead relatives.) Neighbors set up altars for families that had no surviving relatives.

The total number of civilians killed at XOM LANG Sub-Hamlet was 2060, including old people, children, women and young people.

At XOM GO Sub-Hamlet of CO LUY Hamlets, American pirates blew up and burned every hut and tossed grenades into civilian shelters. The sand was soaked with blood; beheaded bodies lay sprawled on the ground. People died without enough time to utter a word! Mothers holding sons' bodies! Grandmothers holding grandsons' bodies. They died unjustly. Fifteen people were killed inside Mr. LE's shelter. They even killed pregnant women. VO THI HAI, who had given birth to a child the night before, was raped and killed, leaving behind a newly-born baby with no milk, with no one to suckle it. NGUYEN THI NGON, 32 years old, near the end of her pregnancy, was mutilated inside her bunker, exposing the stirring, unborn baby. While 30 year old VO THI PHU was feeding her baby, they snatched her baby away and raped her. Later, both were burned to death.

Mrs. KHEO, 65 years old, was shot to death by the bunker entrance and her body was tossed onto the burning fire. Mr. DUONG, 85 years old, was marched out of the bunker when they came. They marched him to every bunker, showing him the sights of the barbaric killings. They offered him poisoned candy, but he caught the bad smell and didn't eat the candy. They searched him and found nothing and released him.

At this place, American pirates killed 92, wounded 10, burned 304 huts, destroyed 78 bunkers and destroyed and burned civilian property worth 900,000 piastres.

Civilian laborers who had come to work or to visit relatives at TU CUNG Hamlet and CO LUY Hamlet were also massacred.

Thus, on 16 March 1968, the US pirates and their lackeys massacred a total of 502 people at TU CUNG Hamlet and CO LUY Hamlet of TINH KHE Village and wounded 50 who survived the first bursts of automatic rifle fire. Among the dead were 67 old people, 170 children, 137 women. All huts, trees and animals were completely burned and destroyed.

This is by far the most typical of the barbaric massacres committed by the US Imperialists against our People.

Like the other earlier massacres by American and Korean pirates at PHUONG DINH, SON TINH; VAN HA, (MO DUC) PHU THO, (NGHIA HANH) BINH HOA, (BINH SON) PHO MINH, (DUC PHO) the TINH KHE Village massacre was the worst crime committed by the US Imperialists and their lackeys before their complete defeat.

The Heavens will not tolerate this! The blue ocean waters will not wash away the hatred. These murders are even more savage than Hitler or TAN THUY HOAN [Translator's Note: TAN THUY HOAN was the Chinese emperor who ordered hundreds of thousands of civilians to build the Great Wall, which resulted in thousands of deaths.]

Shamefully defeated, confused, the enemy is like a wild animal just before dying, due to our thunderous Spring attack. They have become excited and crazy, hoping to shake our spirit and the heroic tradition of our people. QUANG NGAI is the province of proud BA TO, uprising TRA BONG, BA GIA, VAN TUONG, the province of glorious victories that scared the enemy.

With deep hatred in their hearts, the people of TINH KHE, as well as the people and armed forces of QUANG NGAI Province, have turned their sufferings and hatred into a rising, vengeful force.

After the massacre, the people of TINH KHE Village wiped away their tears, hate deep in their hearts, and bravely rebuilt their homes, clearing away all traces of tragedy, growing potatoes, rice.

Immediately after the massacre, TINH KHE guerrillas and other village guerrillas killed 31 enemy soldiers on 17 and 19 March 1968, including 17 Americans. TINH KHE guerrillas personally killed 8 Americans on 17 March. The armed forces of the province have forced the enemy to pay their bloody debt.

During the 15 days from 13 March to 28 March 68, Local Force and QUANG NGAI guerrillas fought many battles, killing 298 enemy soldiers, including 20 Americans, and captured much equipment.

The massacre of the 500 civilians of TINH KHE has increased our hatred. We must attack continuously, rising up to make the enemy pay their debts!

> 28 March 1968
> National Liberation Front Committee
> of QUANG NGAI Province

chapter 18

18–1. Memorandum from Special Counsel Robert MacCrate Attached to Final Report (March 14, 1970)

14 March 1970

MEMORANDUM FOR: Secretary of the Army
Chief of Staff, US Army
SUBJECT: Final Report of Investigation

I would like to record my concurrence in the basic findings of the report and my satisfaction with the manner in which the Inquiry has been conducted by LTG Peers. I am satisfied that every reasonable effort has been made to determine the full facts surrounding the original Army investigation of the incidents and that the report fairly records what was found.

Since joining the Inquiry on December 5, 1969, Mr. Jerome K. Walsh, Jr., and I, as civilian legal counsel, have served as integral members of the Inquiry team. Our advice has been continually solicited in the course of the Inquiry and our suggestions as to issues to be examined and information to be sought have been conscientiously pursued. We fully participated in the interrogation of witnesses, the review of the evidence and the preparation of the report. While there have been many aspects essential to the Inquiry and to a complete report which go beyond a layman's sphere of knowledge, every attempt was made by LTG Peers and members of his team to provide us with the background information required to enlarge our participation.

It became clear to me in the course of the Inquiry that the resources and technical competence of the Army itself were essential to a sound, thorough and effective examination of this matter. I am convinced that it was desirable from the point of view of the public and of all concerned that this matter in the first instance be fully examined by the Army. I believe it has been well done.

Robert MacCrate
Special Counsel

chapter 20

20–1. Fact Sheet on Men in Charlie Company

DCSPER-CSD   FACT SHEET

Mr. Ruberton/54200
12 Jan 70

SUBJECT: Company C, 1st Battalion, 20th Infantry
TO: Chief of Staff, United States Army

Purpose: To provide a review of the background, aptitudes, trainability, and educational level of enlisted personnel assigned to Company C, 1st Battalion, 20th Infantry.

Facts

1. The roster of the company furnished by the Peers' Inquiry Committee contained the names of 136 enlisted personnel. Twenty three were NCOs and 113 other enlisted men. The roster includes three NCOs and eight other men who were attached to the company which are included in this review.

2. Records of five men were not available and all items of information were not available in several cases. However, the results of this review are considered to be representative of the entire company. Norms used in the review pertain to the median which divides the upper and lower half of the group.

3. A review of the records of the 23 NCOs reveals that the majority were above the norm.

—66 percent were enlistees in comparison to 40 percent of Army wide accessions for FY 67, 68 and 69.

—Distribution among the four mental categories was nearly identical to accessions of new men during FY 67, 68 and 69.

—52 percent were above the norm in general learning ability (GT Score 100).

—50 percent were above the norm in Infantry aptitude (IN Score 100).

—87 percent were high school graduates in comparison to 69 percent of Army wide accessions (25 percent had some college credits).

—Median age was 22 years.

4. Review of the enlistees and inductees, less NCOs, shows no significant deviation from the normal cross section of first term enlistees and inductees.

—39 percent were enlistees which is nearly identical to Army wide accessions.

—Distribution among the four mental categories was nearly identical to accessions of new men during FY 67, 68 and 69.

—47 percent were above the norm in overall trainability (AFQT 50 percentile) in comparison to 52 percent of Army wide accessions.

—54 percent were above the norm in general learning ability (GT Score 100) in comparison to 60 percent of Army wide accessions.

—51 percent were above the norm in Infantry aptitude (IN Score 100) which is nearly identical to Army wide accessions.

—70 percent were high school graduates which is slightly higher than Army wide accessions (19 percent had some college credits).

—Approximately 8 percent of the entire company were Project One Hundred Thousand men while Army wide accessions are 12 percent.

—Average age was 21.6 years.

5. Regular Army enlistees (less NCOs) comprised 39 percent of the company. A review of their records reveals that the majority were below the norm in overall trainability and general learning ability. Sixty-one percent were above the norm in infantry aptitude. Fifty-six percent were high school graduates (23 percent had some college credits). Average age was 20.8 years.

6. The inductees comprised 61 percent of the company (less NCOs) and were above the norm in practically every area. Fifty-three percent were above the norm in overall trainability, 59 percent in general learning ability, 79 percent were high school graduates (17 percent had some college credits); 46 percent were above the norm in infantry aptitude. Average age was 22 years.

7. Based upon the foregoing it is concluded that there is no significant deviation in the enlisted personnel of Company C from the normal cross section of first term enlistees or inductees.

20–2. Fact Sheet on Men in Bravo Company

DCSPER-CSD   FACT SHEET

Mr. Ruberton/78540
6 February 1970

SUBJECT: Company B, 4th Battalion, 3rd Infantry
TO: Chief of Staff, United States Army

Purpose. To provide an analysis of the background, aptitudes, trainability, educational level and other information pertaining to personnel assigned to Company B, 4th Battalion, 3rd Infantry.
Facts
1. The roster of the company furnished by the Peers' Inquiry Committee contained the names of five officers and 126 enlisted personnel (27 were NCO's and 99 other enlisted men).
2. Records of the 5 officers were available. Records of 7 enlisted men were not available and several items of information were not available in 10 other cases. However, the results of this analysis are considered representative of the entire company. Norms used pertain to the median which divides the upper and lower half of the group.
3. Review of the 5 officers' records reveals that as a group the officers assigned to Company B at the time of the incident appear to have been above average in educational level, maturity, and manner of performance. Three had college degrees. All but one had service at company level prior to arriving in Vietnam. Two had prior service as enlisted men. Only 2 joined the unit after it had arrived in Vietnam. The average age was 26 years. Three received their commissions through OCS and two through ROTC. None had prior combat experience. None had any significant identifiable weaknesses.

—The Company Commander CPT Michles appears to have been an extremely conscientious, hardworking, and Army career motivated officer. He was dedicated and probably sincerely interested in the welfare of his officers and men.

—His Executive Officer, 1LT Mundy, appears to have been a loyal but plodding worker who had not as yet decided where he was going in life and was not concerned about it. In addition to his reported lack of enthusiasm and force, he probably lacked imagination.

—CPT Willingham, a platoon leader in Company B, and later Commander of Company E, is probably quite intelligent and capable of performing better than average in any job to which he is assigned; but he appears basically not motivated towards a career as an Army officer and is probably self-oriented.

—2LT Lewis' record contains little upon which to base an evaluation. He was a small man physically (5'5", 137 pounds). Although he was described as being enthusiastic by his raters during his service on an instructional committee at Fort Polk, there is nothing to indicate how he performed as a platoon leader in combat.

—1LT Cochran appears to have been a mature, solid, sincere officer trying to do a job. Although he lacked color and dash as a rifle platoon leader, he probably could be counted upon to come through when the going got tough.

—Evaluation of each officer is attached at inclosure 1.

4. Review of the 27 NCO records reveals that they were above the norm in all areas.

—67 percent were enlistees in comparison to approximately 40 percent Army-wide accessions.

—Distribution among the four mental categories was better than accessions of new men in FY 67, 68 and 69. Forty-five percent were in Categories I and II compared to 34 percent of accessions; 15 percent were in Category IV compared to 26 percent of accessions.

—63 percent were above the norm in overall trainability (AFQT 50 percentile) in comparison to 52 percent of Army-wide accessions.

—85 percent were above the norm in Infantry aptitude (IN score 100).

—72 percent were above the norm in general learning ability (GT score 100).

—85 percent were high school graduates or higher in comparison to 69 percent of Army-wide accessions (41 percent had some college credits—3 had college degrees).

—Median age was 23 years.

—Two had combat experience in World War II. One also had combat experience in Korea.

—Awards included—6 BSM, 3 PH, 2 ACM, and 5 GCM.

—17 records indicated that training had been received on the Geneva Convention during the period Jan 67–Jan 68. The other files were either incomplete or no entry was recorded on the Enlisted Qualification Record.

—24 were rated excellent in both conduct and efficiency. Ratings for 3 NCO's were not available.

5. Review of 87 enlistees and inductees, less NCO's, reveals that they were below the norm in several areas.

—29 percent were enlistees in comparison to 40 percent Army-wide accessions.

—Distribution among the four mental categories deviated somewhat from normal accessions. While Categories I and III were similar, Category II was 12 percent below accession level and Category IV 13 percent higher than normal accessions.

—37 percent were above the norm in overall trainability (AFQT 50 percentile) in comparison to 52 percent of Army-wide accessions.

—44 percent were above the norm in Infantry aptitude (IN score 100) in comparison to 50 percent of Army-wide accessions.

—42 percent were above the norm in general learning ability (GT score 100) in comparison to 60 percent of Army-wide accessions.

—74 percent were high school graduates or higher in comparison to 69 percent of Army-wide accessions. (20 percent had some college credits— 2 had college degrees.)

—Average age was 21.6 years.

—None had combat experience prior to duty in Vietnam.

—Awards included—8 BSM, 13 PH, 11 ACM, and 2 GCM.

—63 records indicated that training had been received on the Geneva Convention during the period March 67—March 68. Three received the training in June and August 1968. The other files were either incomplete or no entry was recorded on the Enlisted Qualification Record.

—All men (except 2) were rated Excellent in both conduct and efficiency. One was rated good and one unsatisfactory.

—Approximately 10 percent of the company were Project One Hundred Thousand men while Army-wide accessions are 12 percent (50 percent were enlistees).

6. The only significant differences between the enlistees and inductees (less NCO's) were that the enlistees were higher in Infantry aptitude with 56 percent above the norm, while the inductees had a higher percentage of high school graduates and men who attended college. The two college graduates were regular Army enlistees.

7. Based upon the foregoing it is concluded that:

—The officers were generally above average.

—The NCO's were above average and apparently very well selected with emphasis on quality.

—There was some deviation among the other enlisted personnel from the normal distribution of accessions in mental categories and aptitudes. However, most of the high quality NCO's in the company were a part of the regular accessions. They were selected from the same group of first term enlistees and inductees which accounts for some of the deviation. This is considered normal since the higher quality men are most likely to become NCO's.

—The analysis of the NCO's and other men as a group shows that the enlisted personnel of the company are nearly identical to the accessions that entered the Army during the same period of time.

Appendix

Findings and Recommendations

[Chapter 12 of Volume I of the Inquiry's final report is presented here for the interested reader. The sections on findings against individuals and the peripheral issues are not included.]

I. . . . the findings of the Inquiry are as follows:

A. Concerning Events Surrounding the Son My Operation of 16–19 March 1968

1. During the period 16–19 March 1968, US Army troops of TF Barker, 11th Brigade, American Division, massacred a large number of noncombatants in two hamlets of Son My Village, Quang Ngai Province, Republic of Vietnam. The precise number of Vietnamese killed cannot be determined but was at least 175 and may exceed 400.

2. The massacre occurred in conjunction with a combat operation which was intended to neutralize Son My Village as a logistical support base and staging area, and to destroy elements of an enemy battalion thought to be located in the Son My area.

3. The massacre resulted primarily from the nature of the orders issued by persons in the chain of command within TF Barker.

4. The task force commander's order and the associated intelligence estimate issued prior to the operation were embellished as they were disseminated through each lower level of command, and ultimately presented to the individual soldier a false and misleading picture of the Son My area as an armed enemy camp, largely devoid of civilian inhabitants.

5. Prior to the incident, there had developed within certain elements of the 11th Brigade a permissive attitude toward the treatment and safeguarding of noncombatants which contributed to the mistreatment of such per-

sons during the Son My Operation.

6. The permissive attitude in the treatment of Vietnamese was, on 16–19 March 1968, exemplified by an almost total disregard for the lives and property of the civilian population of Son My Village on the part of commanders and key staff officers of TF Barker.

7. On 16 March, soldiers at the squad and platoon level, within some elements of TF Barker, murdered noncombatants while under the supervision and control of their immediate superiors.

8. A part of the crimes visited on the inhabitants of Son My Village included individual and group acts of murder, rape, sodomy, maiming, and assault on noncombatants and the mistreatment and killing of detainees. They further included the killing of livestock, destruction of crops, closing of wells, and the burning of dwellings within several subhamlets.

9. Some attempts were made to stop the criminal acts in Son My Village on 16 March; but with few exceptions, such efforts were too feeble or too late.

10. Intensive interrogation has developed no evidence that any member of the units engaged in the Son My operation was under the influence of marijuana or other narcotics.

B. Concerning the Adequacy of Reports, Investigations and Reviews

11. The commanders of TF Barker and the 11th Brigade had substantial knowledge as to the extent of the killing of noncombatants but only a portion of their information was ever reported to the Commanding General of the American Division.

12. Based on his observations, WO1 Thompson made a specific complaint through his command channels that serious war crimes had been committed but through a series of inadequate responses at each level of command, action on his complaint was delayed and the severity of his charges considerably diluted by the time it reached the Division Commander.

13. Sufficient information concerning the highly irregular nature of the operations of TF Barker on 16 March 1968 reached the Commanding General of the American Division to require that a thorough investigation be conducted.

14. An investigation by the Commander of the 11th Brigade, conducted at the direction of the Commanding General of the American Division, was little more than a pretense and was subsequently misrepresented as a thorough investigation to the CG, American Division in order to conceal from him the true enormity of the atrocities.

15. Patently inadequate reports of investigation submitted by the commander of the 11th Brigade were accepted at face value and without an effective review by the CG, American Division.

16. Reports of alleged war crimes, noncombatant casualties, and serious incidents concerning the Son My operation of 16 March were received at the headquarters of the American Division but were not reported to higher

headquarters despite the existence of directives requiring such action.

17. Reports of alleged war crimes relating to the Son My operation of 16 March reached Vietnamese government officials, but those officials did not take effective action to ascertain the true facts.

18. Efforts of the ARVN/GVN officials discreetly to inform the US commanders of the magnitude of the war crimes committed on 16 March 1968 met with no affirmative response.

C. Concerning Attempts to Suppress Information

19. At every command level within the American Division, actions were taken, both wittingly and unwittingly, which effectively suppressed information concerning the war crimes committed at Son My Village.

20. At the company level there was a failure to report the war crimes which had been committed. This, combined with instructions to members of one unit not to discuss the events of 16 March, contributed significantly to the suppression of information.

21. The task force commander and at least one, and probably more, staff officers of TF Barker may have conspired to suppress information and to mislead higher headquarters concerning the events of 16–19 March 1968.

22. At the 11th Brigade level, the commander and at least one principal staff officer may have conspired to suppress information to deceive the division commander concerning the true facts of the Son My operation of 16–19 March.

23. A reporter and a photographer from the 11th Brigade observed many war crimes committed by C/1–20 Inf on 16 March. Both failed to report what they had seen; the reporter submitted a misleading account of the operation; and the photographer withheld and suppressed (and wrongfully misappropriated upon his discharge from the service) photographic evidence of such war crimes.

24. Efforts within the 11th Brigade to suppress information concerning the Son My operation were aided in varying degrees by members of US Advisory teams working with ARVN and GVN officials.

25. Within the American Division headquarters, actions taken to suppress information concerning what was purportedly believed to be the inadvertent killing of 20 to 28 noncombatants effectively served to conceal the true nature and scope of the events which had taken place in Son My Village on 16–19 March 68.

26. Failure of the American Division headquarters to act on reports and information received from GVN/ARVN officials in mid-April served effectively to suppress the true nature and scope of the events which had taken place in Son My Village on 16–19 March 1968.

27. Despite an exhaustive search of the files of the 11th Brigade, Americal Division, GVN/ARVN advisory team files, and records holding centers, with few exceptions, none of the documents relating to the so-called investigation of the events of 16–19 March were located.

* * *

II. It is recommended that:

A. You take cognizance of the findings set forth above.

B. The names of the members of the Army . . . , together with information concerning their omissions and commissions, be referred to their respective general court-martial convening authorities for possible disciplinary or administrative action.

C. Consideration be given to the modification of applicable policies, directives, and training standards in order to correct the apparent deficiencies noted. . . .

Index

Abrams, Creighton, 133, 239
Adcock, Michael C., 53, 54
After Action Report, 93, 205
air assault, 28–29
Alpha Company, 95–96, 145, 147, 167, 172
Americal Division, 26, 32, 73, 87, 180–81, 185, 202, 210, 241
  absence of documents in, 142, 143
  chain of command in, 48
  coverup and, 204–5, 207, 208
  11th Brigade assigned to, 27, 37
  operating policies of, 118
  Regulation 525–4, "Combat Operation, Rules of Engagement" of, 32, 118–19, 124
  Vietnamese channels and, 154
Anderson, Colonel, 147
Andreotta, Glenn W., 66, 70n, 71, 72, 243
Anistranski, Charles, 126–28, 129, 130, 155
Apici, Joseph I., 17, 49
Armstrong, John W., 145, 147
Army, U.S.:
  damaged image of, 209
  dismissal of charges by, 221–23, 226–27
  Document Center, 142
  vs. HASC, 20, 22
  internal disorders remaining in, 251

professional ethics and morality in, 250, 251
Regulation 15–6 of, 10–11, 14, 62, 88n, 114
Regulation 350–216 of, 238–39
surveys conducted by, 238, 239
training revisions of, 239
see also U.S. Army, Vietnam
Army Inquiry, *see* Peers Inquiry
Army Legislative Liaison Division (ALLD), 22
Army War College study, 249–50
artillery, SOP for, 32
Artillery Incident Report, 58n, 88, 128, 129, 204
  regulations for, 88n, 95
aviation records, 239–40
Bailey, F. Lee, 77, 79
Balmer, Jesmond D., Jr., 119, 123–24, 130
Barker, Frank A., 18, 67, 69, 74, 86, 87, 93, 101, 102, 103, 107–8, 115, 128, 130, 142, 173, 177, 179, 234–35
  Bravo Company and, 186, 188
  in Calhoun's testimony, 89, 90–91
  cease-fire ordered by, 178, 190
  Combat Action Report of (March 28, 1968), 59, 86, 122, 124, 132, 142, 148, 202, 268–71